ETHICS AND POLITICS

Alasdair MacIntyre is one of the most creative and important philosophers working today. This volume presents a selection of his
classic essays on ethics and politics, focusing particularly on the
themes of moral disagreement, moral dilemmas, and truthfulness
and its importance. The essays range widely in scope, from Aristotle
and Aquinas and what we need to learn from them, to our contemporary economic and social structures and the threat which they pose
to the realization of the forms of ethical life. They will appeal to a
wide range of readers across philosophy and especially in moral
philosophy, political philosophy, and theology.

ALASDAIR MACINTYRE is Senior Research Professor of Philosophy
at the University of Notre Dame, a Member of the American
Academy of Arts and Sciences, and a Fellow of the British Academy.
His publications include *A Short History of Ethics* (1967), *After Virtue*
(1981), *Dependent Rational Animals* (1999), and numerous journal
articles.

ETHICS AND POLITICS

Selected Essays, Volume 2

ALASDAIR MACINTYRE

University of Notre Dame

CAMBRIDGE
UNIVERSITY PRESS

CAMBRIDGE UNIVERSITY PRESS
Cambridge, New York, Melbourne, Madrid, Cape Town,
Singapore, São Paulo, Delhi, Tokyo, Mexico City

Cambridge University Press
The Edinburgh Building, Cambridge CB2 8RU, UK

Published in the United States of America by Cambridge University Press, New York

www.cambridge.org
Information on this title: www.cambridge.org/9780521670623

First published 2006
Reprinted 2007

A catalogue record for this publication is available from the British Library

ISBN 978-0-521-85438-2 Hardback
ISBN 978-0-521-67062-3 Paperback

Contents

Preface

The essays in this volume were written between 1985 and 1999, after I had recognized that my philosophical convictions had become those of a Thomistic Aristotelian, something that had initially surprised me. All of them give expression to that Thomistic Aristotelian standpoint, albeit in very different ways. The first four are concerned with the interpretation and defence of Aristotelian and Thomistic positions. The remaining eight contain only occasional references to Aristotle or Aquinas and sometimes none at all. Nonetheless each arrives at conclusions that are supportive of, derived from, or at least consistent with a Thomistic Aristotelian stance, even though in one case – that of the content of the rule forbidding the utterance of lies – my conclusion is at odds with Aquinas's own. The great majority of present and past Aristotelians are of course not Thomists. And some Thomists have been anxious to stress the extent of what they take to be the philosophical as well as the theological differences between Aquinas and Aristotle. It is therefore important to make the case for understanding Aristotle in a way that accords with Aquinas's interpretation and in so doing it is necessary to distinguish and defend Aristotle so understood from a number of rival Aristotles. The first two essays are a contribution to those tasks. In their original version they were delivered as the Brian O'Neil Memorial Lectures in the History of Philosophy for 1997/98 at the University of New Mexico and I am grateful to the faculty and students of that department for their critical and stimulating discussion.

One point that I emphasize in those essays is that for Aristotle ethics is a part and aspect of politics and that the human good is to be achieved in and through participation in the lives of political communities. This is a familiar and uncontroversial thesis with respect to Aristotle. It is less familiar when made about Aquinas. Yet misunderstanding of Aquinas is inescapable, if we do not remember that on his view it is through achievement of common goods that we are to move towards the achievement of the human good and that the precepts conformity to which is required for the achievement of those common goods have the character of *law*. Aquinas's account of law was in its thirteenth-century context developed as an alternative and rival to accounts that informed the law-making and law-enforcement of such rulers as Louis IX of France and the emperor Frederick II. And, although Aquinas envisages the institutionalization of law in terms that are partly Aristotelian and partly thirteenth century, he provides a considerable part of the resources necessary to ask and answer the question: what would it be to develop a politics of the common good and the natural law here and now?

Yet of course the claim that one and the same set of goods are to be achieved and one and the same set of precepts obeyed in widely different social, economic, and cultural settings is itself in need of elucidation and defence of more than one kind. It seems to follow, for example, from what Aquinas says about the knowledge of the precepts of the natural law that he takes all or at least most human beings to possess that we should expect to find respect for one and the same set of moral rules in most social and cultural orders. What we in fact find is a very high degree of moral diversity. And in "Aquinas and the extent of moral disagreement" I catalogue a number of the more striking examples of radical moral disagreement between and sometimes within cultures. I then argue that, insofar as the various moral stances which result in such disagreement are at odds with the precepts of the natural law, they represent failures in practical rationality, as Aquinas understands it, directing our attention to the sources of those failures.

If practical rationality requires us to conform to the precepts of the natural law, it seems to follow that it must be possible to conform to these precepts without inconsistency. They must never make incompatible demands upon us. Yet, if this is so, it seems that there can be no such thing as a moral dilemma, a situation in which the only courses of action open to someone are such that she must either obey this precept and, by so doing, violate that or avoid the violation of the latter precept by failing to obey the former. I have made a promise to do whatever you ask me to do on your birthday. What you ask me to do turns out to be something that it would be wrong to do. So it seems that now either I must do wrong by doing what you ask or I must do wrong by breaking my promise. There is no third alternative.

Some of the most perceptive of recent moral philosophers, including Bernard Williams, have held that the occurrence of moral dilemmas is a brute fact of the moral life and that any theory that entails a denial of their occurrence must be in error. The debate about these claims is still ongoing and the editors of *Philosophy and Phenomenological Research* invited me to survey the contributions to this controversy in a supplement designed to celebrate the fiftieth anniversary of the founding of that journal in 1940. "Moral dilemmas" is a revised version of my article. In it I conclude – and, when I started to write the article, I was not at all certain that I was going so to conclude – that Aquinas was right in holding that moral dilemmas do indeed occur, but only as the result of some prior action that was itself a violation of some precept of the natural law.

It is the conclusion of the argument developed in the next two essays that puts me on one particular topic at odds with Aquinas. Those essays were Tanner Lectures delivered at Princeton University in 1994 and the published version owes a great deal to those who commented on them on that occasion, Christine Korsgaard, Onora O'Neill, and Quentin Skinner. My aim was to state the case for and against Kant's unqualified and unconditional condemnation of lying, drawing such resources as I could from Mill. For anyone who inhabits a postEnlightenment culture enquiry into fundamental moral issues has to begin with Kant and Mill. It is when and insofar as they leave us resourceless that we have to go elsewhere. And I have argued, most notably in *After Virtue*, that they do at crucial points leave us resourceless. But in my Tanner Lectures I wanted to make sure that I had identified what could be learned from them before trying to go further. What I took and still take myself to have learned from them is this: that Kant is right in his contention that only a categorical and unconditional rule regarding truth telling can inform human relationships, if those are to be relationships between practically rational agents; and that Mill is right in his contention that no rule can be adequate, unless it allows for those occasions when it is not just permissible but a duty to lie.

We do not need to and we should not follow Mill in adopting a consequentialist standpoint. Mill himself was often uneasy with his own consequentialism. But the considerations that seemed to him to make it necessary to take a consequentialist view of lying can be given their due weight by a better formulation of the categorical rule concerning truthfulness and lying than Kant provided. I attempt to supply just such a formulation in the second of these essays, in so doing disagreeing with Aquinas as well as with Kant.

The last five essays address political questions, answers to which are presupposed by any sufficiently developed moral philosophy. The first of them was written as an introduction to the 1995 edition of my *Marxism and Christianity*, first published under the title *Marxism An Interpretation* in 1953, and then in a revised version under its present title in 1968. It reasserts the truth of that in Marxism which has survived every critique and it attempts, although too briefly, to suggest how Marxist, Aristotelian, and Christian insights need to be integrated in any ethics and politics that is able to reckon with contemporary realities.

"Poetry as political philosophy: notes on Burke and Yeats" approaches some of the same questions in another way. It was written for a *Festschrift* for my colleague and friend, the late Donald Davie, an excellent poet and a very great interpreter of poetry. Just because of the claims that I have made for the importance of tradition incautious readers have sometimes supposed that I am or should be sympathetic to Edmund Burke. Davie was a discriminating admirer of Burke and I used this essay to define our differences about Burke as well as to suggest an interpretation of some of Yeats's later political poetry.

"Some Enlightenment projects reconsidered" is an attempt to distinguish that in the political claims of some Enlightment thinkers, most of all Kant, that should still be reaffirmed from that which should now be put in question. About any set of claims as to what norms should govern our normal and political lives we need to ask what it would be for those norms to be institutionalized, to be embodied in practice. It is my thesis in this essay that, effective as the theses and argument of Enlightenment thinkers were in exposing what was unjust and oppressive in various eighteenth-century regimes, the form that their institutionalization has since taken has had outcomes very different from those hoped for by Kant, by the utilitarians, and by other Enlightenment thinkers. The Enlightenment has failed by its own standards.

Some relevant features of the social order and the institutions that we now inhabit are identified in "Social structures and their threat to moral agency." Here two problems are posed. One is that of whether and how far ignorance concerning our own actions, their character and their consequences, is culpable. The other is that of the kind of moral reflection that is required of us, if we are to act as we ought. The type of social context that provokes these questions in a peculiarly contemporary way is that of the growing compartmentalization of each sphere of social activity, a compartmentalization such that each sphere increasingly has its own roles governed by its own norms, with little or no social space preserved for effective critical reflection on the overall ordering of social life.

The final essay, "Toleration and the goods of conflict," asks what we should make of the views advanced on toleration by Locke and by Mill.

The conclusions of my argument are that we badly need to be *intolerant* of the expression of certain lamentable points of view, such as that of those who deny that the Holocaust ever happened, but that we should not make the state the instrument of our intolerance. And I also argue that we can recognize the need for such intolerance without quarreling at all with some at least of Mill's arguments in favor of freedom of expression and of the toleration of opposing standpoints.

Every one of these five essays on the politics of ethics adopts a negative and critical stance to the dominant norms, values, and institutions of the contemporary social order. What may seem to be missing is any statement of an alternative to that order, an alternative that would give expression to some conception of a social and political order that, by embodying the precepts of the natural law, would direct us towards the achievement of our common goods and educate us to become citizens who find their own good in and through that common good. But it is important that the construction of such an alternative cannot begin from any kind of philosophical or theoretical statement. Where then does it begin? Only in the struggles, conflicts, and work of practice and in the attempt to find in and through dialogue with others who are engaged in such struggles, conflicts, and work an adequate local and particular institutional expression of our shared directedness towards our common goods.

Of course every negative critique has positive implications and the more detailed the critique the more detailed these implications are. And of course the same theoretical resources, drawn for the most part from Aristotle, Aquinas, and Marx, need to be put to work both in negative critique and in articulating the goods and goals of particular political and social projects. But philosophical theorizing cannot construct blueprints for designing the future after the manner of Fabian Socialism or Soviet Marxism – or rather, it cannot do so without producing effects very different from those that were hoped for. So that, if at a certain point my thinking on political matters seems to stop short, that is by intention.

Finally, let me reiterate my gratitude to all those whose critical comments upon these essays rescued me from various errors and to Claire Shely for her extraordinary work in preparing this volume. In the introduction to the first volume of my essays I named those to whom I have been greatly indebted for philosophical discussion over extended periods of time. I remain in their debt for the work published here. And I once again add to their names that of my wife, Lynn Sumida Joy, without whom none of this would have been possible.

Acknowledgments

Of the essays in this second volume, number 4 was previously unpublished. I am grateful to the following for permission to reprint essays that have appeared elsewhere:

- the Department of Philosophy at the University of New Mexico for the first and second essays, first published by that Department as the Brian O'Neil Memorial Lectures for 1997/98;
- the editors of the *Journal for Medieval and Early Modern Studies* for the third essay, first published in vol. 26, no. 1, of the *Journal* in 1995, pp. 61–87;
- the editors of *Philosophy and Phenomenological Research* for the fifth essay, first published in the Supplement to vol. L, Fall, 1990, pp. 369–82;
- the Director of the Tanner Lectures for the sixth and seventh essays, which were delivered as Tanner Lectures on Human Values at Princeton University, April 6 and 7, 1994, and which are printed with the permission of the Tanner Lectures on Human Values, a Corporation, University of Utah, Salt Lake City, Utah;
- Duckworth (Gerald Duckworth and Company Ltd.) of London for the eighth essay, first published as an Introduction to the revised edition of *Marxism and Christianity*, 1995, pp. v–xxxi;
- Vanderbilt University Press of Nashville, Tennessee, for the ninth essay, first published in *On Modern Poetry: Essays Presented to Donald Davie*, ed. V. Bell and L. Lerner, 1998, pp. 145–57;
- Taylor and Francis for the tenth essay, first published in *Questioning Ethics: Contemporary Debates in Moral Philosophy*, ed. R. Kearney and M. Dooley, London and New York: Routledge, 1995, pp. 245–57;
- the editor of *Philosophy* and the Royal Institute of Philosophy for the eleventh essay, first published in *Philosophy*, vol. 74, 1999, pp. 311–29;
- Edinburgh University Press for the twelfth essay, first published in *The Politics of Toleration*, ed. S. Mendus, 1999, pp. 123–25.

PART I

Learning from Aristotle and Aquinas

CHAPTER I

Rival Aristotles: Aristotle against some Renaissance Aristotelians

A systematic history of Aristotelianism would be an immense under-taking populated by a great variety of rival Aristotles: Theophrastus's, the Aristotle of the Neoplatonists, a whole range of medieval Aristotles – Farabi's, ibn Rushd's, Maimonides's, Aquinas's – and after them an equally impressive set of Renaissance Aristotles, followed by Coleridge's, Thomas Case's, and the whole variety of twentieth-century Aristotles from Werner Jaeger to Terence Irwin and beyond. I shall deal only with a very small selection from this set of rival Aristotles and even with them I shall be concerned only with a limited set of issues, issues concerning the relationship of moral and political theory to moral and political practice and of both to moral education.

I

Towards the end of the tenth book of the *Nicomachean Ethics* Aristotle argues that arguments by themselves are insufficient to make human beings good. Arguments may encourage and incite those of the young who already have some propensity for virtue – they may have, that is to say, rhetorical power. But with the majority they do not even have this kind of power and indeed it is one of the marks of already achieved goodness to be willing to submit to argument.[1] So practical habituation in the exercise of the virtues has to precede education in moral theory. But it is not just that such habituation is required for those who are to be able to understand and be responsive to argument. It is also that only those who have undergone such habituation will be in a position to theorize well about issues of practice.

To be virtuous is to act in accordance with a mean and to judge rightly about the mean is to judge as the *phronimos*, the practically

---

1 *Nicomachean Ethics* 1179b4–16 and 1180a10–12.

intelligent human being, would judge.[2] The *phronimos* has in the act of practical judgment no external criterion to guide her or him. Indeed practical knowledge of what criteria are relevant in this particular situation requires *phronēsis*. The good human being *is* the standard of right judgment, passion, and action: "In all such matters that which seems so to the good human being is held really to be so" and "virtue and the good human being are the measure in each case."[3] It is in this light that we must understand what Aristotle says about moral perception at the end of the second book. Judgment concerning the mean is a matter of particular facts and judgment concerning these "rests with perception."[4] But the perceptions must be the perceptions of a good human being. Perception is not a source of moral judgment, independently of the character of the perceiver and judger.

Only the good then are in a position to make justified true theoretical judgments about the nature of moral practice. The construction and evaluation of sound moral theories, unlike the construction and evaluation of sound theories in the physical sciences, require more than intellectual virtues. They require a particular kind of initiation into and participation in a particular kind of moral and political practice. And this view puts Aristotle very much at odds with the whole notion of ethics as presently conceived by most members of the American Philosophical Association. Jobs in ethics go to those with the appropriate analytic and dialectical skills and knowledge of the relevant academic literature. If good moral character, understood as Aristotle understood it, is sometimes exemplified by the practitioners of contemporary ethics, it is so only *per accidens*. And if moral and political philosophies can be rationally commended within the arenas of contemporary academic ethics and politics only by appeal to principles and premises that are shared at least by the vast majority of their practitioners, then, if Aristotle is right, it is going to be impossible to succeed in commending moral and political Aristotelianism rationally in the areas of professional academic debate.

Yet of course there are within academic ethics a variety of philosophers, among them myself, who profess what we take to be Aristotelian principles and uphold Aristotelian positions in debate with Kantians, utilitarians, contractarians, and others. In so doing we are recurrently going to be tempted to treat Aristotle's moral and political theory as if it were a theory

2 *NE* 1106b36–1107a2.   3 *NE* 1176a15–18.   4 *NE* 1109b22–23.

that could be understood and presented independently of the contexts of practice, as though its positions could be made adequately intelligible to those who do not understand themselves as participants in the relevant kind of practice. But, if we attempt to avoid yielding to this temptation, we will be confronted by more than one set of problems. The first of these arises when we try to answer the questions: what is the kind of practice in which Aristotelian theory claims to be rooted? And where can we find examples of it?

Part of Aristotle's own answer to these questions ought to be treated as more unsettling than it usually is. Aristotle tells us that ethics is a part of politics and a clear implication of this is that we cannot adequately understand the claims made in the *Nicomachean Ethics* except in the context provided by the *Politics*. Contemporary academic practice generally presupposes that Aristotle was mistaken in this view of his own work. Almost always the *Ethics* is read in one set of courses by one set of students, usually in departments of philosophy by teachers with a philosophical training, while the *Politics* is more often read in quite another set of courses by quite another set of students, usually in departments of political science by teachers with a training in political theory. This divorce of the *Ethics* from the *Politics* has of course a long history. And one of its effects has been to enable us to ignore the fact that the ethics of the *Nicomachean Ethics* is the ethics of and for a citizen of a *polis* and that the social practice articulated by Aristotelian theory is the practice of a *polis*. So the claim can very plausibly be made: no ethics except as part of politics and no politics except as the practice of a *polis*.

Yet Aristotle's was after all one of the last generations of Greeks to inhabit a *polis* – and he was not a citizen. His pupil Alexander helped to write the epitaph of the *polis*. And the notion of reviving the *polis* at some later time – not only a recurrent phantasy of some eighteenth- and nineteenth-century romantics, but a phantasy recurrently imputed to Aristotelian critics of modernity, such as myself, no matter how vigorously we disown it – has always been absurd, as the emperor Hadrian unintentionally demonstrated, when he attempted to restore the *polis* by imperial edict. So that we may be inclined to infer that, since there is and can be no *polis*, there can be no Aristotelian politics and, since there can be no Aristotelian politics, there can be no Aristotelian ethics.

I shall argue against this conclusion. But I shall also suggest that we are only entitled to reject it, if we have been able to give an account of what kind of practice it is that, after the *polis* has disappeared, is able to supply the social context required for an Aristotelian ethics and politics. In order to give such an account, I will first consider and criticize one important wrong-headed attempt to do so, that of certain Renaissance Aristotelians. If I am severely critical of that account, it is only in order to put that criticism to constructive use in providing what I hope will be a more adequate account.

In addressing this question "What is the practice to which Aristotelian moral and political theory is the counterpart?" it is important not to lose sight of a second major problem about the relationship of theory to practice. Consider how theory and practice will be related in a *polis* that is, by Aristotle's standards, well ordered. Each successive generation of the young will be habituated in virtuous practice and the kind of teaching and institutional framework necessary to provide this habituation will have been established by legislators guided by Aristotelian theory. Such legislators will be regarded as well qualified to make use of theory in framing laws and devising institutions, just because they themselves have in their youth been educated into that same practice of which their theory is the articulation.

Suppose that we now enquire of them what grounds they have for their allegiance to Aristotle's rather than to any rival type of moral and political theory. On a variety of issues their answers will have to appeal either to the nature of practice or to judgments made by those who are regarded as excellent by the standards of practice. As Aristotle remarks, after having considered a variety of theoretical arguments about the nature of happiness and the concurrent opinions of "the wise," ultimately "in matters of practice truth is judged on the basis of what we do and how we live."[5] But with this it becomes difficult to avoid a charge of question-begging circularity. For when this or that theoretical contention is put in question, we are to appeal to practice; but the practice to which we are to appeal was itself elaborated in accordance with the canons of the very same theory, so that the test seems not to be a genuine one.

Suppose, for example, that someone puts in question Aristotle's account of courage as a virtue in order to test Aristotle's claims that the virtue of courage can only be possessed by those who also possess the virtue of *phronēsis* and that courage and *phronēsis* together can only be possessed by those who possess the other moral virtues. We test these claims by examining practices and by considering actual examples of courage, distinguishing in so doing genuine courage from various simulacra of

5 *NE* 1179a18–19.

courage – the apparent courage of the experienced soldier or of the spirited personality, for example – and primary and paradigmatic cases of courage from secondary and marginal cases. The problem is that, unless we draw our examples from the practice of the morally well educated, we can have no grounds for confidence in our choice of examples, but, if we do draw our examples from the practice of the morally well educated, then we have to recognize that their habituation into courage was prescribed in accordance with Aristotle's theory, so that the distinctions that they make in practice will mirror the distinctions defended within the theory. Hence it seems that those examples cannot be adduced as providing confirmation for the theory. Circular justifications, as Aristotle himself taught us, are no justifications.

Any protagonist of Aristotle's standpoint in ethics and politics has therefore at least two obligations to discharge. She or he must not only be able to give an account of the kind of practice in which Aristotelian theory needs to be rooted and without which it is incomplete, but also to provide a rational justification for the whole body of theory-and-practice which does not involve this kind of empty circularity.

II

Some Renaissance Aristotelians took both obligations seriously. They did so by presenting the justification of theory as itself an entirely theoretical matter and by presenting good practice as the systematic application of theory. As teachers of moral and political philosophy such Aristotelians were in one way remarkably like us, in another way very different. They were like us in their mode of teaching: they commented on texts, they discussed and evaluated rival interpretations of passages, they analyzed arguments, and they explained their disagreements with rival views. The differences between the content and form of their lecture courses and ours are relatively insignificant compared with the differences between both and, say, standard thirteenth- or early fourteenth-century discussions of Aristotle.

They differ from us however in a striking way. For they presented as the aim of their teaching and they claimed as the effect of their teaching the moral improvement of their students. Reading the *Nicomachean Ethics* and listening to lectures on it are activities, so they insisted, that will issue in the development of the moral virtues. I choose as a notable example of someone advancing these claims, Francesco Piccolomini. Piccolomini was born in Siena in 1523 and died there in 1607. After teaching at Siena,

Macerata, and Perugia, he was appointed as professor of natural philosophy at Padua, where he taught from 1560 until 1598. In 1583, when he was sixty years old, he published at Venice his *Universa philosophia de moribus*, a work that has not yet been translated. It is a remarkable book, both for its originality and its independence of mind, the same independence of mind that Piccolomini exhibited in his extended controversy with Zabarella on philosophical and scientific method. Although Piccolomini is always deferential to Aristotle, and although his book is generally and by intention Aristotelian, it does not take the form of an exposition of or commentary upon the *Nicomachean Ethics*, but that of an independent enquiry by Piccolomini into the place of the virtues in civic life. And he is not always Aristotelian, sometimes knowingly, sometimes not.

Piccolomini avowedly departs from Aristotle at the beginning and again at the end of his book. At the beginning[6] he contrasts his method with that of Aristotle. Aristotle's method was that of resolution, his is to be that of composition. Where Aristotle was concerned to resolve civil – that is, political – science into its constituent parts, Piccolomini is concerned to begin from the parts of civil science, so as to exhibit our movement from the habits needed for civic life, the virtues, to a developed apprehension of our final good and then to use that apprehension as a standard to guide right action, action in accordance with the virtues. "That is requisite, since the right ordering (*rectitude*) of human actions is to be sought from the highest good as from a rule and measure."[7] The first principles on the basis of which Piccolomini conducts his project of composition are to be the same first principles that emerged from Aristotle's resolutive enquiry.

So there follow in order sections on the matter of the virtues, on the principles of the virtues, on what Piccolomini calls semivirtues, that is, states of continence, on the moral, intellectual, and heroic virtues, on "a certain use of virtue," namely friendship, and on various means that may assist virtue in being effective, such as good fortune, external goods, honor, and physical beauty. All this is an extended prologue to two final chapters, one on the highest good and one on the relationship of virtue to the highest good, a topic of consequence not only to individuals, but also to cities and peoples.

Piccolomini's second avowed departure from Aristotle is more radical. In his discussion of Aristotle's account of the highest good he accuses Aristotle

---

6 Introductio, cap. XXXII.   7 Ibid., cap. XXXII.

of contradicting himself, since, according to Piccolomini, Aristotle assigns unqualified superiority to the contemplative life, but only by ignoring what he himself has said about the active life. If we follow that account, we have to recognize that in some respects the good to be achieved by the active life is superior. "Which grade of the highest good is more grounded in steadfast character and more lasting (*constantior et firmior*)?"[8] Piccolomini asks, and he replies that the effects of the practice of the virtues of the active life, the part that habituation plays in their acquisition and the fact that their exercise is less open to interruption by external circumstance than is the contemplative life all support his conclusion about the superiority of the active life.

It is true that in the progress towards the good through different levels of virtue, natural, moral, and civil, rational, heroic, and divine, the ultimate end is still that of achieving contemplative wisdom, understood in Christian terms. But Piccolomini's whole emphasis is upon a training in the virtues directed towards the ends of the active life. To become a good citizen of heaven, guided by Christian theologians, may be our ultimate end, but what should preoccupy us here and now, especially if we are nobly born and well prepared for higher education, is how to become a good and successful citizen of Venice, guided by Aristotle and by his contemporary exponents.

Piccolomini's praise of the active rather than the contemplative life is of course not new. It was already found in that earlier Aristotelian, the Florentine Leonardo Bruni. Like Bruni's, it is closely related to concerns deriving from his civic allegiance, concerns that he shares with his intended readers. The audience to whom the *Universa philosophia de moribus* is the most obviously directed fall into three classes. The first are his fellow-scholars. Piccolomini was unusually learned, both in ancient philosophy and in the literature devoted to commentary on Aristotle. And he was well aware that at many points he was making and defending scholarly claims, whether about the relationship of Aristotle's views to those of Plato or the Stoics or about the interpretation of this or that Aristotelian text, claims that were highly contestable. This gives a scholarly dimension to his work that is lacking in the writings of some earlier Renaissance Aristotelians, such as Bruni. But his fellow-scholars were not Piccolomini's only intended audience. For what he supplied his readers with was in effect a detailed syllabus for university lecture courses on

---

8 Ibid., section nine, XLIII.

Aristotle's ethics and politics, designed for and addressed to the Venetian students of the University of Padua. Yet oddly enough Piccolomini never himself delivered such lectures. All his own teaching was on natural philosophy. But here he sets out the lecture course that he might have given. So that in the background there are not only his scholarly rivals, but also the past and future students of the university, while in the foreground there is a third and primary audience. Piccolomini dedicated the *Universa philosophia de moribus* to the Venetian senate and it is the senate whom he addresses directly. Both in his dedicatory introduction and in his discussion of prudence[9] he cites as examples of those who have excelled in prudence the present and past members of that body. What he is offering to the members of the Venetian senate is both explanation and prescription. How is the enduring greatness of the Venetian Republic to be explained? A number of Venetian historians had addressed this question and Piccolomini's claim that it is to be explained in key part by the virtues that have informed Venetian civic life was already in one way a familiar one. The dominant mode of enquiry in sixteenth-century Venice had been historical, not philosophical, a kind of history designed to teach moral and political lessons through narrating episodes from the Venetian past. What the story of the Venetian past demonstrated, according to such official historians of the Republic as Andrei Navagero, Giovan Pietro Contarini, and Paolo Paruta, was that it was the peculiar excellence of Venetian institutions that not only accounted for their stability and their enduring excellence, but also for the preservation of Venetian liberty.

Piccolomini agreed with them. His treatment of the question, which is the best practically achievable type of constitution, is much briefer than Aristotle's and this is clearly because he takes it that the history of Venice rather than Aristotle's text has provided the definitive answer to this question. Just as Aristotle had argued, the best practicable constitution is a constitution of a mixed type, combining elements of monarchy, aristocracy, and democracy, as Venice does. But for Piccolomini the interesting question is not whether Venetian institutions are excellent, but what has made them so. And here he has his own avowedly Aristotelian answer.

The Venetian historians had acknowledged the importance of the virtues. Indeed they take it for granted. What was original to Piccolomini was his catalogue and analysis of the relevant virtues and his further prescriptive claim that the cultivation of those virtues now requires an education in civil science, the very same education that is available

---

9 Ibid., section five, cap. XXXVI.

at Padua. Excellent institutions are the result of the cultivation of the virtues and the virtues are to be understood by and inculcated through the teaching of the exponent of civil science, the moral and political philosopher. Venice needs philosophy.

It is in defending this latter claim that Piccolomini's Aristotelianism begins to look very different from Aristotle's. After all, Aristotle had, as I already noticed, declared that it would be a mistake to teach moral philosophy to the adolescent young. And it seems to follow that, if Aristotle is right, lectures on the *Nicomachean Ethics* and the *Politics* would be quite inappropriate matter for undergraduate teaching. Yet such teaching was the stock in trade of many Renaissance Aristotelians, including Piccolomini, and this without any sense of a disagreement with Aristotle. They were of course aware of the relevant passages in Aristotle. Indeed that Aristotle had said what he did was a Renaissance commonplace. In *Troilus and Cressida* Shakespeare has Hector compare Paris and Troilus to "young men, whom Aristotle thought/unfit to hear moral philosophy" on the grounds that they are moved by "the hot passion of distemper'd blood." So how did such Renaissance Aristotelians reconcile the text of Aristotle with their own educational practice? They did so in two ways, both exemplified by Piccolomini. They provide glosses on *Nicomachean Ethics* 1095a2–8 designed, if not to remove, at least to make less obvious their difference from Aristotle. And they provide an account of moral education, revised so that it assigns to the teaching of moral and political philosophy a function other than and greater than that which Aristotle assigned to it.[10]

Piccolomini makes his prescriptive case to the senators about the need for teaching moral philosophy to the young in the course of his discussion of the nature of *paideia* (Latinized as "paidia"), which he understands as preliminary to a genuine education in the virtues. After rejecting an assortment of what he takes to be false opinions,[11] he assigns to *paideia*[12] the task of preparing the young so that they may later become fit students of civil science. *Paideia* comprises not only intellectual, but also practical instruction, a combination of appropriate teaching with friendly advice and preliminary, although only preliminary habituation in right action. And this provides just the kind of experience that prepares one both for a training in the arts and in civil science.

---

10 II, ii, II. 164–69.
11 Francesco Piccolomini, *Universa philosophia de moribus in decem gradus redacta*, Venice, 1583, V, 12.
12 Ibid., V, 13.

Piccolomini is in effect saying to the Venetian senators that what is supplied to the young in the households and primary and secondary schools of Venice from the ages of six to fifteen should be regarded, at least for the Venetian elite, as preparation for subsequent instruction in civil science. The education provided in the Venetian schools is only a beginning, a prelude. And in this Piccolomini challenged the established Venetian view that education within the household and the schools was sufficient for the teaching of the virtues to all those who were to become good servants of the Venetian state. In the schools, so the established view ran, it was through the *studia humanitatis*, the study of ancient, especially Latin rhetoric and literature, that the virtues were to be inculcated. As early as 1446 a school for the boys who served the Great Council had been established and subsequently public education was expanded, especially after a law of 1551 provided for the appointment of larger numbers of teachers.

The ideology that had received its expression in that law was expounded by Giovita Ravizza, a teacher in the most distinguished of the humanistic schools, the Scuola di San Marco, in his *De liberis publice ad humanitatem informandis*, published in the same year, dedicated to the Doge and to one of the sponsors of the new law. Most of Ravizza's book was concerned with practical details: curriculum, library provisions, teacher training, and the first known proposal for a school lavatory. But in the last chapter Ravizza defined and discussed the ends to be achieved by these means, the moral improvement of the students, through the cultivation of *bonae litterae*, whereby the *sententiae* and the examples of ancient virtue teach the students to pursue the very same virtue.[13]

What matters is not only what the Venetian public schools taught, but what they did not teach. What Grendler said about Renaissance teaching in general held true in Venice: "Renaissance pedagogues neither taught a separate subject called moral philosophy nor read specific texts for that purpose. Instead they extracted moral lessons from curricular texts."[14] (The one notable exception to this generalization, noted by Grendler in a footnote, is however Venetian. In 1587 – a year in which teachers in Venice were required to make a profession of faith to a representative of the Patriarch, and accompanied it in most cases with an account of their teaching – eight teachers did report that they taught Cicero's *De Officiis*.

---

13 Paul F. Grendler, "Venetian Schools in the High Renaissance," chapter 2 of *Schooling in Renaissance Italy*, Baltimore and London: The Johns Hopkins University Press, 1989, pp. 63–66.
14 Ibid., p. 263.

But since there were at the time about one hundred and fifteen teachers in private Latin schools, in addition to the teachers in the public schools and the church schools – the public schools educated only 4 per cent of the pupils – those teachers were a very small minority. The importance of the public schools for my present argument is that they were directly under the charge of the Venetian magistrates.[15])

When therefore Piccolomini in the tenth part of the *Universa philosophia de moribus* concluded that the teaching of moral philosophy is of crucial practical importance for the Venetian republic, and when in the fifth part he treated the *paideia* of the public and private schools as having only a preliminary moral function, he was challenging the well-established and near universal opinion of those whom he was addressing, that familial instruction and education in the *studia humanitatis* were together practically sufficient to provide the virtues needed for Venetian public life.

The argument that Piccolomini advanced in order to convince them is an interesting one. Its three premises are all Aristotelian. One concerns the ends for the sake of which a republican polity, such as the Venetian, exists: "A republic has two ends, the one proximate, that we reproduce fittingly, are fed and preserved in security, the other ultimate, that we flourish (*bene simus*)."[16] A second premise concerns the relationship of virtue to power: "Virtue is that which renders a human being fit for *imperium* and therefore that *imperium* is most beneficial in which human beings endowed with virtue rule over others."[17]

From these it follows that the ends of the republic are best served by a polity in which rulers are educated into the virtues. Which virtues do they need? Since the task of magistrates is to enact and enforce laws, rulers need above all that virtue without which law cannot function properly, prudence. Piccolomini's third premise states that prudence is prior to law: "Prudence is the principle, parent and mistress (*domina*) of the law, not law of prudence."[18] (Moreover the individual who is well-fitted for magistracy will be neither too rich nor too poor: "A moderate fortune is the most desirable"[19] and this once again for Aristotelian reasons.)

In order for a republic to be assured of virtuous rulers it must therefore provide for their education in prudence. And this cannot be achieved[20] without the providential action of God, the exercise of intelligence, the

---

15 Ibid., ch. II. 16 Piccolomini, *Universa philosophia*, X, 13.
17 Ibid., X, 110. 18 Ibid., X, 19. 19 Ibid., X, 20. 20 Ibid., X, 31.

influence of households, families, and especially parents, and the educational activities of the republican city. But the right establishment of this education, "since it is the office of prudence, by excellent right belongs to civil science," that is, to political and moral philosophy. So, just as Piccolomini had already concluded in his account of the virtues, political and moral philosophy is to be the keystone of effective practical education into prudence and what can be achieved in the household and the high school is only preliminary to its study.

How is moral and political philosophy to accomplish this task? There are three elements in the development of virtue, that which is supplied by nature, that which is due to direction by philosophical theory (doctrine), and that which is the outcome of moral habituation.[21] But, so Piccolomini continues, as Plato, Alexander, Simplicius, and Averroës all agree in contending, it is philosophy that is of the first importance. "Philosophy as superintendent brings about sound morals" (*"Philosophia inspectrix parit probos mores"*). Why does philosophy have this preeminent place in moral instruction? Piccolomini gives us his answer in a later passage, where he discusses the functions of each of the three elements. "Nature forms appropriately what belongs to the body, habituation corrects desire, education forms reasoning."[22] Each of these three extends into the sphere of the others. Bodily nature can affect desire and reasoning, habituation bodily nature and reasoning, reasoning bodily nature and habituation. But reasoning is of the highest importance and needs to be instructed by philosophy, if it is to issue in prudence: "The mistress of this education is civil philosophy: by forming prudence, it prescribes laws to particular inclinations."[23] What then is Piccolomini's conception of prudence?

Prudence is the virtue that enables us to make use of theoretical knowledge of the human good to pass judgment on whatever inclinations we may have in particular situations. It is this ability to apply theory to practice that enables us to answer the question: would it tend towards the achievement of the human good to act on this desire here and now? Lacking a theoretical knowledge of the human good, for the acquisition of which the study of moral and political philosophy is generally necessary, we would be unable to give true answers to this question. The difference between Piccolomini's view of prudence and Aristotle's is remarkable and what is equally remarkable is that this difference was unremarked by Piccolomini.

---

21 Ibid., V, 17.   22 Ibid., X, 33.   23 Ibid., X, 33.

On Aristotle's account *phronēsis* is indeed concerned with particulars. Without it we could not discern what justice or courage or generosity requires of us in this or that particular set of circumstances. But it does not have to involve *any* application of theoretical knowledge. According to Aristotle, three conditions must be satisfied for an action to be the virtuous action of a virtuous agent, that is, to be the kind of action that the *phronimos* would perform. First, the agent must know that what he or she is doing is just, or courageous, or generous, or whatever. Secondly, he or she must do what he or she does for the sake of the action itself, must act justly or courageously or generously on this occasion, that is to say, just because in this situation this action is what justice or courage or generosity requires. And thirdly, in so doing, the agent must give expression to a settled disposition of character.[24] Note that, as a condition to be satisfied for ascribing the possession of some virtue, Aristotle takes knowledge to be the least practically important of the three elements of virtuous activity.

To become a virtuous agent what one needs then is not generally theoretical instruction, but training that will result in the relevant kind of habituation so that one becomes disposed in particular circumstances not only to act, but also to judge and to feel as the virtues require. One therefore needs a teacher who possesses the virtue of prudence and is able to communicate a practical ability that is not fully articulable in theoretical terms, one that even some apt learners may not be able to articulate at all, or scarcely at all. So the only sense in which a moral teacher provides a standard or criterion is that in which she or he *is* in her or his own actions the standard or criterion.

We also make a mistake if we suppose that effective practical teachers of the virtues have as the subject matter of their teaching *ethics*. There is, on Aristotle's view, no such separate and distinctive subject matter for practical instruction. We learn how to act virtuously, while engaging in and learning how to act well in the activities of everyday social life. So we learn how to act courageously, for example, as part of learning how to live the military life – although not only the military life – and we learn how to act generously as part of learning how to manage or to share in managing the income and expenditures of a household. It is the good military instructor and the good teacher of domestic economy who teach us how to be courageous and to be generous. Virtues and vices are

24 *NE* 1105a31–33.

exercised as adverbial modifications of our actions in all our roles, functions, and crafts and, although there is such a thing as the teacher of theoretical ethics – it too is a craft – there is no distinct role for someone who might be thought of as a teacher of the virtues.

Aristotle's standpoint is thus very different from Piccolomini's. Where for Aristotle philosophy has the task of understanding the relationship between the actions and the practical reasoning of practically intelligent, particular agents in particular situations, for Piccolomini it is philosophy that itself educates us into that prudence which issues in right action. And where for Aristotle philosophy has the task of understanding how good laws, for both the enactment and the administration of which prudence is required, foster virtues in citizens, for Piccolomini it is philosophy that itself educates us into the kind of prudence that issues in good laws. Moral and political philosophy has been transformed into the keystone of education. It is true that Piccolomini never rules out the possibility of someone happening to become prudent and virtuous without having had a philosophical education. Just because nature and habit sometimes supply what is lacking by way of reason, occasionally good character emerges, independently of any acquaintance with moral and political philosophy.

Piccolomini's radical departure from Aristotle is all the more worth taking note of because something of much the same sort is found in the writings of some other Renaissance Aristotelians, ranging from Leonardo Bruni to John Case of Oxford University, who published his *Speculum quaestionum moralium, in Universam Ethicen Aristotelis* in 1585, two years after Piccolomini's book had appeared. In his *Isagogicon moralis philosophiae* of 1425 Bruni had recommended the *Nicomachean Ethics* to Galeotto Ricasoli, formerly commandant of the Florentine militia, as an indispensable guide to practice. Without knowledge of the first principles afforded by moral philosophy Ricasoli will be condemned "to live randomly." "All our error springs from this that we live without a defined end." And the knowledge of this defined end is to be provided by philosophy. John Case takes a similar view. Indeed his account of the place of moral philosophy in the practical education of moral agents is such that he has the problem of how philosophical knowledge and practical intelligence, prudence, are to be distinguished,[25] so closely has he assimilated them. He answers that moral philosophy stands to

---

25 John Case, *Speculum quaestionum moralium, in Universam Ethicen Aristotelis*, Oxford, Joseph Barnes, 1585, Book VI, ch. 5, p. 258.

prudence as genus to species. The exercise of prudence is in the application of the prescriptive generalizations of moral philosophy not to types of action – that falls within philosophy – but to particular circumstances.

In comparing Piccolomini's interpretation of Aristotle to that taken for granted by Bruni and that expounded by Case, and so suggesting that Piccolomini's views are in some important respects representative of the moral and political philosophy of Renaissance Aristotelianism, I do not mean to diminish or denigrate the distinctiveness of Piccolomini's achievement. Part of what makes his work distinctive is the Venetian flavor of his Aristotelianism. Anyone who aspires to identify her or his moral and political stances with those of Aristotle in any time and place has the task of explaining what that Aristotelianism amounts to in her or his particular local circumstances, in the context of the particular institutional framework that she or he inhabits. This task must have seemed in one way easier for Florentine and Venetian Aristotelians of the fifteenth and sixteenth centuries than it did to either their medieval predecessors or their modern successors. They after all inhabited city-states, just as Aristotle did. They did not have to interpret Aristotle's account of the *polis*, so that it had application to medieval kingdoms, as Aquinas had done, or to the institutions of modern nation-states, as A. C. Bradley was to do. And they were not haunted, as we moderns are, by a fear of anachronism.

So Piccolomini had no hesitation in treating the Venice of his day as in large measure an embodied Aristotelian polity and correspondingly in construing Aristotle in Venetian terms. Yet perhaps it was precisely in insisting upon this close fit between Aristotelian moral and political philosophy and sixteenth-century Venetian realities that Piccolomini assisted, quite contrary to his own intentions, in discrediting Aristotle's morals and politics, as perhaps in parallel fashion Case in England quite unintentionally contributed to the downfall of Aristotelian moral teaching. How so?

In the case of Piccolomini part of the answer lies simply in two discrepancies between on the one hand Aristotle's preferred type of polity and the virtues of its citizens and on the other the actualities of Venetian society and the qualities of character valued by Venetians. First, there is a contradiction at the heart of Piccolomini's enterprise. For he treats the Venetian senators of his own day explicitly and their predecessors by implication as models of virtue and more especially of prudence. Yet he also insists that a philosophical education is generally, even if not always, a prerequisite for the acquisition of prudence. But the Venetian senators of his own and past generations had not in fact received anything like the kind of philosophical education that Piccolomini commends. They would instead have been schooled in the *studia humanitatis*, educated exclusively in ways that were, on Piccolomini's view, insufficient to supply what is needed for a moral education. So the Venetian senators whom Piccolomini addresses are in their own lives counterexamples to the principal thesis that he urges them to accept. And Piccolomini seems not to have noticed this.

Secondly, if we were to classify Venice in terms drawn from Aristotle's *Politics*, it would have to be as one of those commercial oligarchies of which Aristotle is severely critical. An important and valued trait of character in the citizens of commercial oligarchies generally and of Venice in particular is acquisitiveness. What was valued among Venetians was a kind of acquisitiveness that was informed by adventurousness, yet also tempered by prudence, not the prudence of *phronēsis* or of medieval *prudentia*, but prudence in the modern sense, a self-regarding care for one's own interests that safeguards one from disasters incurred by too adventurous a spirit. Yet acquisitiveness, so necessary for successful capitalist development, is to be found in the Aristotelian scheme of the virtues only as "*pleonexia*," "*Mehrundmehrwollhaben*," as Nietzsche translated it, the vice of injustice.

In this light Piccolomini's enterprise seems Quixotic. For he was attempting to get his fellow citizens to understand themselves in Aristotelian terms, while their habits, their inclinations, and their institutions all presented significant obstacles to achieving this goal. And, since other sixteenth-century Aristotelians faced very much the same difficulties in their enterprise, the question of why Renaissance Aristotelianism as a moral and political enterprise failed may not be too difficult to answer. The problem may rather be why it flourished in so many places for as long as it did.

III

Yet something more needs to be said about the defeat of Aristotelian morals and politics in the early modern period. At the beginning of this essay I argued that anyone who claims that Aristotelian morals and politics have contemporary relevance is under an obligation to specify just what kind of practice it is within which in his particular time and place the form of an Aristotelian moral and political life can be realized. And I have now argued that Piccolomini, like a number of other

Renaissance Aristotelians, recognized and attempted to discharge that obligation, but was mistaken in supposing that the established institutional and habitual modes of sixteenth-century Venetian life were congruent with and hospitable to a genuinely Aristotelian morals and politics. I have also suggested that at least some other Renaissance Aristotelians made similar mistakes. Yet the outcome of my overall argument is not a claim that the root cause of the failure of Renaissance Aristotelianism was that the social, cultural, moral, and political ethos of the age was too inimical to its reception. Something like this latter thesis has been advanced by J. B. Schneewind in "The Misfortunes of Virtue,"[26] although with reference to the seventeenth rather than to the sixteenth century. Among the misfortunes that, on Schneewind's view, prevented an Aristotelian conception of the virtues from surviving beyond the seventeenth century three stand out and all of them have to do with the cultural ethos, an ethos friendly, so Schneewind claims, to the natural law ethics of Grotius and Pufendorf, but hostile to the virtue ethics of Aristotle.

The first of these is what Schneewind, following Thomas Reid, takes to be an incompatibility between Christian conceptions of divine law and Aristotelian virtue ethics.[27] Schneewind's wonderfully brief and compressed treatment of this large question in two paragraphs may tempt us to be unjustly dismissive. We should reject this temptation. For Schneewind is certainly right in at least this: there are both Protestant and Catholic strains influential within sixteenth- and seventeenth-century Christianity that view Aristotelian ethics as incompatible with Christian orthodoxy. But this does not explain very much, since in the periods in which Aristotelian ethics had flourished among Christians, the same antiAristotelian claims had been made, although less influentially. A second misfortune of virtue ethics was, so Schneewind claims, the appeal that Aristotelians make to the standard provided by the character and actions of the *phronimos* and to the insights of the *phronimos*. Once again Schneewind's way of putting his point may get in the way of our recognizing the truth in what he says. "The Aristotelian theory may have been suited to a society in which there was a recognized class of superior citizens, whose judgment on moral issues would be accepted without question. But the Grotians did not believe that they lived in such a world."[28] One does not have to accept this eccentric notion of the *phronimoi* as a class whose judgments others ought to accept, but could

---

26 *Ethics* 101, 1, October 1990, pp. 42–63.
27 Ibid., pp. 44–45.   28 Ibid., p. 62.

have no good reason to accept, to recognize that it is true that at a certain point in time *phronēsis* was no longer included in the standard catalogue of the virtues and that "prudence" and its cognates underwent just that change of meaning which I noticed in passing earlier. But once again we may need to look in a different direction for an explanation.

A third misfortune that Schneewind supposes Aristotelian virtue ethics to have encountered in the seventeenth century arose from its inability to deal adequately with moral disagreement and conflict. For such an ethics moral disagreement must, so Schneewind asserts, derive from a flaw in the character of at least one of the contending parties and Schneewind infers that if I, as an Aristotelian, am involved in such disagreement, I will always be minded to accuse my opponents of defective moral character, rather than trying to resolve the disagreement rationally.[29] Yet this is seldom, if ever, the type of reason advanced by sixteenth- and seventeenth-century antiAristotelians for rejecting Aristotle's account. Indeed the major moral and political conflicts of the seventeenth century were not resolvable in Aristotelian terms, if only because the protagonists of the major contending positions had by then formulated their disagreements in terms that presupposed the falsity of Aristotle's morals and politics.

Schneewind's case is then that Aristotelian morals and politics had become socially irrelevant: "We need not think that Grotius and Pufendorf had refuted Aristotle; for the cultivated Europe of their age . . . they displaced his understanding of morality with another one,"[30] one that spoke to the condition of those whose moral vocabulary was no longer Aristotelian and who lacked the presuppositions on which Aristotelian arguments would have relied. And this is true. But it still leaves the displacement of Aristotelian morals and politics to be adequately explained. I am suggesting that the moral to be drawn from the story of Piccolomini is that, by the time that the scene was set for Grotius and Pufendorf to make their impact, Aristotelians such as Piccolomini and Case had already contrived their own defeat. Had Grotius and Pufendorf never written or had their works fallen stillborn from the presses, Aristotelian moral theory would still have been discredited, not by hostile external critics, but by the Aristotelians themselves. How so?

Piccolomini, like Case and some other Aristotelians, placed upon the Aristotelian moral philosopher the burden of a function that no

29 Ibid., p. 62.   30 Ibid., p. 48.

philosopher qua philosopher could ever discharge. For he presented the moral philosopher as one whose role as analyst and enquirer into moral theory is subordinate to and undertaken for the sake of discharging the role of moral teacher. But the teaching of moral philosophy never of itself transforms the character of its students. And, if we had not already learned this from long practical experience, we should have been able to learn it from the *Nicomachean Ethics*. There are many kinds of moral educator and the education that they provide is of various kinds: parents, aunts, school teachers, pastors, drill sergeants, workmates, friends, and saints. They succeed by inculcating habits, eliciting desires, redirecting sentiments, punishing us for, among other things, acting only so as to avoid punishment, and providing examples and role-models, so that Aristotle's phrase "judging as the *phronimos* would judge" begins to find practical application in and to their pupils' experience. But they *never* succeed in forming character or directing lives by presenting theoretical arguments and analyses. And, if they attempted to do so, they would discredit themselves, just as Piccolomini and a number of his Aristotelian contemporaries did.

From this I have already drawn two conclusions. The first is that Renaissance Aristotelianism in morals and politics was defeated by its own pretensions rather than by the arguments of its rivals or by an inhospitable social and cultural climate. The second is that those characteristics of Renaissance Aristotelianism in morals and politics that ensured this defeat were precisely those in which it differed from and had misinterpreted Aristotle. It was not after all Aristotle who was rejected in the moral and political debates of the Renaissance, but rather a simulacrum of Aristotle, an ingenious philosophical invention. What should we learn from this?

We have been set a problem. On the one hand Aristotle insisted that the kind of knowledge of our ultimate end that is provided by his philosophical enquiries is of practical relevance and importance. It is no piece of *mere* theory. On the other he made it equally plain that what directs us towards that end in our particular practical judgments and actions is not theoretical reflection, but a kind of habituation. How are those two related? To this question I turn in a second essay.

CHAPTER 2

Rival Aristotles: Aristotle against some modern Aristotelians

I

Aristotelian moral philosophers of the Renaissance generally had no doubt that what directed right action was a knowledge of the ultimate end of human beings. Knowledge of that end provides us with one set of premises for our practical reasoning, knowledge of this or that particular agent's particular circumstances another. Conjoin those sets of premises and from them the agent will by sound inferences be able to reach a true conclusion about what is to be done. Those philosophers thus affirmed versions of what Sarah Broadie has denounced as "the 'Grand End' view of practical wisdom."[1] The virtuous agent on this view (Broadie ascribes it to John Cooper, Anthony Kenny, and myself: I am not sure that she is quite right about any one of us, but she would certainly have been right in ascribing it to Leonardo Bruni or Francesco Piccolomini or John Case) begins from what Broadie calls a "grand picture" of "the human good without restriction," a vision "invested with a content different from what would be aimed at by morally inferior natures."[2] "A choice shows practical wisdom only if . . . given the facts as seen by the agent, enacting the choice would lead to the realization of his grand picture" and "his grand picture is a true or acceptable account of the good."[3]

Broadie is not claiming that those who hold the Grand End view believe that rational agents on all occasions explicitly argue from premises about the Grand End to immediate practical conclusions. But she does take it that, on the Grand End view, practical reasoning can be reconstructed and justified, only if choice and action can be shown to aim at the Grand End. This thesis she herself of course rejects and she takes Aristotle

---

1 *Ethics with Aristotle*, New York: Oxford University Press, 1991, pp. 198–202.
2 Ibid., p. 198.   3 Ibid., p. 198.

to reject it. The ends towards the realization of which our deliberation is directed are, on her view, immediate and heterogeneous, "anything that a person finds desirable without having to think about it."[4] But since I am here concerned with what Broadie denies rather than with what she asserts, I need not develop her view further.

John McDowell's account of what Aristotle understood by deliberation differs significantly from Broadie's. But he does agree with her in rejecting much of what she rejects. More particularly he rejects the following interpretation of Aristotle's account of deliberation. "The end proposed, doing well, is a universal, and the problem is to arrive at an instance of it. That can suggest that deliberation of this sort requires arriving at, or otherwise availing myself of a blueprint in universal terms and applying it to the circumstances at hand. But this picture does not fit Aristotle."[5]

It is true, he agrees, that "grasp of the universal that forms the content of a correct conception of doing well" is involved in doing well. But that grasp, according to McDowell's Aristotle, "need not be isolable, even in principle, as a component in the propensity to put the end of doing well" into practice in specific situations.[6] Our grasp of the end of doing well is not something external to our dispositions and the actions that issue from them. The question of the correctness of those actions for those "with a properly formed character" who "have learned to see certain actions as worth undertaking on the ground that they are noble" is resolved into "a series of piecemeal questions, whether this or that action is correctly seen as noble." And these questions "arise within the conceptual and motivational outlook" produced by the right kind of upbringing. To suppose that an external validation is needed "reflects a kind of anxiety that is peculiarly modern."[7]

Broadie and McDowell, rejecting what the one calls a Grand End and the other a universal blueprint, put themselves at the opposite end of the spectrum of interpretations of Aristotle's views on practical rationality from such Renaissance Aristotelians as Bruni, Piccolomini, and Case. Where Bruni, Piccolomini, Case, and others think that they have learned from Aristotle that knowledge of the ultimate end is of indispensable practical relevance to individual moral agents in their deliberations as to how to act here and now, Broadie and McDowell treat such knowledge as

---

4 Ibid., p. 233.
5 "Deliberation and Moral Development in Aristotle's Ethics" in *Aristotle, Kant and the Stoics. Rethinking Happiness and Duty*, Cambridge: Cambridge University Press, 1996, p. 21.
6 Ibid., p. 24.   7 Ibid., p. 30.

irrelevant to such agents. This does not of course at all preclude its having another kind of relevance.

Richard Bodéüs has suggested what that might be.[8] Bodéüs, like Broadie and McDowell, distinguishes sharply between the kind of practical intelligence that agents need in particular situations and knowledge of the ultimate end of human beings, although his characterization of that contrast is very much his own. His focus is on the nature *of phronēsis*: "Aristotelian prudence . . . has the function of inquiring into (particular) means and not that of theoretical enquiry about the (general) end"[9] and it is the possession of moral virtue that, by directing the agent towards her or his good, differentiates the *phronimos* from the *deinos*, the merely clever or crafty deviser of means. Moral virtue does indeed involve correct opinion about the principles of good action, but what is involved here is not a theoretical grasp of the end, but what Bodéüs characterizes as "a form of intuitive knowledge."[10] What then is the point of theoretical enquiry about the human end?

Bodéüs answers this question by an interpretation of what Aristotle says about education in the closing passages of the *Nicomachean Ethics*, where Aristotle reiterates what he had said earlier,[11] that only those who already have virtuous habits are able and willing to listen to sound reasoning about moral and political matters. "For Aristotle, therefore, the knowing (*to eidenai*) acquired through teaching by discourses amounts to an external regulator, useful only for the learner whose actions obey reason, an internal regulator."[12] But, we may ask, if the virtuous agent already obeys reason, what useful knowledge can she or he acquire from arguments and discourses? Bodéüs replies that what theoretical enquiry provides is what is needed by the legislator and more generally by those who superintend the *polis* and the household. The function of the *polis* and the household is to make good citizens and good human beings through enacting good laws and administering them well. The sciences of ethics and politics provide the knowledge necessary for achieving this end, by teaching us how to bring into being and sustain that framework within

---

8 *The Political Dimension of Aristotle's Ethics*, tr. J. E. Garrett, Albany: State University of New York Press, 1993; originally *Le philosophe et la cité*, Paris, Publications de la Faculté de Philosophie et Lettres de l'Université de Liège, 1982.
9 Ibid., p.33.
10 Ibid., p. 35.
11 *NE* 1179b24–31; see 1095a10–11.
12 Bodéüs, *Political Dimension*, p. 53.

which the right kind of habituation into virtue of the young will take place. And the intended audiences of the lectures that became the *Nico-machean Ethics* and the *Politics* are those with not only the right kind of habituation, but also the necessary experience to qualify them as potential legislators, judges, heads of households, and the like.

Bodéüs, then, like Broadie and McDowell, makes knowledge of the ultimate end of human beings irrelevant to their practical deliberations on what to do here and now in this or that particular situation, once they have been well trained. In so doing all three have emphasized an import-ant truth, both about how Aristotle is to be understood and about universal practical experience. It is clear that, according to Aristotle, practical habituation is in all cases necessary for the acquisition and exercise of the moral virtues and therefore for *phronēsis* (since there is no *phronēsis* without moral virtue and no moral virtue without *phronēsis*), and that it may be and sometimes is sufficient for the acquisition and exercise of those virtues. A *phronimos* who happens *never* to reflect on the ultimate end of human beings is not a contradiction in terms. And, for many of us at least, our own experience of the best human beings that we have known attests that human goodness and inarticulateness about, indeed lack of interest in reflection upon ultimate ends can indeed be found together.

Moreover, even if we argue, as I shall presently do, that on any plau-sible view of practical reasoning reflection on the ultimate good for human beings must play some part in that reasoning, even if not for every practical reasoner, it is clear that one aspect of Broadie's condem-nation of Grand End views is undeniable. We do not proceed by *first* acquiring a vision of the Grand End and only secondarily deducing from it what we ought to do. Not even Piccolomini or Case believed quite this (I think that for them the acquisition of knowledge of the end and acquisition of the virtues proceed *pari passu*), although Bruni writes as if he did. And Broadie is clearly in the right in rejecting this both as an interpretation of Aristotle's views and as an account of practical experience.

Yet, even when this has been said, there are sufficient grounds for rejecting any dichotomous reading of Aristotle that makes the practical reasoning of agents in particular situations one thing and a theoretical knowledge of the human good quite another, so that the latter cannot enter into the former, so that reflective reasoning about the human good cannot itself become practically and immediately relevant. And I shall suggest that, if Aristotle had held the kind of view imputed to him by

Broadie, McDowell, and Bodéüs, he too would have made an important mistake about practical reasoning.

I begin by suggesting two different kinds of doubt about the dichotomous reading of Aristotle. First, there are those passages in which Aristotle asserts the practical utility of theoretically grounded knowledge of the good and this in a way that does not obviously lend itself to Bodéüs's interpretation. In his critique of Plato in Book I of the *Nicomachean Ethics* Aristotle made it clear that the human good must be characterized, so that it is true of it that it is attainable.[13] And earlier he has already remarked that knowledge of it will make a great difference to life, since it will provide us with a mark to aim at.[14] Add to this that it is the greatest of goods and it is difficult not to conclude that the knowledge of it which Aristotle is engaged in providing for us must be, on his view, of very real practical utility. And there is further evidence that this is how Aristotle understood his own enquiry.

Richard Kraut, in the course of arguing against Broadie's view,[15] has drawn attention to a passage from Book I of the *Eudemian Ethics*:

Since we have established that every one that has the power to live according to his own choice should set up for himself some object of the good life to aim at, honor or reputation or wealth or education (since evidently it *is* a mark of much folly not to have organized one's life with regard to some end) it is therefore most necessary first to decide . . . in which of our [activities] the good life consists and what it is without which human beings cannot achieve it.[16]

To anyone who suggests that Aristotle nowhere says this quite so straightforwardly in the *Nicomachean Ethics* we should reply not only that nothing in the *Nicomachean Ethics* is inconsistent with this, but also that we could scarcely have a better characterization of the project undertaken by Aristotle in the first book of the *Nicomachean Ethics*. So that it should be unsurprising that Aristotle tells us in Book II that his theoretical enquiry does not have as its final aim the acquisition of theoretical knowledge, but rather that "we are enquiring . . . in order to become good,"[17] an assertion suggesting strongly that the acquisition of theoretical knowledge about ends and means may on occasion itself be a means for becoming good.

---

13 *NE* 1096b31–35.   14 *NE* 1094a22–24.

15 In "In Defense of the Grand End," *Ethics* 103, 2, January 1993; I am much indebted to Kraut's article and to his writings in general.

16 *NE* 1214b6–14.   17 *NE* 1103b28.

Secondly, if we accept from Bodéüs the thesis that legislators for and rulers over cities and households need theoretical knowledge of the human end, it seems difficult to avoid the conclusion that others too may need it for their individual purposes. Note first that, on Aristotle's account, any theoretical knowledge possessed by legislators and judges can only become practical through the exercise of *phronēsis*, either the *phronēsis* of the legislator or that political *phronēsis* which is exercised in implementing decrees through deliberation and action.[18] Both of these make use of the findings of the science of politics. Later on in Book X Aristotle remarks that it seems fitting for each of us to guide our own children and friends into virtue and that to achieve this it would be well for individuals to become what legislators are.[19] This parallel between what individuals need in order to live as they should with their friends and children and what the legislator needs in order to contrive the right kind of life for the *polis* fits very well with Aristotle's earlier claims that one cannot be concerned about one's own good without being also concerned about the good of one's household and the good of one's political community[20] and that those who understand what is good for themselves and for human beings in general are also considered good at managing households and cities.[21] There is after all, on Aristotle's view, no such thing as the good of the individual qua individual, apart from and independent of the good of that individual qua member of a household and qua citizen. But, if this is so, then any sharp contrast between the *phronēsis* needed by the individual qua individual and the theoretical knowledge needed by the individual qua legislator breaks down. In both capacities individuals need to exercise *phronēsis* and on occasion also some theoretical knowledge.

These two sets of passages then seem to present insuperable obstacles for any dichotomous interpretation. And this is perhaps just as well, since, were one of the dichotomizing interpretations correct, Aristotle's account of practical reasoning would be seriously defective. To understand why this is so, I turn now to an examination of the nature of practical reasoning and of the virtue of *phronēsis*.

---

18 *NE* 1141b23–28.   19 *NE* 1180a30–34.
20 *NE* 1142a8–10.   21 *NE* 1140b7–11.

II

Phronēsis is the virtue of those who know how to do what is good, indeed what is best, in particular situations and who are disposed by their character traits to do it. To do what it is good and best to do in a particular situation is to act *kata ton orthon logon*;[22] it is to judge and to feel and to act in accordance with the mean of virtue and that mean is determined by right reason.[23] How then do we employ right reasoning in doing what is best?

There is no set of rules to invoke, nothing therefore that corresponds to Kantian maxims or to the rules of a rule-utilitarian. It is true that on Aristotle's account there are certain kinds of action that ought never to be performed: acts of homicide, theft, adultery, lying. But to know this is to know only what we are all and always precluded from doing. It is not to answer the question of how it is best for me to act here and now in these particular circumstances.

Part of what precludes answering this question by applying a rule or a set of rules is that part of the agent's task is to select, from a multiplicity of potentially relevant considerations arising out of the agent's past history, the agent's relationship to others, and the particularities of the agent's present situation those that are actually relevant to the agent's immediate choice of action. And to do this the agent has to be able to draw upon past experience both of what causes what under particular circumstances and of the range of heterogeneous goods, goods as various as those of, for example, courage, justice, glory, pleasure of assorted kinds, wit, and honor, in order to identify what the key differences are between the different courses of action open to her or him. Insofar as appeal to some particular rule is on occasion among the relevant considerations in identifying such differences, the judgment that it is relevant cannot itself be derived from any rule.

Two kinds of mistake can be made by an agent in the course of deliberating: "either about the universal or about the particular; either that all waters that weigh heavy are unhealthy (*phaula*) or that this water weighs heavy."[24] An agent who makes either kind of mistake will fail to judge *kata ton orthon logon*, since right reasoning requires that the agent's reasoning must be true and the agent's desire rightly directed.[25] The

---

22 *NE* 1103b32.   23 *NE* 1138b21–25.
24 *NE* 1142a22–23.   25 *NE* 1139a23–24.

agent's judgment that it is this or that here and now that it is good for her or him to do expresses the agent's desire. The premises from which that judgment derives must be true, if judgment and action are to accord with right reasoning. But, although these conditions must be satisfied, if either vice or incontinence[26] is to be avoided, we need not suppose and should not suppose that the agent who deliberates well does so by first constructing a piece of practical reasoning and then acting on it. It is rather that the action itself gives expression to the conclusion of a piece of practical reasoning[27] and that what makes the action adequate or inadequate as an answer to the question "What is it best for me to do now?" is the adequacy or inadequacy of the reasoning to whose conclusion it gives expression.

Phronēsis involves, but is not to be identified with, a certain kind of perception, not the sense-perception by which we are acquainted with particulars, but a kind of seeing that, analogous to the mathematician's perception that a triangle is one of the ultimate components of a certain sort of figure.[28] What such perception enables us to grasp are the universal and the particular *together*. Our grasp of the universal arises out of our grasp of the particular and seeing the particular in this or that light is what perception affords. Such perception, says Aristotle, I call *nous*.[29]

What Aristotle thereby makes clear is that any attempt to contrast a conception of the agent as having an intuitive grasp of what it is that is to be done and why with a conception of the agent as arguing from premises to a practical conclusion, and even more any attempt to present these as in opposition to one another, is a mistake. *What* the rational agent grasps intuitively in acting as she or he does can only be articulated in the form of an argument and it is only through evaluating that argument that we can evaluate the agent's judgment and action. But, if this is so, at once questions arise.

III

If practical judgments and actions give expression to deductive arguments, insofar as they are rational, then standard questions about the soundness of those arguments may always be apposite. What types of inference are

---

26 *NE* 1147b20–29.   27 *De Motu Animalium* 701a8–13.

28 *NE* 1142a27–30.

29 *NE* 1143b2–5; I am very much indebted to David Wiggins's interpretative translation in "Deliberation and Practical Reason" in *Essays on Aristotle's Ethics*, ed. A. O. Rorty, Berkeley: University of California Press, 1980.

involved? And are the arguments valid? (There are of course important issues about the nature of the rules of inference in practical reasoning. But here I put these on one side.) Are their premises true? And how do we know this? From what further premises can these be derived as conclusions? Aristotle remarked that "The syllogisms of practice have as their first premise (*archē*): 'Since the end (*telos*) and the best is of such and such a kind', whatever it may be (let it be, for the sake of argument, whatever one pleases) . . ."[30] If he is right, then one condition of the soundness of a particular agent's particular argument on a particular occasion is not only that one at least of his premises in that argument follows as a conclusion from a statement of what *the* end and *the* best is, that is, of what the human good is, but also that that statement is true. So that there is, on Aristotle's view, this possibility of appeal to an external standard to confirm or disconfirm an agent's conviction that she or he has indeed a genuine intuitive grasp of what it is is good and best for her or him to do.

Aristotle goes on in the same passage to say that what the end and the best is is not evident, except to a good human being. "For badness distorts and causes us to be deceived about the first premises (*archas*) of action."[31] That is to say, intellectual and moral defect will be closely associated. But it does not follow that an agent suffering from such defect might not become aware of this by comparing her or his actions and judgments with those that would, on the basis of a theoretical understanding, be required in order to achieve one's ultimate end qua human being.

Consider first what might prevent someone from making this comparison. Aristotle in his discussion of the Spartan constitution criticizes not only the Spartan constitution, but also the Spartan character, in which he identifies two serious flaws. The Spartans make their laws with an eye only to part of virtue, the courage of the soldier when at war, rather than to the whole of virtue. And they understand even that virtue only as a means to the goods that are obtained and preserved by military courage, so encouraging greed for those goods.[32] Notice that the Spartans themselves have no means of identifying these errors, let alone of correcting them. Why not?

The answer is that their whole mode of life and the upbringing of young Spartans to prepare them for that mode of life exclude respect for the goods of reflective thought. Spartan deliberation is – of course – laconic. The Spartans do not look beyond the ends immediately presented

30 *NE* 1144a31–33.   31 *NE* 1144a34–36.
32 *Politics* 1271b2–17.

to them as desirable, ends which they have been habituated to regard as the only desirable ends. They are the victims of their upbringing just because it has deprived them of the ability to reflect, either individually or collectively, upon the limitations of that upbringing. To identify those limitations and to understand why they are limitations and what their causes are is possible only from an external standpoint.

Let us then cautiously propose the hypothesis that one of the marks of a good upbringing is that it is a type of upbringing that does not imprison one, but allows one to view it from some other standpoint. And consider in this light Aristotle's discussions of justice both in the *Politics* and in the *Ethics*. On Bodéüs's account, indeed on any plausible account, Aristotle's intended audience for his lectures would have been composed of future legislators, political leaders, and heads of household. And they would have been drawn from different Greek cities and very likely also from Macedonia and from different parties and groupings within these cities. Both in the *Ethics* and in the *Politics* Aristotle emphasizes the disagreements as well as the agreements that democrats and different types of oligarch have over justice[33] and argues for his own view as a corrective to their partial and one-sided views.

But these partial and one-sided views would have been the views of some members of his audience. Aristotle argues with and against them not just in order to correct their philosophical account of justice, but also in order to transform their practice. That is, he advances arguments that are designed both to reveal the inadequacies of their upbringing and to correct them. And he offers them the standpoint of theoretical enquiry as one external to their upbringing from which that upbringing can be criticized to practical effect.

Three features of this project deserve special attention. First, although what justice requires in the *polis*, in the household, and in one's relationships to one's friends is not the same, the virtue of justice in an individual is such – excluding, as it does, *pleonexia* and requiring, as it does, a desire for fairness – that failure in one of these spheres seems bound to entail failure in the others. Indeed the unity of the virtues, on Aristotle's view, is such that failure in justice would surely have to involve failure in certain other virtues whose scope is less political than that of justice. So to correct the effect of someone's upbringing by arguments about justice is going to involve a significant transformation

---

33 *NE* 1131a24–9; 1161a10–1161b10; 1301a25–1301b4.

of their overall character. And to say this is to reiterate the point that a moral character for Aristotle cannot but have a political dimension. "A good human being, but no good at politics" is a verdict incompatible with Aristotle's ethics and politics.

Secondly, what kind of knowledge must someone have in order to transform character in this way? Not only knowledge of justice, for, even when it has been argued that such and such is just, the question can always be raised as to whether what is just *is* always good. In the *Rhetoric* Aristotle cites examples of this kind of debate, considering the case of someone who argues that "the just is not wholly good, for were it wholly good, whatever happens justly would be good, but to be put to death justly is not desirable."[34] What will such a person, or someone who aspires to respond to the argument, have to know? Aristotle has already answered this question: "About justice, whether it is good or not, we must argue from the characteristics of the just and the good."[35] It is difficult to suppose that the *Rhetoric is* not, in this as in other respects, self-referential, a lecturer reflecting not only on other people's discourses, but also on his own, as to how what he has to say about justice and the good may be said not only with sound argument, but persuasively.[36] So the study of the good is required for the study of justice.

Thirdly, those who are able to be persuaded by this kind of argument, in such a way that it has an effect on their character and actions, must already have a well-formed character. Aristotle insists that those who do not as yet have a tolerably well-formed character, either by reason of their youth or their failure, as they age, to mature, are immune to rational argument. We should not infer that those with an already well-formed character will have no need of further argument to lay bare possible limitations and defects to which even a well-formed character may be prone. What kinds of limitations might these be?

The discussion of the Spartans should already have suggested an answer, one that needs to be spelled out in terms of the twofold character of practical reasoning. The practical reasoner asks and answers two questions: "What is it good and best for me to do here and now in this particular situation?" and "Does each of the various types of good that it is open to me to pursue, achieve and enjoy have its due place in my life or

34 *Rhetoric* 1397a20–22.   35 Ibid., 1396a31–33.

36 See Larry Arnhart, *Aristotle on Political Reasoning*, DeKalb: Northern Illinois University Press, 1981, especially chapters 3 and 6 and Eugene Garver, *Aristotle's Rhetoric: An Art of Character*, Chicago: University of Chicago Press, 1994.

do some goods have too large a place and others too small a place, so that although what I pursue are in general goods, they are not goods for me with my particular character and responsibilities at this particular stage of my life?"

These questions cannot be answered in independence from one another. The answers that one gives to the first will always presuppose some particular set of answers to the second. For in judging on a range of particular occasions that it is best to do such and such in these circumstances and so and so in these other circumstances we presuppose some classification and rank ordering of goods, some underlying judgment about what place this or that type of good ought to have in our lives and in human life in general. Each of us has, I take it, just such a rank ordering. And for me to become aware of what my rank ordering is for me to become aware of the hierarchy of ends towards the achievement of which my activities are directed, a hierarchy that gives expression to my conception both of what the good life for human beings in general is and what the good life for me is. So that, when I ask whether or not this or that type of good has its due place in my life, I also put in question some range of my practical judgments on particular occasions about what it is best for me to do here and now.

We all of us then begin our adult lives with some classification and rank ordering of goods, some hierarchy of ends, some implicit or partially explicit conception of the human good that we have acquired from our upbringing and from the culture into which that upbringing was an initiation. But the range of goods to which we need to be responsive changes as we pass through the different stages of life, something that Aristotle recognizes in his discussion of who should serve the *polis* as a soldier and who as a judge. Aristotle's answer is that it should be the same individuals, but at different stages in their lives, but he goes on to remark that the activities of soldiers must be such that they prepare citizens for what they will have to do when the time of soldiering is over.[37] And it is not only here that Aristotle recognizes that what is good for one at one stage of life is not the same as what is good for one at another. In the *Rhetoric* he remarks that what is excellence in the bodies of the young is not the same as excellence in the bodies of the mature adult or the trained athlete or those who are old.[38]

---

37 *Politics* 1329a2–17.   38 *Rhetoric* 1361b7–14.

It will therefore be a sign of *phronēsis* [39] to recognize that the pursuit of different goods should have a different place in one's activities at different ages. And it will be a grave defect and limitation in someone to continue to pursue at some later time goods the pursuit of which was appropriate only at some earlier stage. It will be an even greater defect and limitation not to be able to engage in the relevant kind of self-criticism. What sort of argument would such self-criticism need to deploy? They will be of the kind that Aristotle supplies, often in abbreviated form, both in the *Nicomachean Ethics* and in the *Rhetoric*. In the latter he proceeds from arguments concerning the definition of goodness to the evaluation of goods and evils as greater or lesser, and next to the goodness of the virtues, of pleasure, and of a variety of activities and capacities. He then discusses what may appear to be goods, when not in fact such. In the former he proceeds initially in the opposite direction, beginning from a classification of types of good in order to move towards an account of what it is to be unqualifiedly good and of what is unqualifiedly good. And what emerges in both discussions are a number of rank orderings of goods in terms of the "for the sake of" relationship.

So Aristotle provides us with standards for the rational evaluation of our present rank orderings of goods. In order to apply those standards I need both a knowledge of myself, of my abilities, my character and my circumstances, and a knowledge too of the full range of goods that I am not presently pursuing, but that it might be good for me to achieve. This latter knowledge the Spartans notably lacked; but a lack of awareness of the full range of goods of which we need to be aware may be found even in those with a much less constricted upbringing than the Spartans. Aristotle himself considers in various places the goods peculiar to a wide range of occupations: those of the soldier, the athlete, the philosopher, the tragic or comic poet, the holder of political office, and the musician, but he notoriously excludes from citizenship and therefore from full moral education both those whose labor is manual and women, and in so doing he also excludes from view – and in so doing exhibits his own errors and self-deceptions – the goods to be achieved by farming and other forms of manual labor and the goods of those household activities, including the upbringing of small children, which he understands as proper occupations only for women.

---

39 *Politics* 1329a14–16.

Here once again, in identifying the defects of Aristotle's own moral standpoint, the importance of his emphasis on the unity of the moral and the political life emerges. Just because I cannot deliberate about my own good without deliberating about the good of my political community and vice versa, so too the criticism of my own character as unresponsive to some particular set of virtues and excellences always raises the question of whether it is only myself or also my political community that fails, as the Greek *polis* failed in its constraints upon women and its subjection of slaves. And, when we ourselves judge some alien standpoint from without, as Aristotle judged the Spartans and as we judge Aristotle, then the relationship between our judgment of individual character and our judgment of the standards that structure the social and political life within which that kind of character flourishes is characteristically easier to discern than it is in our judgments about ourselves.

It is in the self-scrutiny that is involved in deliberating about character that we have to bring together considerations that arise from the contingencies of our own particular circumstances and considerations that are grounded in the knowledge provided by theory. To say that any agent who seriously and persistently asks the questions "What place should the pursuit of this or that good have in my life?" and "What kind of human being should I become?" has to draw upon considerations grounded in philosophical theorizing about the nature of the human good is not of course to say that such agents have themselves to become fully fledged moral philosophers or even to apply themselves to the study of moral philosophy. To think so was the mistake of such Renaissance Aristotelians as Piccolomini. But it is to say that, if an agent were to articulate the rational grounds for her or his rank ordering of goods in this way rather than that, he or she would have to become to some significant extent a moral philosopher.

What philosophical enquiry achieves, on the view that I am ascribing to Aristotle, is an outline sketch of what it would be for any rational animal to achieve its specific good, constructing by dialectical argument an account of what *eudaimonia* cannot consist in, that is, in such lives as the life of moneymaking, the life of sensual pleasure, or the life for which political honor is a sufficient end, and what it must be, a life of activities that give expression to the several moral and intellectual virtues, a life of friendships and of engagement in political activity, a life that moves towards a perfected understanding of that life and of its place in the universe. What such philosophical enquiry also constructs is a specification of the forms of deductive argument by which we would, if everything relevant to our judgments, passions, and actions were made explicit, move from premises concerning the nature of the good life for rational animals and the function of the virtues in achieving the ends of such a life through intermediate steps concerning what particular virtues require in particular types of circumstance to ultimate conclusions about what it is good and best for me to do in *these* circumstances here and now.

What such a theoretical account, the kind of account given in the *Nicomachean Ethics*, the *Politics*, and the *Rhetoric*, does not supply and cannot supply is the knowledge of how to apply this knowledge to my particular circumstances. And it cannot do so, because in morals and politics we do not begin with theory and then, only secondarily, find application for theory in practice. If we attempt to do this, then either that attempt will be empty and fruitless, as by and large it was with the Renaissance Aristotelians, or it will lead to distortions of practice, as it sometimes does when contemporary practitioners of so-called Applied Ethics conceive of the relationship of theory to practice in this way. How then does theory become practical?

It does so as the terminus for the rational justification of practical judgment and action. We cannot but begin from the immediacies of practical judgment, from enquiring more or less reflectively what reasons we have for doing this rather than that and whether they are sufficiently good reasons. We then on occasion find that we have to ask what makes a sufficiently good reason sufficiently good and how it is distinguished from insufficiently good reasons. And, if we press this question systematically, we shall find that good reasons for doing this rather than that are also good reasons for becoming this kind of person rather than that, for acquiring this or that kind of character. Since what discriminates one kind of character from another is how goods are rank ordered by the agent, and since each rank ordering of goods embodies some conception of what the good life for human beings is, we will be unable to justify our choices until and unless we can justify some conception of the human good. And to do this we will have to resort to theory as the justification of practice.

Rationality however does not necessarily, nor even generally, require that we move to this point. I may on many types of occasion judge rightly and rationally that it is here and now desirable and choiceworthy that I do so and so, without having to enquire whether this type of action is genuinely desirable and choiceworthy for someone such as myself. I may on many types of occasion judge rightly and rationally that this type of action is desirable and choiceworthy for someone such as myself, without having to enquire whether the type of character that it exemplifies is genuinely good character. And I may judge rightly and rationally on many types of occasion that this type of character is indeed better than that, without having to enquire about the nature of the human good. Yet insofar as my judgment and action are right and rational they will be such as would have been endorsed by someone who had followed out this chain of enquiry to the end (in two senses of "end"). It is always as if the rational agent's judgment and action were the conclusion of a chain of reasoning whose first premise was "Since *the* good and *the* best is such and such . . ." But it is only in retrospect that our actions can be understood in this way. Deduction can never take the place of the exercise of *phronēsis.*

The rational moral agent therefore always may, but seldom needs to end up as a moral and political philosopher. Yet moral and political philosophers always have to begin from their own experience as rational moral agents and, if they have had a defective upbringing, or if for some other reason the formation and the development of their character has gone astray, then they will also be defective as moral philosophers and no amount of reasoning will help them. For "reason is not the teacher of first principles, whether in mathematics or with respect to actions; it is virtue that is the teacher of correct belief about first principles."[40] With this remark my argument has returned to the point from which it commenced, where I took note of Aristotle's claim that the good human being is the standard of right judgment, passion and action and that therefore only the good are in a position to make justified true theoretical judgments about moral practice.

I noted in that initial discussion that this involves a conception of the moral philosopher that is very much at odds with that current in contemporary universities, where what is required of us as moral and political philosophers is only that we should be academically qualified, and where enquiry into the moral character of candidates for academic appointments would be thought at best irrelevant, at worst persecutory. And, because the office of the holder of an academic philosopher in our society is what it now is, such enquiry would in fact be irrelevant and perhaps persecutory.

The fact is that the role and function of the moral and political philosopher, as they emerge in Aristotle's thought, are such that there seems perhaps to be no place for a genuinely Aristotelian moral and political philosopher in the contemporary conventional academic landscape or indeed the contemporary cultural landscape. And this may seem

40 *NE* 1151a17–19.

to confer a paradoxical character on my own enterprise. But it is also instructive, for it directs our attention to one cause of this alienation, the dominance in our culture of a very different conception of the relationship of theory to practice from that presupposed by Aristotle's theory.

For Aristotle the moral and political philosopher is to function within the *polis*, contributing to the common good of the *polis* by articulating for the citizens of the *polis* the ends that they must achieve, if they are to flourish, so that they may understand better what those ends are and how, as rational animals, to direct themselves towards their achievement. Moral and political philosophy are to make explicit the nature of our directedness towards our ends and the function of various capacities and excellences in achieving them and so to provide us both as agents and as educators of agents with standards of justificatory argument. But those standards can never displace – indeed they presuppose – the standard of excellence provided for both agents and educators by the good human being.

For some Renaissance Aristotelians, such as Piccolomini, by contrast, the moral and political philosopher has or deserves to have the commanding place in moral education simply in virtue of that philosopher's command of the relevant theory, something that no one else can contribute to the life of political societies. The moral life, for those with the appropriate education, consists in key part in the application of a theoretical knowledge of the human good to the complexities of everyday moral and political practice. The moral and political philosopher is thus a civic functionary, one without whom the young could not be adequately prepared for the discharge of their own civic responsibilities. But the setting of this standard, so I argued earlier, prepared the way for discrediting these pretensions of sixteenth-century Aristotelians. Professors of moral philosophy were all too evidently unable to render themselves credible figures in the role of moral teacher. And it was as professed moral teachers that Philip Sidney was to mock them in *An Apologie for Poetrie*.

The role of the professor of moral philosophy survived into the modern period only by discarding these pretensions. It became embedded in institutional structures and relationships that characteristically distance those who enact that role from the arenas of practice outside higher education. And that distance is a function not only of the ways in which philosophical theorizing about morals and politics is now conceived, but also of contemporary modes of practice. Early on in my argument I asked the question: "What kind of practice is it to which Aristotelian moral and political theory is the counterpart?" I now offer a sketch, although only a bare sketch, of an answer to it in order to highlight the differences between the mode of social and political practice presupposed by Aristotelian theory and the dominant modes of practice in contemporary politics and society. Three areas of difference are of particular importance.

First, because the practice of an Aristotelian community must be one informed by shared deliberation, it must be a type of practice in which there is sufficient agreement about goods and about their rank ordering to provide shared standards for rational deliberation on both moral and political questions. This is of course compatible with the occurrence of extended and significant disagreements, but it still requires a type of community that exhibits a common mind in its practice arising from its shared goals. By contrast the societies of modernity presuppose that we have agreed to disagree about a wide range of questions about goods and that politics is one thing and morals quite another. Is it therefore impossible to find such communities of Aristotelian practice anywhere in contemporary milieus? An answer is suggested by considering a second area of difference.

If there is to be practice that involves widely shared participation in deliberation, and if that deliberation is to be effective in decision-making, then communities of practice will have to be small-scale local communities whose members are able to call each other to account in respect of their deliberative standards. And they will have to avoid those destructive conflicts of interest that arise from too great inequalities of wealth and power. Their structure is thus incompatible with that of the dominant institutional forms of modernity, those of the centralized large-scale nation-state and of the large-scale market economy. But they may be and indeed sometimes are exemplified to a significant extent in the forms of various local enterprises: households, fishing crews, farming cooperatives, schools, clinics, neighborhoods, small towns.

Thirdly the activities of such communities will presuppose shared standards of rational justification that are independent of the de facto interests and preferences of their members. Those standards define the community's common good and the fundamental bond between their members will be allegiance to that common good. This means that the self-understanding of members of such communities has to be incompatible with substituting for that fundamental bond any notion of civic unity as arising either from some shared ethnic or religious or other cultural inheritance – important as these may be – or from the shared interests and preferences of its members.

I have in this and the preceding essay presented three rival versions of Aristotle's morals and politics, indeed rather more than three, since such Renaissance Aristotelians as Piccolomini and Case did not on a number of issues agree among themselves, and those contemporary Aristotelians with whom I have been disagreeing each have their own highly distinctive views. And there are of course there yet other versions of Aristotle, both in the Renaissance and in recent discussions, not to speak of the Aristotelians of the Islamic, Jewish, and Christian Middle Ages and the Peripatetics of the ancient world. But I have also in these lectures argued in favor of one particular interpretation and this interpretation is one that has been explicitly or implicitly rejected by a variety of distinguished scholars and commentators.

Am I then suggesting that there are or could be conclusive arguments that might settle disputed questions in favor of my view and against rival views? Like other interpreters, I often write as if it were so. Like other interpreters, I even more often wish that it were so. But it is for the most part not so. Aristotle's text underdetermines its interpretation. It does of course provide us with genuinely conclusive grounds for rejecting some interpretations. But the possibilities that remain open are too numerous, too diverse, and each of them too well-supported for us not to recognize that we are confronted with the claims of a number of rival Aristotles, each of them constructed in part as a result of the different questions that different interpreters bring to their reading of the texts, of the different importance that interpreters attach to particular passages and of the different ways in which they extrapolate from texts that very often cannot be read intelligently without some extrapolation.

Aristotle is not alone in this respect. There are rival Platos, rival Kants, rival Wittgensteins. The history of philosophy is a history of interpretations and of interpretative debates. And therefore, whatever grounds for confidence we may have in upholding one particular view against others, that confidence always needs to be tempered by caution, by great respect for those from whom we have learned through our disagreements, and by the knowledge that in these matters no one has the last word.

CHAPTER 3

Natural law as subversive: the case of Aquinas

That the thirteenth century in Europe was a time of extended conflict and debate does not differentiate it from other times and places. But the character and intensity of some of its conflicts and debates are worth remarking, if only because they gave what turned out to be enduring definition to some rival and alternative modes of moral and political thought and action. So if we begin by situating the moral and social thought of Aquinas in the context of such conflicts and debates, rather than – as is usually done – by abstracting it from and ignoring those contexts, we will perhaps be better able to understand its continuing and distinctive relevance. Which conflicts and debates do I have in mind?

They are conflicts between rival claimants to jurisdiction in particular areas and over particular types of issue, second-order conflicts about who has the legitimate authority to resolve a variety of first-order conflicts. Sometimes they are between ecclesiastical and secular authorities, sometimes between one ecclesiastical authority and another or between one secular authority and another. Examples of the former are those between feudal lords or kings and bishops, most notably those between emperor and pope; examples of the latter include those between local feudal lords and royal officials and those between bishops and the superiors of religious houses. A central question characteristically is, to what higher authority, if any, may someone appeal against the verdict of whomsoever it is that locally has the power to impose authority? Unsurprisingly these conflicts extend from this question into theological and philosophical debate about how different kinds of authority are hierarchically ordered.

Such conflicts were generated in part by the growth and strengthening of centralizing tendencies in both ecclesiastic and secular affairs. The papacy of Innocent III had achieved at the Fourth Lateran Council in 1215 an unprecedented expression of political as well as of theological unity in the church. The kingdom of Sicily under Frederick II provided an example of a polity in which royal courts of law had no limits set to their jurisdiction. In both France and England a progress in the imposition of royal authority was evident, and turning-points in making that progress irreversible were in France the legislative enactments of Louis IX and in England those of Edward I. Each of these increasingly empowered systems of secular and ecclesiastical law had within it its own conception of the hierarchy of authorities, each to greater or lesser degree challenging both the conceptions of its rivals and those conceptions embodied in older local systems of law, systems that had derived their authority from local custom and tradition and now represented a barrier to the royal supremacy.

The story of how these tendencies developed is one usually told in retrospect from the standpoint of those political, legal, and administrative institutions which finally emerged victorious. And because those same institutions, the institutions of the nascent nation-state, are continuous both in their history and in their claims to legitimacy with the institutions through which political hegemony is still exercised in our own contemporary social order, that this story should be told from such a standpoint is usually taken for granted. Indeed we are sometimes told that it is no more than idle and undisciplined speculation to ask, what else could have happened? What other possibilities might have been, but were not realized? The prohibition upon asking such questions is always ideological in its effect. For, if effective, it functions to conceal from view the fact that our predecessors did in the past confront real alternative possibilities, that there were roads not taken which might have been taken, and that the character of the roads that were in fact taken cannot be fully understood unless it is recognized that taking them involved a rejection of or a defeat for those other possibilities. The present could have been other than it is and to assume differently may always hide from us some of its important characteristics.

One partial remedy for this tendency to treat the outcomes of past conflicts as inevitable and preordained is to consider not only their actual political, legal, and institutional history but also that of the accompanying theoretical debates. Why so? I will suggest an answer to this question by arguing that at the level of theoretical enquiry Aquinas defined, both for his contemporaries and for us, a set of legal, political, and moral possibilities for structuring communal life, practically as well as theoretically alternative to those which were in fact realized, and I have argued elsewhere that this alternative was and is rationally and morally superior to that which was in fact realized in and by the emerging nation-state and its later bureaucratic heirs.[1] I will do so by contrasting the answers given by Aquinas to a set of questions about law with the answers to the same questions which were given or presupposed by the legal procedures and enactments of Frederick II in Sicily and of Louis IX in France.

In his definitive work on the history of conceptions of the natural law,[2] Michael Bertram Crowe presented Aquinas's account of law as a theoretical construction responsive to the theses and concerns of a variety of earlier theorists: Augustine and indirectly Cicero, Ulpian, Gratian, Peter Lombard, and his own teacher, Albertus Magnus. My account is intended to supplement rather than to correct Crowe's narrative. Aquinas was indeed engaged theoretically with the contentions of Roman and canon lawyers, of theologians and of philosophers. But the nature of his theoretical engagement will perhaps be misunderstood, if it is abstracted from the practical aims of his writings about law. Aquinas characteristically wrote with specific intentions for specific sets of readers. And among the preoccupations of those for whom and to whom he wrote about law, the recent legal and administrative innovations of Frederick II and Louis IX, very different as these were from one another, must have been central.

As for Frederick II, I shall be concerned with the laws decreed at the Diets of Capua and Messina in 1221 and with the Constitutions of Melfi, promulgated in 1231, the former of these four years before Aquinas was born, the latter when he was six years old and already an oblate at Monte Cassino. Aquinas, we need to remember, had been born in the castle of Roccasecca in Caserta, a province of the kingdom of Sicily bordering the papal states. Just before he entered the abbey at Monte Cassino at the age of five, the peace of San Germano had been concluded between Frederick II and Pope Gregory IX, and so the abbey was no longer under imperial military occupation.

In 1239, when Aquinas was fourteen, the pope excommunicated Frederick, and in the ensuing war the abbey was once again occupied by imperial forces. By an edict of June 1239, all religious not born in the kingdom of Sicily were expelled from the kingdom, leaving behind at Monte Cassino only eight monks. Unsurprisingly, it was about this time that Aquinas was transferred, presumably by direction of his parents, to the *studium generale*, later to become the University of Naples, which

---

1 Chap. 9, "Aquinas on Practical Rationality and Justice" in MacIntyre, *Whose Justice? Which Rationality?*, Notre Dame, Ind.: University of Notre Dame Press, 1988.
2 Michael Bertram Crowe, *The Changing Profile of the Natural Law*, The Hague: Martinus Nijhoff, 1977.

Frederick had founded as the first European university under entirely secular control in 1224, requiring his subjects not to attend any other university. When we add to these episodes in Aquinas's early life the fact that his brothers Aimo and Rinaldo both began as soldiers for the emperor and at later stages changed to papal allegiance, it becomes difficult to suppose that in thinking about law, he could have been ignoring those practical problems of rival claims to jurisdiction which informed the conflicts of papacy and empire. His later refusal of papal appointments, on one occasion as abbot of Monte Cassino and on another as archbishop of Naples, have suggested to some of Aquinas's biographers a strong and consistent desire not to become personally entangled in those conflicts.[3]

As for Louis IX, I shall be concerned with the laws and administrative reform of the ordinance of 1254 and with those later decrees which were sequels to that ordinance. In 1254 Aquinas was *baccalarius Sententiarum* in the University of Paris, living in the Priory of St. Jacques, whose buildings had in part been the gift of Louis IX and whose friars were supported by the king's alms. It was a period in the life of that university when tensions and conflicts were of a high order between the secular masters of the university (who claimed direct papal protection and privileges in asserting their right to govern the university) and the Dominicans and Franciscans (who also acted under direct papal authority and license, in defending themselves against the attempts by the secular masters to restrict their teaching). There were also conflicts between the latter and the bishop of Paris. Louis IX acted in these conflicts as protector of the Dominicans, sending royal archers, for example, so that a Dominican master could safely deliver his inaugural lecture for the year, in September 1255, at a time of university rioting and violence.[4]

The ordinance of 1254 was followed by a renewal of royal *enquêtes* into the local administration of justice by the king's local representatives. The teams of *enquêteurs* commonly included either a Dominican or a Franciscan, whose evaluations of secular justice would have recurrently involved them in the conflicts between feudal right and local customary law on the one hand and the sovereignty of the royal courts on the other. Those who spoke up for feudal right and customary law, whether in formal declarations of the French barons or in rebellious chansons, identified their

3 James A. Weisheipl, *Friar Thomas D'Aquino: His Life, Thought, and Works*, Garden City, N.Y.: Doubleday, 1974, p. 8.
4 Ibid., chap. 2, " 'Sententiarius' in the City of Philosophers."

continuing enemy the "clerks," those clergy and lawyers, including the Dominicans, who were the king's instruments in extending the authority of the royal conception of justice.[5] Since, when Aquinas wrote the *secunda pars* of the *Summa Theologiae* in 1269–72, he was once again teaching in Paris, and since his detailed treatments of law in the *prima pars* of the *secunda pars* and of justice in the *secunda pars* of the *secunda pars* are most plausibly understood as written with an eye to the practical guidance of pastors, confessors, and others engaged with the problems of justice in everyday life, it would be odd if he had not had in mind among these the members of his own Dominican order who had repeatedly confronted these particular French problems of rival and conflicting jurisdictions.[6]

It is easy to understand that Aquinas could not but have been deeply critical of the legal doctrines and enactments of Frederick II, enemy of the papacy and protagonist of secular power. But it might too easily be supposed that he could not have been in any fundamental disagreement with Louis IX, who not only sustained the work of the church, but exhibited both in his political and in his personal actions those remarkable qualities of moral and religious character which were responsible not only for his canonization only twenty-six years after his death, but also for the French medieval folk-memory of him as the paradigmatic good king. Aquinas himself had, on at least one occasion, dined with Louis IX, seated next to the king, even though, as the story has it, he was preoccupied on that occasion with his own thoughts. Yet in fact the practical implications of Aquinas's conception of law were very much at odds with that king's legal enactments and administration, and this at a fundamental level. Let me therefore begin with what it is that puts Aquinas in opposition to Louis IX and only later turn to his disagreements with Frederick II.

Louis IX was morally sophisticated as well as devout. He understood the distinction between the natural virtues and secular life on the one hand and the requirements of the Catholic faith on the other. He cultivated and celebrated the secular virtue of *prud'homie*, the virtue of the person of honor, as assiduously as he practiced the religious virtue of humility.[7] Nonetheless, those French monarchical institutions which he inherited and his own personal belief and devotion combined to make it

---

5 Jean Richard, *Saint Louis: Crusader King of France*, ed. Jean Birrell, chap. 9, "The Government of the Kingdom and Its Reform," Cambridge: Cambridge University Press, 1992, pp. 155–83.

6 On Aquinas's dissatisfaction with current Dominican manuals and teaching on moral matters see Leonard E. Boyle, *The Setting of the Summa Theologiae of St. Thomas*, Etienne Gilson Series, vol. 5, Toronto: Pontifical Institute of Mediaeval Studies, 1982.

7 Richard, *Saint Louis*, pp. 77, 332.

impossible for Louis IX to conceive of his role in other than theological terms. The justice that he aspired to enact and to administer was the justice of which the Scriptures speak. The king of France, according to the influential Peter of Fontaines, had the imperial power to make law, the power originally conferred on the Roman emperor by the senate in the *Lex regia*, and from the theologians the king had learned that his was a sacred office. So Jean Richard has remarked upon the contrast between the king's "personal humility" and "the quasi-infallibility claimed for his justice and his administration, with the support of the theologians and the legists."[8]

The image which Richard conveys is of a king who understands himself as drawing upon the teaching of the Scriptures and of the church in order, through his unique authority, to require from his subjects and to enforce upon them through law the religion and the morality of those teachings. So he not only involved Franciscans and Dominicans in the administration of secular justice, and provided for the punishment both of heretics and of those who gave them shelter, but in the ordinances of 1254 he also legislated against any cursing or swearing that "tended to the contempt of God, Our Lady, and all the saints," prohibited his officials from engaging in games of chance, any games played for money, and, surprisingly, chess, made it a crime to manufacture dice, ordered taverns to become places of hospitality only for travelers, excluding local people, and attempted to abolish both usury and prostitution.[9] By the ordinances of 1254 Louis IX made it plain to his subjects that the identification of some type of activity as involving or encouraging, or even being indirectly associated with some vice, was sufficient to justify enacting its prohibition or taking administrative measures to abolish or control it. And in the precepts which he wrote for the instruction of his son, he enjoined him to "banish from his land the public sins of blasphemy, fornication, games of chance, and drunkenness," as well as heresy.[10]

It is therefore striking that, when Aquinas poses the question whether it belongs to the human law to repress all vice, he replies trenchantly in the negative.[11] Indeed, Aquinas's thirteenth-century readers, who had learned

---

8 Ibid., p. 248.
9 For sources generally see Richard, *Saint Louis*, pp. 333–44; for the text of the ordinances see *Ordonnances des rois de France de la troisième race*, ed. E. de Laurière, vol. I, Paris, 1723; for the actions of the *parlements*, see *Les Olim ou arrents rendus par la cour du roi*, ed. A. Beugnot, Paris: Didot frères, 1839.
10 Richard, *Saint Louis*, p. 158.
11 *Summa Theologiae*, Ia-IIae 96, 2.

from question 92 that the purpose of law is to make human beings good, by habituating them in the performance of those types of actions which are required by the virtues, and had found this thesis reiterated in question 95, may well have been a little surprised by his answer. Aquinas offers them two reasons for his negative answer.

The first concerns the part that law plays in moral education. Law is designed for the instruction and correction of those who are still deeply imperfect in the virtues, and of them too much should not be asked too soon. Moral education will be ineffective if it sets too high a standard too quickly. Hence, legislation should concern "only the more grievous vices," especially those that harm others and undermine social life: "murder, theft, and the like." Aquinas's second reason is that attempts to impose the requirements of the virtues unrestrictedly and unqualifiedly are self defeating. They provoke in too many of the imperfect just those evils which they were designed to prevent. Aquinas thus disagrees both with later puritans and with later liberals. Like those puritans and unlike those liberals he understands the law as an instrument for our moral education. But, like those liberals and unlike those puritans, he is against making law by itself an attempt to repress all vice. And so he is in strong disagreement with Louis IX. But the disagreement is not only in his conclusion, it is in his way of reaching that conclusion.

Louis IX appealed to theological, indeed to specifically Christian, premises to support his legal and administrative conclusions. Aquinas appealed to natural reason, not only for his account of the purpose and function of law, but also for the standard to which all positive legal enactments and administrative measures must conform, if they are to be appropriate law rather than merely an expression of the will and interest of those who enact and administer. It follows that to be a legitimate ruler one need not be a Christian. And this Aquinas explicitly asserts, saying that dominion (*dominium*) and hierarchy (*praelatio*) are instituted by *ius humanum* and that *ius divinum* does not take away *ius humanum*, which is from natural reason.[12] That human law is from natural reason has radical implications.

In Aquinas's view the authority to make human law belongs either to a whole people or to someone acting on behalf of a whole people.[13] Those with such authority have to promulgate the laws that they make, if those laws are to have the authority of laws.[14] But promulgation, even by someone with the requisite authority, is, though necessary, not sufficient

---

12 Ibid., IIa-IIae 10, 10.   13 Ibid., Ia-IIae 90, 3.   14 Ibid., 90, 4.

to confer upon a decree or statute the authority of law. For "every law laid down by a human being has the nature of law only insofar as it is derived from the law of nature. But if in some respect it is in disagreement with the natural law, it will not be law, but a corruption of law."[15] And who is to say what the natural law is? The knowledge that enables us to do this is possessed by any person capable of adequate reasoning and, so far as the common principles of the natural law are concerned, by every rational being.[16]

At this point it is worth reminding ourselves what the grounds are, on Aquinas's view, for respecting the precepts of the natural law and how it is that, on that view, we come to know those precepts. We come to know them practically as precepts whose binding authority is presupposed in any situation in which learning and enquiry between rational individuals about their individual and common goods can be advanced and by any relationship in which individuals can conduct themselves with rational integrity. Which of those precepts is peculiarly relevant will depend in part at least on what type of situaton or relationship is in question and what threats there are to its rational possibilities. But the violation of *any* precept of the natural law always constitutes such a threat: for example, the unqualified truthfulness required for learning, the unqualified fidelity required for marriage, the unqualified respect for the boundaries between the sacred and the secular which is so necessary for rational integrity in relationship to either are to be understood as also involving respect for the natural law as such.

Just because even in situations in which there is serious, even skeptical enquiry about the precepts of the natural law, willing conformity to those precepts is a precondition of rational and serious enquiry, it turns out that we cannot but presuppose allegiance to them in our activities. We know them, at least primarily, not as conclusions but as presuppositions of our activities, just insofar as those activities are or aspire to rationality. As Aquinas says, the generalizations apprehended by *synderesis* are known prior to any particular practical inferences.[17]

The natural law, that is to say, defines the requirements of justice, and unjust law fails as law.[18] Whether a particular positive law has authority over us is therefore something to be discerned by rational persons. We are not intelligible to ourselves or to each other, except as those who recognize that good is to be done and pursued and that evil is to be avoided. And we

15 Ibid., 95, 2.   16 Ibid., 93, 2.   17 *De Veritate*, 16, 2.
18 *Summa Theologiae*, Ia-IIae, 95, 2.

discover that we are directed towards certain goods, as beings, as animals, and as rational animals. The exceptionless precepts of the natural law are those which, insofar as we are rational, we recognize as indispensable in every society and in every situation for the achievement of our goods and of our final good, because they direct us towards and partially define our common good.[19] It is to rulers that a care for the common good is especially entrusted. But how they and everyone else must act if the common good is to be achieved is not something known in any special way by, let alone only by, rulers.

Aquinas followed Aristotle in holding that there is indeed a particular virtue or excellence specific to ruling. Insofar as someone is ruled over and not a ruler, she or he does not share in that excellence. But "every human being, insofar as rational, has part in ruling according to the judgment of reason," and political prudence, which is the virtue specific to the ruler, has its analogue in the prudence of those ruled over.[20] More than this, Aquinas follows Aristotle in arguing that "the virtue of a good human being also includes the virtue of a good ruler."[21] So that insofar as human beings have the capacity to become good, they also have the capacity to exercise the prudence of a ruler. Those human beings who do happen to become rulers therefore have no special capacity, which differentiates them from plain persons, whose capacity for prudence and whose knowledge of the natural law is theirs in virtue of their human nature.

So plain persons can never lose their capacity for judging when they ought and when they ought not to obey the human laws enacted by their rulers. Such laws may be unjust, when they are not conducive to the common good, when they are imposed by someone without the requisite authority to do so, and when, although designed to promote the common good, they place a disproportionate burden on some for the benefit of others. Such laws no one is bound to obey. What each person has to judge is whether disobedience to unjust laws may not cause scandal or some greater harm, to a degree that gives one good reason to conform out of prudence, rather than from a respect for justice. But laws may also be unjust in that they prescribe or encourage defiance of the law of God by, for example, promoting idolatry. Such laws one is always bound to disobey.[22] The knowledge of the natural law which plain persons possess provides them with the grounds to which they need to appeal in their

---

19 Ibid., 94, 2.
21 Ibid., 47, 11.

20 *Summa Theologiae*, IIa-IIae, 47, 12.
22 *Summa Theologiae*, Ia-IIae, 96, 4.

debates with other plain persons about how they should respond to the enactments of positive law.

This is a more fundamental point of difference between Louis IX and Aquinas than any matter of the content of particular laws, and it gives further significance to Aquinas's criticism of any use of the law, such as that of the king, to repress all vices, which that criticism would not otherwise possess. The king's project required and was itself an expression of an attempt, and a remarkably successful attempt, to develop royal control, both legally and administratively, over the whole life of the French people.[23] That the people are the source of a ruler's authority to make laws, something central to Aquinas's legal theory, became as a result of that attempt something practically obscured and ignored. The incipiently bureaucratic extension of centralized authority and power, designed by Louis IX to remedy injustices perpetrated with the sanction of local feudal jurisdictions, could not but have the effect of professionalizing law enforcement and administration. The reality of the king's own devotion to justice is not in question. He understood himself as answerable to divine judgment in a way that few rulers have done. But the inquests and reforms which gave expression to that devotion constituted one decisive moment in the process of handing over the enforcement of positive law, at the level at which plain persons encounter it, to lawyers and to administrators, to professional specialists with their own training and their own monopoly of expertise. The deference to royal authority of contemporary French teachers of law, which I noticed earlier, is one aspect of the relationship between that authority and professional lawyers; its other aspect is the extent to which the royal authority becomes translated into the authority of lawyers and administrators over plain persons. The contrast with Aquinas's thesis that authority as to what the law is, on fundamentals at least, rests with plain persons and that the most important things that lawyers and administrators know about law, they know as plain persons and not as lawyers and administrators, is striking.

Moreover it follows that those who do not recognize what the natural law is and how it functions cannot understand what the common good is either. If, either as rulers or as lawyers and counselors, they put their own authority in place of the authority of the natural law, they exhibit both their failure to understand the common good and their lack of the virtue of political prudence. By failing to understand what they are capable of understanding, but only as plain rational persons, they have failed both

23 Richard, *Saint Louis*, p. 177.

politically and legally. It is thus one of the central truths of politics, if Aquinas's account of the natural law and the common good are correct, that those who arrogate to themselves an exclusive professionalized authority of a certain kind by that very act of arrogation discredit their own claims to legitimate authority.

Aquinas's reflections upon Roman law and canon law had thus led him in an opposite direction from that taken by the most influential teachers of law in the universities. Nowhere is this more apparent than in his treatment of custom. Local custom was that to which the enemies of royal centralization characteristically appealed. But the conflict was not only between "respect for ancient custom" and "a monarchy propagating Roman law."[24] As Richard stresses, the great barons were equally concerned to assert their own authority in their own fiefs against local custom. The appeal to custom was therefore one that placed its proponents in opposition to all the great wielders of power – royal, baronial, and even, we need to add, ecclesiastical. With whom then does Aquinas stand? In a passage in which he begins by quoting Augustine on how customs are to be considered a law – he had earlier cited Isidore to the same effect – and by reiterating his contention that human law proceeds from the human will, regulated by reason, Aquinas argues that laws can be changed and published by repeated actions, as much as by speech, and indeed that from actions repeated so that they have become customary "something can be established which has the force of law."[25] Even when a free people has given the authority to make laws to a ruler, prevailing custom has the force of law, until it is changed. But Aquinas had argued earlier that change of law is of itself prejudicial to the common good, because custom brings about obedience to laws and abolishing a custom lessens the binding force of law.[26] One therefore would need the strongest of reasons to interfere with local custom.

The law teachers of Orleans aspired in their theory to balance the claims of Roman law and those of custom. But in the acts of those influenced by them on the king's council, such as Peter of Fontaines,[27] himself the author of a collection of customs, *Conseil à un ami*, custom never seemed to be a barrier to extensions of royal authority. And the extension of that authority was characteristically justified not by reference to local French custom, but rather to the *Lex regia*, embodying the legal fiction of the king of France as another Augustus Caesar. We therefore

24 Ibid., 214.   25 *Summa Theologiae*, Ia-IIae, 97, 3.   26 Ibid., 97, 2.
27 Richard, *Saint Louis*, p. 174.

find Aquinas's theory deeply at odds with the practical understanding of law and power embodied in the policies and legislation of Louis IX on three central matters: on the relationship of law to moral education, on the relative authority of rulers and their bureaucratic and legal agents on the one hand and of plain rational persons on the other, and on the weight to be assigned to local custom. In each case what put Aquinas at variance with Louis IX put him as much or even more at variance with Frederick II.

The resemblances and the differences between the French king and the imperial ruler of the kingdom of Sicily are important. Attention to the resemblances helps us to correct Ernst Kantorowicz's brilliant exaggeration of Frederick II's uniqueness.[28] Attention to the differences helps to correct David Abulafia's exaggerated correction of Kantorowicz's exaggeration.[29] In the Constitutions of Melfi, which, as I noted earlier, Frederick promulgated for his kingdom of Sicily in 1231,[30] we find the same moralistic attempt to repress all vice that we find in the ordinances of Louis IX and also the same extension of the power of centralizing royal authority and of its incipiently bureaucratic agencies at the expense of local custom. Abulafia rightly stresses both the heterogeneous and the far from fully worked out character of the laws of the Constitutions of Melfi and also, following Hermann Dilcher, the heterogeneity of the sources of those laws: Byzantine, Lombard, Norman, canonist, and Spanish, as well as Roman. But this makes the unity of purpose discernible in this assemblage of assorted parts more, rather than less, impressive. Blasphemy, games of chance, adultery, prostitution, and the dispensing of love-potions were made punishable offenses, and the keeping or frequenting of taverns were made grounds for exclusion from civic life, in a way that would have had to incur Aquinas's condemnation of misuses of law to repress all vices, just as did the legislation of Louis IX. Local custom was allowed the status of law only insofar as it had acquired royal, or rather imperial approval, in a way that was quite incompatible with Aquinas's understanding of the legal force and authority of custom. But these crucial features of the content of the laws laid down in the

---

28 Kantorowicz, *Kaiser Friedrich der Zweite*, Berlin: G. Bondi, 1927, translated by E. O. Lorimer as *Frederick the Second. 1194–1250*, London, 1931; with a second volume of notes and excursus, *Ergänzungsband*, Berlin: G. Bondi, 1931.

29 David Abulafia, *Frederick II: A Medieval Emperor*, Oxford: Oxford University Press, 1992.

30 For the text see J. L. A. Huillard-Breholles, *Historia diplomatica Friderici secundi*; vol. I, Paris: Plon, 1852, pp. 1–178; the only and not uniformly reliable translation is James M. Powell, *The Liber Augustalis*, Syracuse, N.Y.: Syracuse University Press, 1971.

Constitutions of Melfi are much less important than their conception of imperial lawmaking authority or the attempted centralization of power which was central to Frederick's project.

How then is authority conceived in the Constitutions? Frederick is treated throughout as the contemporary Augustus Caesar, possessing in his own person the authority ascribed to a Roman emperor, just as was Louis IX. But in his case this is far more than a reinvocation of the *Lex regia*. The *Prooemium* of the Constitutions is a theological narrative according to which divine providence provided for the punishment and correction of fallen human beings by instituting princes to rule over nations. Supreme among those with this divinely ordained mission is the Roman emperor, sole source of justice and peace for those over whom he rules. The imperial authority is thus not, as in the *Lex regia*, from the senate and the Roman people, but immediately from God. The emperor unites in his own person both supreme spiritual and temporal powers, protector of the church as well as of civil order, and independent of papal or any other ecclesiastical authority in his spiritual as well as his temporal role. (It is worth remembering that Pope Gregory IX had invaded the kingdom of Sicily as recently as 1229.)

In this respect of course Frederick II and Louis IX parted company. Louis's devotion to the Catholic faith committed him to recognize not only the independent authority of the papacy, but also that he himself owed the church obedience in its own sphere. But for my present purposes what matters about the theology of the Constitutions of Melfi is not primarily the attempted subordination of papal to imperial authority. It is that the investing of that imperial authority with a sacred and numinous quality was designed to place actions performed and judgments uttered in the name of that authority quite beyond appeal and quite beyond question. So in reissuing the law of his maternal grandfather, Roger II, Norman ruler of Sicily,[31] according to which any questioning of the judgments, projects, and enterprises of the king was forbidden, Frederick II made of such questioning a crime "Sacrilegii . . . instar," like to sacrilege. Legal commentators would later distinguish these crimes of quasi-sacrilege from sacrilege properly so-called. But the point of the comparison with sacrilege is clear: putting in question or appealing against imperial decrees in any way is presented as a form of rebellion against God. And later the emperor is described as himself at once "father

---

31 Huillard-Breholles, *Historia diplomatica*, Book I, title 4.

and son, lord and minister of justice,"[32] himself, as it were, embodying justice in all its aspects, something to which Kantorowicz drew our attention.

Any appeal to the precepts of reason, as understood by plain persons, as providing a definitive account of justice, is therefore, from the standpoint of the Constitutions of Melfi, not merely null and void but also at once a grave theological error and a punishable offense. And of this offense anyone would have been guilty who had made her or his own either the key theses about law advanced by Aquinas in the Ia-IIae or those passages in the IIa-IIae in which Aquinas asserts that plain persons have the rational capacity to judge the actions of princes as just or unjust and, when they are unjust, to resist them by whatever appropriate means.[33] Aquinas was therefore a prime example of those whom Frederick took to be impious defenders of sacrilege.

The *Prooemium* to the Constitutions concludes by declaring that they should have force and authority both inside and outside courts of law. The laws were not there for those who merely happened to seek redress or protection. They were to be actively enforced, and the agents of their enforcement, always with the authority to prevail over local custom, were to be the royal officials. Those who held the office of justiciar were no longer to be local notables. No justiciar could officiate in a district where he was a feudal lord, thus putting an end to any confusion of the royal interest with local feudal interests. And the ranks of the royal officials were increasingly to be filled by those trained in the law at the University of Naples, founded by Frederick only seven years before the Constitutions of Melfi for just this purpose.

It is then perhaps no accident that someone with Aquinas's mature beliefs should in his early education have had firsthand experience of the teaching of that university. Aquinas was, of course, from Frederick's point of view, one of its educational failures. But it was not Frederick's appeal to secular reason – insofar as Frederick did so appeal – that was incompatible with Aquinas's standpoint. On questions concerning political authority and the common good what was incompatible with Aquinas's standpoint was Frederick's theological invocation of revealed truth. And so it was also with Aquinas's disagreements with Louis IX. It is the rulers who speak as theologians, Aquinas who speaks as a philosopher. But perhaps what separated Aquinas from both rulers will become adequately clear, only

---

32 Ibid., Book I, title 31.
33 *Summa Theologiae*, IIa-IIae, 69, 4.

if we focus attention upon the detail of some one particular issue. An illuminating example is the treatment by each of matters concerning *jongleurs*, that is, traveling singers, players, and entertainers.

For a long time *jongleurs, joculatores*, jesters, had had a bad name. As they traveled through the countryside, performing at country fairs, at festivals and other celebrations, minor crime waves, so it was said, traveled with them. They were reputed to lead disorderly lives. Their songs were often subversive, providing a voice, sometimes the only voice, for popular dissent and complaint. They were the social kin of the Goliard poets, themselves objects of many accusations from "respectable" people. Jacques Le Goff has reminded us "that the term *joculator*, or *jongleur*, was at the time the epithet used for all those who were considered dangerous, whom one wanted to banish from society."[34]

The issues raised by the activities of *jongleurs* had a special importance for thirteenth-century universities. Such universities in general, as Le Goff stresses, had the tasks of recruiting and educating the new governing elites.[35] In that capacity they were designed to be instruments of political order. But intermittently they were in fact places of conflict and disorder, and the disorders were often of a type with which *jongleurs* were characteristically associated. It is not just that poor students sometimes earned their living as *jongleurs*.[36] More importantly, in the often bitter and occasionally violent university conflicts which divided Dominican and Franciscan teachers from those drawn from the secular clergy, both students and their teachers from the burgesses of university towns, and ecclesiastical from civil authority, the voice of the *jongleur* was on occasion an important element.

So it was at Paris in 1253, when the Dominicans and Franciscans refused to join other teachers in suspending classes as a protest against the behavior of the civil authority over a lethal brawl between students and sergeants. In the ensuing disputes both Pope Alexander IV and Louis IX finally made decisions condemning the chief enemy of the friars, William of Saint-Amour, who was thereby deprived of his chair. Aquinas himself had participated as a major figure in this affair, arguing the case for the friars. He was therefore, even if not by name, one of the targets of an attack on the Dominicans for their part in it, in a mocking ballad, *La discorde de l'université et des Jacobins*, by the *jongleur*, Rutebeuf, himself a former Parisian student. And this was only the first in a series of satirical

34 Jacques Le Goff, *Intellectuals in the Middle Ages*, trans. T. L. Fagan, Oxford: Blackwell, 1993, p. 26.
35 Ibid., p. xv.   36 Ibid., p. 26.

and rebellious chansons aimed at all those in authority.[37] Aquinas thus had firsthand experience of the *jongleur* as a source of disorder.

It is therefore instructive to compare Aquinas's attitude to *jongleurs* with those of Louis IX and Frederick II. Both rulers behaved very much as we might expect. Louis IX identified the performances of such songs as a danger to the Christian faith and in 1261 forbade altogether the kind of gathering at which *jongleurs* performed, in this following the example of the pope,[38] with the effect of driving the *jongleurs* towards destitution. Forty years earlier at the Diet of Messina in 1221 Frederick had already legislated not only to regulate traveling entertainers but also to decree that "players and wandering minstrels should be outlaws if they dare to disturb the Emperor's peace with ribald songs."[39] Neither Louis nor Frederick could see in the activity of the *jongleur* anything but a source of disorder; but not so Aquinas, even though the Dominicans had been an object of Rutebeuf's attacks.

For Aquinas has a quite different conception of order, that of the order of a community directed towards its common good through the discharge of those functions necessary for the achievement of that good. And it is one of those essential functions that is discharged by players and entertainers. The most general word that Aquinas uses in articles 2, 3, and 4 of question 168 of IIa-IIae, when speaking of them, is *histriones*, players. But when he cites the *Life of St. Paphnutius* as an authority, his reference is to a *joculator*, a *jongleur*. So it is the same class of persons who alarm Frederick and Louis whose function in life Aquinas takes to be required by virtue and reason.

Aquinas praised the activities of play in a number of contexts. In the prologue to his commentary on Boethius's *De Hebdomadis* he draws an analogy between play and contemplation. Earlier in the *Summa Contra Gentiles* he had distinguished play for the sake of the pleasure internal to it with play for the sake of studying better afterwards.[40] It is, however, play for the sake of its own pleasure which, on the view which Aquinas develops in question 168, is needed to restore the soul from the fatigue of even its highest work, contemplation. And hence he argues in the second article of that question that there is a virtue in words and actions which are "*ludicra vel jocosa*," provided, of course, as with all virtues, that

---

37 Richard, *Saint Louis*, pp. 232–36.
38 Ibid., 235; see also E. B. Ham, *Rutebeuf and Louis IX*, Chapel Hill: University of North Carolina Press, 1962.
39 Kantorowicz, *Kaiser Friedrich*, p. 121.
40 *Summa Contra Gentiles*, 3, 2.

it is exercised at appropriate times and does not involve injury to others or – Aquinas quotes Cicero – "what is discourteous, insolent, scandalous, obscene" (although every good *jongleur* presumably knows and knew that what is discourteous or scandalous offstage is not the same as what is so on stage). Aquinas identifies this virtue with Aristotle's *eutrapelia*. To lack this virtue is to fail in reason. "It is against reason for someone to be a burden to others, for example, by offering nothing for their delight and by hindering the delight of others."[41]

Play and the delight taken in play are therefore necessary to the exchanges and interchanges, the *conversationes*, of human life. And there are therefore *officia* through which what is needed may be supplied. These are the *officia* of players and entertainers, including *jongleurs*, and theirs is a legitimate full-time occupation.[42] They need time for prayer and they need to discipline their passions, but Aquinas would have said this of every occupation. The reference to the discipline of the passions has, however, specific importance. This whole discussion by Aquinas is in the context of his account of the virtue of temperateness. And one way to fail in temperateness is by inadequate, as well as by excessive, appreciation of what players and entertainers provide. Hence, for Aquinas, a society without *jongleurs*, or their functional equivalent, would be a defective society, one defective in respect of the achievement of its common good. The common good requires, and hence the natural law requires, the making of jokes and the staging and enjoyment of entertainments. When those with political power and authority, such as Louis IX and Frederick II, fail to recognize this by their actions, plain persons have the capacity for understanding that the laws that those rulers make are void as law, because they are contrary to reason and virtue. The contrast between Aquinas's standpoint and that of the two sovereigns could not be plainer. It is in their attitudes to jokes and jesters that the failure of rulers and of their counselors and lawyers to understand what rational plain persons have the capacity for understanding is made evident.

Yet at this point I need to attend to what may seem to be an inescapable objection to Aquinas's position, as I have interpreted it. For, it may be said, the arguments of the relevant articles of question 168 of the IIa-IIae, like the arguments by which in general Aquinas reaches the particular moral conclusions of the IIa-IIae, are parts of a complex and sophisticated deductive structure, the structure of an Aristotelian science, and can only

41 *Summa Theologiae*, IIa-IIae, 168,4.
42 Ibid., 168, 3.

be evaluated as such. But the evaluation of the conclusions of such a science requires developed intellectual virtues, and these are not possessed by many plain persons. Hence, the capacity to judge whether a given precept is or is not a precept of the natural law does not belong to plain persons qua plain persons, but only to members of some intellectual elite. The force of the objection is obvious and, so far as I know, there is no discussion of it anywhere in Aquinas's writings. But the issue was later discussed in detail by Suarez,[43] who in this part of his argument took himself to be following Aquinas. It would, of course, be a mistake to ascribe Suarez's theses and arguments to Aquinas. But what Suarez asserts does seem to follow directly from Aquinas's conclusions. And J. B. Schneewind has recently appealed to Suarez's text to support his contention that, on any Aristotelian or Thomist view, judgments as to morals and law are the preserve of an elite and, in the case of Suarez, a theological elite.[44]

Suarez considers the precepts of the natural law to belong to three different classes (chapter 7). First, there are the primary and general principles, that good is to be done and evil avoided, that one should not do to another what one would not want done to oneself, and the like. Secondly, there are the more definite and specific precepts which enjoin a life which embodies justice, the worship of God, temperateness, and the like. A third class of precepts Suarez subdivides. They are the precepts which are not evident without a certain amount of rational reflection and inference, and they are divided into those which are more easily recognized and these less so. The first class, recognized by the greater number of persons – those, we may suppose, with any capacity for inference at all – includes the precepts prohibiting adultery, theft, and like acts. But there are other such precepts the apprehension of which is "not easily within the capacity of all," and Suarez gives three examples: that fornication is intrinsically evil, that usury is unjust, and that lying can never be justified. What do these precepts have in common?

They are all examples of exceptionless precepts to which objection had perennially been made that there occur hard cases in which exceptions to them ought to be excused or permitted or required. Such claims were therefore in Suarez's day, as in our own, the subject of ongoing debate, in

---

43 Francisco Suarez, *On Law and God the Lawgiver*, trans. G. Williams, A. Brown, and J. Waldron, Oxford: Oxford University Press, 1966, 2: pp. 7, 8.
44 Schneewind, "Modern Moral Philosophy: From Beginning to End?" in *Philosophical Imagination and Cultural Memory*, ed. Patricia Cook, Durham, N.C.: Duke University Press, 1993, p. 87.

which plain persons needed to find an answer to sophisticated objections to these exceptionless precepts of the natural law. Notice, however, that Suarez does not say that these precepts are not within the capacity of everyone, but only that they are not easily within the capacity of everyone. And what Suarez goes on to say in the next chapter makes it clear what he means.

Schneewind rightly quotes Suarez as saying there that the ignorance of the multitude *can* be invincible in respect of those precepts which require sophisticated reflection and inference. And therefore for this latter type of precept alone is it possible for someone unsophisticated to deny them without culpability. Who might such persons be? They would have to be persons who had never been exposed to the relevant counterarguments on behalf of the precepts of the natural law, arguments that they would have been incapable of thinking up for themselves. But what they would need, in order for their hitherto invincible ignorance to be overcome, is just that and no more than that: a sound argument or a set of sound arguments, to whose conclusions they would then be able to give rational assent.

Suarez then does not, as Schneewind mistakenly supposes, assert anything which entails a denial of the capacity and authority of plain persons, as rational beings. What he does is to clarify the Thomistic claim about that capacity. It is not that – which is plainly absurd – *any* plain person whatsoever could have independently thought up, for example, the arguments of question 168 of the IIa-IIae about *histriones* and *joculatores*. Rather, all plain persons as such have the capacity for recognizing the truth of the premises for which Aquinas argues and, confronted by those arguments for the conclusions at which Aquinas arrives, plain persons have the capacity for recognizing their soundness. The role of the philosopher and the theologian in supplying the needed arguments is therefore an important and even in some cases an indispensable one. But with respect to the precepts of the natural law what Schneewind alleges about Suarez – "that the theologian is the ultimate source of knowledge on law" – could not be any part of a Thomist position and is not Suarez's position. It is, Suarez says clearly, through the natural light of understanding that all the precepts of the natural law are promulgated.[45] And the natural light of understanding is afforded, in one way or another, to all plain persons. Philosophers and theologians are themselves in respect of the natural law no more than unusually reflective plain persons, able to present their reflections to others for the rational verdict of those others.

---

45 Suarez, *On Law*, Book I, chap. 6.

Philosophers and theologians do of course have their own special interest in, and also a special knowledge of the application of the natural law through its secondary precepts to the areas of their own professional activities, just as players and *jongleurs* do in respect of theirs. Where such areas are concerned – in the case of philosophers and theologians the activities of teaching and of enquiry – what matters is that law should embody and reflect the rational consensus of the practitioners of those activities, and not a set of rules imposed by external authority. External authority has legitimate tasks to perform, but they are a matter of ensuring that the conditions in which a rational consensus of practitioners can emerge and have its own internal authority is secured. Consider in this light the differences in their founding and formative years between the University of Naples and the University of Paris and the different attitudes to law expressed in each university, attitudes which exemplify the very same conflict that divides Frederick's standpoint from Aquinas's.

Frederick II had founded the University of Naples to be an instrument of his own imperial purposes. David Abulafia has emphasized that "the basic aim of the university was to train notaries and judges for the royal or lesser service; it was an intensely practical institution, whose founders believed in the importance of practical training, and its intellectual vivacity was thereby restrained."[46] Both masters and students were made means to external imperial ends, required to assent to both the injunctions and the conclusions of external authority rather than to give expression to their own rational consensus. But with the University of Paris it had been quite otherwise, and in the thirteenth century that university had succeeded to a remarkable degree in embodying in its practice just those conceptions of the common good and the natural law which Aquinas defended in his theory. Stephen C. Ferruolo, in his narrative of the founding of that university,[47] has shown that not only was it from the consensus of the masters in the schools that the impulse towards the foundation of the university arose, but that when Robert Courson, the papal legate responsible for the statutes of 1214 and himself a former master, framed the statutes, he did so with a close eye to the conclusions reached by the masters themselves on a variety of moral, curricular, and other university questions. The statutes embodied, to a highly significant degree, a rational consensus, and the nature of the authority which they

46 Abulafia, *Frederick II*, p. 264.
47 Stephen C. Ferruolo, *The Origins of the University: The Schools of Paris and Their Critics, 1100–1215*, Stanford, Calif.: Stanford University Press, 1983, esp. the conclusion.

conferred was made plain in the procedures for administering and enforcing them. Anyone accused of violating any rule was liable to excommunication, if they had not appeared within fifteen days either before the whole university of masters and scholars or before some smaller group appointed by them to represent it. Here external authority performs its due function of upholding the legitimacy of internal authority. What makes that internal authority legitimate? And why are fundamental issues of law at stake in these university contexts? These are questions that Aquinas's theory has already answered for us.

We need to remind ourselves once again of his definition of law as consisting of precepts of reason promulgated by due authority and directed towards the common good.[48] The University of Paris as a university of masters and scholars not only serves the common good of a wider community, but as a community it has its own specific and particular good, the common good of the university. It is this latter good which can be apprehended practically only by those engaged in the relevant set of practices of teaching and enquiry, and, although passions and interests were, as they always are, apt to distract and corrupt, the subsequent history of the university was marked by continuing debate and conflict over how the common good of the university is to be understood and what its relationship to the larger common good is. And it was generally, if not always, recognized by the participants in those conflicts that only by appeal to that common good could a standard of law be upheld within the university, something that since the thirteenth century has been perennially forgotten or ignored both by governments and by university administrators.

Yet this use of the example of the University of Paris should itself raise further questions about Aquinas's conception of law. As with other medieval European universities, the appeals to ecclesiastical and secular authority to uphold the order of the university presuppose a systematic set of exclusions not only from the university but in the society at large of those outside the communion of the Catholic Church: Jews, heretics, pagans. And the formalization and enforcement of those exclusions during the preceding two hundred and fifty years had been carried through at times with persecutory savagery. Who was responsible for that savagery? Richard W. Southern wrote of "ecclesiastical office-holders" that "they were responsible for some terrible acts of violence and cruelty," but that they "were less prone to violence, even against unbelievers, than

---

48 *Summa Theologiae*, Ia-IIae, 90, 1, 2, 4.

the people whom they ruled."[49] R. I. Moore has more recently reversed this verdict, concluding "that heretics and Jews owed their persecution in the first place not to the hatred of the people, but to the decisions of princes and prelates."[50] In either case, whether the enforcement of exclusions by persecutory violence was primarily the work of rulers, ecclesiastical or secular, or was primarily the work of the ruled, there is reason to question Aquinas's standpoint. For if the ruled are recurrently prepared to use persecutory violence, then is not the rationality of plain persons as a source of their recognition of law put in question? While if it is the rulers, ecclesiastical or secular, who generate such violence, does not this suggest that Aquinas's views provide a critique of the dominant conceptions of law that is a good deal less radical than it should have been?

What makes at least one aspect of Aquinas's standpoint vulnerable to this latter question is twofold: first, his approval of a conception of the relationship of the church to secular power, embodied in the bull *ad abolendam*, according to which it is a duty of Christian rulers to punish heresy, on occasion by death,[51] and, secondly, the absence of any recognition of the possibility of a political common good shared by individuals and groups of differing religious belief. The first brings Aquinas uncomfortably close to the doctrines of the *Liber Augustalis*. The second suggests that he failed to recognize adequately differences between theological and political categories, in so doing assenting to the same set of exclusions as his contemporaries, and in this respect he was at one with Frederick II and Louis IX.

Yet what is striking and most to the point for my present argument is that, whenever Aquinas gives expression to this shared thirteenth-century *weltanschauung*, he does so exclusively by appeal to arguments drawn from Christian theology, including canon law – arguments of a kind later to be rejected by Catholic teaching authority – and never in any way by appeal to the natural law. Unbelievers – in contrast to lapsed believers – are not to be compelled to assent to Christian belief; established political dominion and authority legitimate on occasion the rule of unbelievers our believers; there should be no limitation of parental authority in Jewish households, so that Jews can bring up their children as they judge right, since "injustice should be done to no human being."[52] These are all

49 Richard W Southern, *Western Society and the Church*, Harmondsworth: Penguin, 1970, p. 19.
50 R. I. Moore, *The Formation of a Persecuting Society: Power and Deviance in Western Society, 950–1250*, Oxford: Blackwell, 1987, p. 123.
51 *Summa Theologiae*, IIa-IIae, 11, 4; and see Moore, *The Formation of a Persecuting Society*, p. 8.
52 *Summa Theologiae*, IIa-IIae, 10, 8; 10, 10; 10, 12.

examples of how the natural law is held to impose constraints on the use of theological exclusions for political ends.

What I therefore conclude is that, insofar as Aquinas is faithful to his own conception of natural law, he finds himself at odds with the persecutory activities of centralizing power and, where he is, lamentably, but understandably, identified with those activities, it is never on the basis of that conception. But what then of the other objection, that plain thirteenth-century persons in Western Europe were much too responsive to summonses to antiheretical or antisemitic passion for it to be plausible to treat them as the rational agents of Aquinas's legal and political theory?

What needs to be emphasized in responding to this question is a feature of Aquinas's account of natural law that I noted earlier. The function of law is primarily to educate, and education is a matter of transforming the passions, so that the habits through which they receive expression in action are virtues. Such education takes place, on Aquinas's Aristotelian view, in and through ongoing communal practices, and the recognition of natural law is a matter of how such practices are structured. The rationality of plain persons is to be elicited by and exhibited in their participation in communal practices, practices which require a shared recognition of their common good as a political bond, a type of bond very different from that provided in local societies by ethnic or religious or other prejudice. So Aquinas's theory is as much at odds with local prejudice – as contrasted with local custom – as it is with centralizing power. But this may seem to say that it is at odds with so much of thirteenth-century political and social reality, that it was not merely eccentric to its age, as my argument has already suggested, but perhaps even deserving to be stigmatized as utopian. I have suggested elsewhere that Utopianism rightly understood is no bad thing.[53] But this is a thought that cannot be pursued here.

(An earlier version of this essay was delivered as the first of three Agnes Cuming Lectures at University College, Dublin, 1 March 1994. I am indebted to members of the audience for their critical and constructive commentary. I am also indebted for extended discussion of these issues to John Roos, whose essay on "The Historical Context of Thomas Aquinas's Political Teaching" (delivered at the International Medieval Congress at Western Michigan University, 9 May 1994) develops some of the same themes, and for critical questioning to David Aers.)

---

53 Alasdair MacIntyre, *Three Rival Versions of Moral Enquiry*, Notre Dame, Ind.: University of Notre Dame Press, 1990, pp. 234–35.

CHAPTER 4

Aquinas and the extent of moral disagreement

I shall ask two questions in this essay: what kind of difficulties do the facts of moral disagreement pose for Aquinas's account of the natural law? And, if those difficulties can be met, what are the implications for our understanding of moral disagreement? I begin therefore first by setting out Aquinas's account of the natural law, to some degree expanding it, and next by cataloguing what I take to be the incontrovertible facts of moral disagreement.

I

The first principles, the fundamental precepts, of the natural law, on Aquinas's view, all give expression to the first principle of practical reason: that good is to be done and pursued and evil is to be avoided. The goods that we as human beings have it in us to pursue are of three kinds: the good of our physical nature, the good, that is, of preserving our lives and health from those dangers that threaten our continuing existence; the goods that belong to our animal nature, including the good of sexuality and the goods of educating and caring for our children; and the goods that belong to our nature as *rational* animals, the goods of knowledge, both of nature and of God, and the goods of a social life informed by the precepts of reason (*Summa Theologiae* Ia-IIae 94, 2).

There are therefore several distinct precepts of the natural law, each a precept of reason directed to our common good that enjoins the achievement of one or more of these shared human goods or forbids what endangers that achievement. Notable examples are: never take an innocent life or inflict gratuitous harm; respect the property of others; shun ignorance and cultivate understanding; do not lie. To say that they are precepts of reason is to say that to violate them knowingly would commit me to asserting "It is good and best for me here and now to act in such and such a way; but I shall act otherwise." What my actions express, if

I knowingly violate the precepts of the natural law, is an incoherence that parallels the incoherence of someone who asserts "It is the case that this is how things are; but I shall believe otherwise." To say of these precepts that they are directed to the common good is to say that the goods that they enjoin are goods that are indeed goods for each of us, qua member of this family or that household, qua participant in the life of the particular workplace or that particular political community. And they are therefore goods that we can achieve only in the company of a variety of others, including not only those others with whom we share the life of a family and household or the life of a workplace or a political community, but also strangers with whom we interact in less structured ways.

The precepts that in this way give expression to the first principle of practical reason Aquinas calls the primary precepts of the natural law. They are not to be derived from any more ultimate precept and therefore are known noninferentially. About them Aquinas makes four assertions: that they are one and the same for everyone, that they are unchanging and unchangeable, that they are known to be what they are by all human beings insofar as they are rational, and that knowledge of them cannot be abolished from the human heart. Each of these assertions needs further explanation and in some cases qualification. The primary precepts of the natural law are indeed one and the same for everyone, but there are also secondary precepts and these vary with circumstances. What does Aquinas mean by a secondary precept? Secondary precepts of the natural law (IIa-IIae 92, 4, 5) are those through which primary precepts find application in and to particular circumstances. A primary precept of the natural law, for example, requires those in political authority to provide whatever may be necessary for the security of their community from external foes. But what is so necessary varies from one set of circumstances to another, depending on the nature of current external threats, the level of weapons technology at that time and place, and the resources possessed by this particular community. So the application of a primary precept will often be in and through a set of legally, socially, and culturally ordered institutions which implement that primary precept through secondary injunctions. The primary precepts of the natural law remain the same in every society and culture, but the socially and culturally embodied forms through which they receive expression do not.

Primary precepts are known and their authority is recognized by human beings in virtue of their rationality. But Aquinas invites us to understand this with two qualifications. One concerns the *amens*, the mentally defective or disordered human being. Such lack the use of their reason *per accidens*; some bodily impediment has prevented the actualization of their rational potentialities. So they are to be accounted rational, but they may well not be aware of precepts of which the normally rational are aware, and they are not culpable for this failure (IIIa 68, 12; IIa-IIae 46, 2). Another qualification is this: there will in the case of each primary precept be some types of case, relatively rare in occurrence, in which the application of primary precepts to particular situations raises difficult questions. A primary precept of the natural law requires us, for example, not to deprive a legitimate owner of her or his property. But what of the problematic case where "it would be harmful and therefore unreasonable to restore goods held in trust, for example, if they are claimed for the purpose of aggression against one's country" (IIa-IIae 92, 4)? Such difficult cases require a sometimes complex spelling-out of the primary precepts through a series of secondary precepts. And how good we are at this task of elucidation and supplementation will vary from individual to individual, depending upon how practically wise each is. So Aquinas's claim is that everyone rational does indeed know what the primary precepts of the natural law are and that they are to be obeyed, but not that everyone knows how to apply them in detail or how to translate them into some set of secondary precepts.

There is of course another way in which our grasp of primary precepts can fail. On particular occasions each of us may and all of us do allow some impulse of desire to blind us to what the primary precepts require here and now. Some strong desire proposes to us a good that is other than and whose achievement is incompatible with that of the particular good that the primary precepts of the natural law require us to acknowledge and to attempt to achieve here and now. Temporarily we allow ourselves to ignore those precepts. Failing to attend to them, we flout them, although it was in our power to attend and to obey. But such failures, although endemic in sinful human life, are temporary and involve no tendency generally to deny the authority of the relevant precepts. But what then of more extended and widespread lapses?

Aquinas appeals to evidence provided by Julius Caesar – as it happens, not a reliable witness – for an example of a lapse by a whole culture: "in some reason is perverted by passion, or bad habit, or bad natural disposition; thus formerly theft, although expressly contrary to the natural law, was not considered wrong among the Germans" (92, 4). Aquinas does not tell us *how* his explanation of this failure to apprehend a particular precept of the natural law is to be understood, so that the question of how this type of cause could produce this kind of effect remains for the moment at least unanswered. But Aquinas does take this kind of failure to be rare and exceptional, occurring only "in some few cases." And to note this is also to note what seems on a first reading to be a plain implication of Aquinas's overall account: that agreement in acknowledging what it is that the precepts of the natural law enjoin and prohibit and in according them authority is, if not universal, so widespread that dissent from it can be expected to be an occasional and exceptional phenomenon, always requiring special explanation. But do the facts concerning moral disagreement bear this out? They do not.

II

Consider five types of moral disagreement. The first concerns the inviolability or otherwise of innocent human life. In every culture there is of course some kind of prohibition of homicide. But there have been societies in which infanticide is regarded as a justified means for controlling family size. And Aristotle, considering the ancient Greek practice of exposing unwanted infants, so that they will die, expressed a view that was not just his own when he said that we should not allow deformed infants to grow up (*Politics* vii 1335b 19–21). In our own culture there are many who, although they would condemn the killing of a newly born child, think that a pregnant woman who decides to procure an abortion of the same infant a few months earlier, does no wrong. All these dissent from a precept of the natural law that instructs us that no active intervention intended to terminate an innocent human life is morally permissible.

A second type of moral disagreement is more general, concerning relationships between ends and means. There are those of us who hold that, if some type of action is evil, then no action of that type is morally permissible, whatever predictable beneficial consequences may flow from it. An example is the use of torture on a prisoner, something widely viewed as wrong. Suppose however that that prisoner very probably, even if not certainly, possesses information about planned terrorist acts, so that by torturing her or him it is probable that the deaths of many innocent people can be prevented, and this is our only chance of achieving this good end. May we then torture that prisoner? Those who hold that a means otherwise evil cannot be justified by any end, no matter how good, are committed to answering "No." But the answer "Yes" will be given by those who hold that the goodness of an end always can and sometimes does outweigh what would otherwise be evil in the use of some means. This latter position seems to entail that no type of action is ever morally prohibited as such. For it will always be possible to envisage some set of circumstances, such that in *that* situation the evil of this particular means would be outweighed by the goodness of the end. So there is here the largest of disagreements with all those who, like defenders of a Thomistic account of natural law, or, like Kant, do believe that some types of action are forbidden as such.

A third type of disagreement concerns human sexuality and our intentions in engaging in sexual relations. That sex affords pleasure and sometimes very great pleasure is, I take it, uncontroversial. When Aquinas wishes to give an example of the reasoning of an incontinent human being (Ia-IIae 77, 2), it is the pleasure of fornication that provides him with a premise. The question is: what is the relationship between intending in one's sexual activity to beget, if possible, children for and within a marriage and intending to enjoy the pleasure of that activity? Is the latter intention legitimate when wholly divorced from the former? Here attitudes characteristic of modernity clash with attitudes central to all the great theistic traditions and it is from different answers given to these questions that the most fundamental disagreements concerning sexuality derive.

A fourth type of disagreement hinges on the place given to certain concepts in our shared moral discourse. An example is the place given to the concepts of honor and loyalty in the lives of seventeenth- and eighteenth-century aristocrats in Europe and twentieth-century gangsters in Chicago. These of course are not the only cultures in which concepts of honor and loyalty have been at home. But the issue is always whether considerations of honor or of loyalty or of both are or are not held to be overriding in respect of other precepts, justifying in the case of the European aristocrats the avenging of an insult by the infliction of death, perhaps in a duel, and in the case of the Chicago gangsters the assassination of informers who had betrayed their associates.

Fifthly, and in this catalogue finally, there are disagreements that derive from different and incompatible conceptions of justice. Here again just one example must serve to focus our attention. There is a moral tradition concerning economic justice, running from medieval theorists of the just price and the just wage to those modern trade unionists who have demanded "a fair day's wage" in exchange for "a fair day's work." But there are also those who, in the light of what they take to be conclusions of economic theorizing, argue that such expressions as "just wage" and "just price" cannot be given a coherent meaning and that the notion of fairness has application only in relationship to the fulfillment of contracts freely entered into, not to the terms of such contracts. This is of course only one area among a number in which conflicts between rival conceptions of justice are such that the concept of justice appears to be indefinitely contestable.

Each of the contending parties in the conflicts generated by these disagreements characteristically presents us with their view as embedded in some more general standpoint. They appeal, that is, to some set of first principles that provides them with what they take to be a justification for their particular moral claims concerning the taking of human life or sexuality or economic justice. Implicitly or explicitly they ground their first principles in some account of human nature and action, and more especially in some account of how the reasons that justify actions are related to the causes of actions, an account whose truth is presupposed by their practical claims. And in the conflicts between these rival points of view appeals to the primary precepts of the natural law seem to take their place as no more than the expression of one more contending standpoint. Furthermore because each of these contending points of view has within it its own standards and mode of justification there appear to be no common, shared standards sufficient to decide between such rival claims. So at a certain point in debate between the adherents of rival views, argument gives out and is replaced by the mere and usually shrill assertion and counterassertion of incompatible first principles.

There are therefore two respects and not just one in which Aquinas's account of the natural law seems questionable when viewed in the light afforded by these facts of moral disagreement. It is not only that, if Aquinas's account is true, we should, so it seems, expect to encounter a much higher degree of uniformity in moral belief and moral judgment than we actually find. It is also that on Aquinas's account the primary precepts of the natural law satisfy the requirements of practical reason and all sets of precepts incompatible with them fail to do so. We should therefore, it may also seem, expect that in rational enquiry and debate the superiority of those precepts would generally become evident without any great difficulty. But this too is not the case. So there is a problem. It appears that on the basis of the argument so far *either* we must revise our assertions about the nature and extent of moral disagreement *or* we must reject Aquinas's account of the natural law. My task in the rest of this essay will be to show that we do not in fact confront these stark alternatives and that, far from it being the case that Aquinas's account of the natural law is incompatible with the facts of moral disagreement, it enables us to understand their significance. To do so we have to make a new beginning.

What are the questions to which the precepts of the natural law supply an answer? And what is the condition of those for whom these questions have become urgent and inescapable? Characteristically and generally human beings first encounter judgments about goods as small children in situations in which what is for their good is sharply contrasted with what they are about to do or have just done at the immediate prompting of some desire. "Don't eat, drink, do that. It's bad for you." And the same contrast is also central when the young are later initiated into a variety of practices as students or apprentices.

Everyone of us initially brings to the practices in which we engage a set of motivations grounded in our antecedent desires: we want to please our parents or teachers, we want rewards of income and prestige that excellence or at least competence in this or that particular type of activity may bring, we want to present ourselves to others in a favorable light. But what successful initiation into every particular practice requires, whether it is farming or fishing, or playing football or chess, or participating in a theatre company or a string quartet, or house-building or boat-building, is that one should come to recognize the goods internal to that practice and the standards of excellence necessary to achieve those goods. So our desires have to be redirected and transformed. And in the course of this education of the desires we have to learn that it is never sufficient to explain or to justify our actions by citing some desire. For the question always arises as to whether it is good for me here and now to act from this desire rather than from that and what has to be explained or justified is why I in this particular situation choose or chose to act from this desire and not from that.

We distinguish, that is, between what it is good to do or to achieve and what we currently happen to want and our reasons for action, if they are good reasons, always involve implicit, if not explicit reference to some good or goods that can be achieved by acting in this particular way rather than in that. This distinction between goods and objects of desire is one that is primarily embodied in our everyday practice, including our practical discourse, and only secondarily in our theoretical reflections about our practice. And it is also at the level of everyday practice that we face the question of what place to give in our lives to the multifarious kinds of good that we have learned that it is possible for us to achieve. Every individual life does of course already express some answer to this question. Each of us, by living as we do, gives expression, usually implicitly and

unreflectively, to some conception of how, with our particular characteristics in our particular circumstances and under our particular constraints,
it is best for us to live. That is, we give expression to some conception of
what for someone with *these* characteristics in *these* circumstances and
under *these* constraints human flourishing is, just by the way in which we
assign to some goods a larger and more important place in our lives, to
others a smaller place, and to some none at all. What rationality requires
of us is that we ask what good reasons there are for taking the conception
of human flourishing that has been embodied in our actions and
relationships up to this point to be the most adequate conception that
is available to us. Is the account of human nature presupposed by our
conception true?

Aquinas argued that each of us does in fact pursue some single final
end, some single ultimate good (Ia-IIae 1, 5). He makes it clear that this
thesis is not incompatible with the fact that each of us does and cannot
but pursue multiple ends, multiple goods. But our single final end is
revealed in the way in which we organize those goods, in which good or
goods it is to which we give the highest place, in what we are prepared to
sacrifice for what, in our priorities. We all of us then presuppose in our
practice one and the same concept of human flourishing and one and the
same concept of an ultimate good towards the achievement of which that
practice is directed. But we disagree, as our various conflicting beliefs and
modes of life show, about what it is that we take that ultimate end to
consist in, about what it is that we take human flourishing to be. So
Aquinas catalogues at least twelve different conceptions of what the
human good is, each of which would dictate a different way of life, eleven
of which he takes to be in error (Ia-IIae 2, 1–8; 3, 6; 4, 6–7). It is at this
point in his overall argument in the *Summa Theologiae*, long before his
discussion of the natural law, that Aquinas takes notice of the facts of
fundamental practical disagreement as arising from disagreements about
the nature of the ultimate human good.

We each of us then, insofar as we are rational, find ourselves compelled
to ask the question of whether the particular conception of our ultimate
end that we have hitherto presupposed in our activities is indeed rationally
justifiable, when we compare it to alternative conceptions of that end, and
to press enquiry into that question systematically. Can we expect such
rational enquiry to resolve disagreement? The answer that Aquinas gives
is: not necessarily.

In the opening *quaestiones* of the first part of the second part of the
Summa Aquinas does of course advance what he – and those of us who

follow him – take to be compelling philosophical arguments against a range of competing conceptions of the ultimate end of human beings and for a conception in which the imperfect happiness that is the best that can be had in this present life directs us towards a conception of a happiness that is possible only beyond this present life in a perfected relationship to God. Did he expect such conclusions to be treated as philosophically unassailable? The answer is "No." He was well aware that it is of the nature of philosophy that no conclusion is ever treated as unassailable. "Human reason," he wrote, "is very defective in matters concerning God. A sign of this is that philosophers in their researches, by natural investigation, into human affairs, have fallen into many errors and have disagreed amongst themselves" (IIa-IIae 2, 4). Continuing disagreement is a permanent condition of philosophy.

Is it then the case that there is no remedy for such disagreement, apart from the gift of faith in divine revelation? This would be a premature conclusion, one that depended on a failure to ask what *practical* rationality requires of us by way of a response to the facts of disagreement. It is the word "practical" that is important here. Fundamental moral disagreements are indeed matter for theoretical, philosophical enquiry, just because in such moral disagreements each contending party presupposes a view of human nature for which *truth* is claimed. And Aquinas follows Aristotle in taking truth to be the aim and end of specifically theoretical enquiry (*Metaphysics* II 993b 20–1; *Commentary on the Metaphysics* II lect. 2, 290). But disagreements concerning the truth of this or that theoretical account of the human end first come to our attention, not directly but indirectly, in the form of practical disagreements, disagreements about how we ought to act here and now. It is initially in the course of deliberation about what to do here and now that we encounter disagreement and what rationality requires is that we deliberate further with others about how such disagreement should be resolved, including among those others those with whom we most deeply disagree. Why so?

IV

It is insufficiently often remarked that deliberation is by its very nature a social activity, that the central deliberative questions are not of the form "What should *I* do here and now?" and "How should *I* live?," but of the form "What should *we* do here and now?" and "How should *we* live?" Of course I always have to decide for myself how to act, but, when my relationships with others are in good order, my conclusions as to how it is best for me to act will often be one of a set of decisions, by others as well as by myself, which give expression to a common mind that we have arrived at together in our shared deliberations. Both Aristotle and Aquinas observe *that* this is so. Both are too brief in their accounts of *why* this is so. "In important matters we deliberate with others," wrote Aristotle, "not relying on ourselves for certitude" (*Nicomachean Ethics* III 1112b10–11). Aquinas expands a little further on this remark:

"Council" ("*consilium*" translating "*boulē*"), he says, "means sitting together from the fact that many sit together in order to confer with one another. Now we must take note that in contingent particular cases, in order that anything be known for certain, it is necessary to take several conditions or circumstances into consideration, which it is not easy for a single individual to consider, but which are considered with greater certainty by several, since one takes note of what escapes the notice of another." (Ia-IIae 14, 3)

What Aquinas stresses in this passage is the one-sidedness of each individual's point of view and perspective and how that one-sidedness can be overcome by learning how to view this or that particular subject matter from the standpoints of a number of others. But this remark could have been made just as aptly about theoretical as about practical thinking. Its peculiar importance for practical reflection derives from the relationship between goods and desires. I have already pointed out that we have to learn to distinguish between genuine goods and other objects of desire, but this is not something that is learned once and for all at some early stage in our lives, so that the distinction thereafter becomes easy to make in everyday life. We have to recognize that we always remain liable to suppose that we want this or that because and only because it is good, when in fact what will primarily be satisfied by our obtaining or achieving this or that is our desire for pleasure or power or money or some such.

In the opening *quaestiones* of the First Part of the Second Part of the *Summa*, as I also noticed earlier, Aquinas catalogues a number of misconceptions of our final end. Pleasure, power, and money are all items in this catalogue and it is important to remember that to take any one of these to have precedence in the hierarchical ordering of our goods is not only to make an intellectual mistake, but also to yield to a practical temptation presented by desire, a temptation that often presents itself in subtle and disguised forms. Indeed it is sometimes when the goods that we are pursuing are genuine goods that we are least able to recognize that we are pursuing this or that not so much because it is good as because its achievement will satisfy our desire for, say, power. This is when we most need the ruthless correction of our judgments by others who can see in us what we cannot see in ourselves and that is why deliberation not conducted in the company of such others is deliberation on which we would be unwise to rely. We should always therefore treat solitary deliberation as peculiarly liable to error.

Of course others are sometimes a source not of deliberative correction, but of deliberative corruption. We need from others, as they need from us, the exercise of the virtues of objectivity. Lacking that objectivity, others may reinforce our phantasies and collaborate in our misconceptions. So it is not just that deliberation will fail unless it is social, but also that the social relationships in question have to be governed by norms of objectivity. And we can only hope to resolve deliberative disagreements rationally with others who agree with us in respecting certain norms of objectivity. Yet at this point in the argument we have to confront another apparent difficulty.

v

Deliberation, as Aristotle asserted (*Nicomachean Ethics* III 1112b13–14) and Aquinas repeats (Ia-IIae 14, 2), is about means and not about ends. When we deliberate about what means to adopt in order to achieve some end, we take for granted, for the moment at least, that this particular end should be our end, that it *is* the good to be pursued by me or by us here and now. We may of course pause and ask whether this is indeed so, but, if we do, it will be, because we are now considering the achievement of this particular end, this particular good, as a means to some further end, either a means that will be causally effective in producing that end, as traveling across the Atlantic is a means to arriving in Paris, or a means that, as a part of some whole, plays its part in constituting that whole, as moving my pawn is a means to implementing a winning strategy in a game of chess. Debate about means, disagreement about means, always presupposes agreement about that particular immediate end to which means now have to be chosen. And although, as I have just noted, that immediate end can itself be considered as a means to some further end, and therefore provide subject matter for deliberation, there is one end that by its very nature can never be a means, namely the ultimate end, that which provides all our practical reasoning with its first premises.

That end, therefore, *that* good can never be subject matter for deliberation. But, if this is so, what I said earlier must now appear questionable. For I asserted on the one hand that, following Aquinas, I was going to

consider moral disagreement as rooted in disagreements about our ultimate end and I proposed to show that such disagreement is to be resolved, if
at all, through participation in the rational deliberation of everyday
practice. But now it emerges that, on Aquinas's view – and I also take
that view – practical deliberation is concerned with means and not with
ends qua ends, and therefore apparently not with our ultimate end. So
how is it possible for engagement in deliberation to involve reflection
upon our ultimate end, whether in agreement or disagreement?

Here we need to consider what it is to have practical knowledge of our
ultimate end. We do not begin, as theoretical enquiry does, with some
partly articulated, highly general conception of that end that can be stated
in propositional form. It is rather that we begin by discovering a directedness in our particular actions and in our particular deliberations, so that
we find ourselves inclined, first by nature, then by habituation acquired
through education by others, to move towards certain types of goal,
ordered and understood in certain specific ways. A good deal therefore
turns on how we are educated into good or bad habits, including the habit
of recognizing what it is that has been inadequate in our education so far
and finding resources to correct such inadequacy. What should prompt us
to undertake such self-questioning is precisely the discovery of disagreement with others as to whether this or that particular judgment or action,
choice or project, is or was the best to undertake in this or that particular
set of circumstances.

Disagreement therefore has a positive function in the moral life, that of
stimulating us to reflect upon the sources of our immediate practical
disagreements, by identifying the immediate premises from which those
disagreements derive, and, if necessary, the further chain of reasoning that
led us to argue from these particular premises about this particular
situation. Some of our disagreements of course turn out to be relatively
superficial, concerning perhaps the character of this or that immediate
situation. (This does not mean that they will always be easy to resolve.)
Others may derive from rival understandings of this or that particular
virtue: we disagree about what courage, say, or justice requires of us. But
some of our disagreements, and these the most basic, turn out to derive
from rival and conflicting conceptions of the ultimate human good, rival
views of the kind of direction in which our lives should proceed and of the
place that a variety of goods should have within the overall pattern of our
lives. So theoretical disagreements about the nature of the end of human
life emerge from immediate practical disagreements in the context of
shared deliberation. It is indeed only as they emerge in this way that their

practical significance is clear. The practical need to resolve our deliberative disagreements compels us to turn to questions of a theoretical kind, but those questions, although theoretical, now also have for us a practical import. So long as our shared deliberations proceed towards agreed conclusions with only incidental and resolvable disagreements, for so long practice can remain innocent of theory. But when disagreements turn out to be systematic and irresolvable in the context of immediate deliberation, then the identification of their character, let alone any attempt to resolve them, has to involve a resort to theoretical enquiry.

VI

When we are on particular occasions confronted by systematic and so far irresolvable disagreements that arise out of shared practical deliberation, but extend beyond it to questions about the nature of the human good, we always face the possibility that shared deliberation with these particular others will no longer be possible. The community that has hitherto been able to participate in joint rational decision-making may be fractured by such irresolvable disagreements. It may no longer be possible for its members to arrive by means of shared practical reasoning at a common mind about how it is best for them to act together. Instead they will have to base their communal decision-making either on inherited patterns of authority that are endowed with nonrational legitimacy or on some implicit or explicit social contract whereby individuals and groups, each trying to maximize their own advantage, arrive at some arrangement about the allocation of costs and benefits. In both cases it will be inequalities of power that determine the outcomes of decision-making processes. Power rather than practical reason will now have the last word. Is there then any way of avoiding these consequences of radical disagreement? How does practical reason require us to act when we confront the possibility of such consequences and their concomitant evils?

Practical reason requires of us, when we do encounter systematic and apparently irresolvable disagreement with our own point of view, that we do not assume that we are in the right, that it is *our* claims that are well grounded and *our* account of human nature that is true. We have initially no grounds for so judging. It may be that we are in the right or it may be that those who hold the opposing view are in the right or it may be that neither of us is. We have therefore to resort to enquiry as to what the truth about these matters is, in company with those others who hold opposing views. In so doing two crucial truths about the human good immediately become evident.

They are that no account of the human good can be adequate that is not vindicated and sustained by continuing enquiry that takes truth to be its end and good, and that therefore the good of truth must be a constitutive part of the human good. Shared participation in the practice of enquiry presupposes at least this measure of agreement about the human good. The conception of truth that is relevant here is that which Aquinas identified by the expression "*adaequatio rei et intellectus*" (*De Veritate* I, 1): the adequacy of a mind to a subject matter about which it enquires and of that subject matter to that mind. Truth, that is, is a relationship to be achieved between a particular intellect and some object about which it judges, a relationship that satisfies two conditions: first, how the thinker conceives of the object has become identical with how that object is and, secondly, that the thinker conceives of the object as she or he does, because and only because that is how the object is. For a mind to move towards truth thus understood involves its discarding anything in itself that involves projecting on to the object the agent's antecedent thoughts or hopes or fears or needs or purposes. And such progress towards truth can be achieved only if three further conditions are satisfied.

First, we have to accord to the good of truth a place that does not allow it to be overridden by other goods. I do not of course mean by this that the pursuit of truth always takes precedence over all other types of activity. That would be absurd. There is a time to enquire and a time not to enquire, but instead to catch fish or to sing the blues or whatever. Enquiry has to find its due place, a place that will vary with circumstances. I do mean that a more adequate understanding in respect of truth is always to be preferred to a less adequate, no matter how profitable it may be to remain with the less adequate or how painful it may be to exchange it for the more adequate. It is this kind of respect for truth that natural scientists endorse, when they insist that the misrepresentation of data or the ignoring of relevant data may justify the expulsion of an offender from the scientific community.

Secondly, however, for those of us for whom practical disagreement has made it necessary to engage even minimally in theoretical enquiry, enquiry has to find *some* continuing and significant place in our lives. If such enquiry requires of those who engage in it conformity to certain rules, then we will have to make those rules our rules. If the goods of such enquiry cannot be achieved without the acquisition and exercise of certain virtues, then we will have to make those virtues our virtues. Moreover

since practical and theoretical rationality both require us to avoid inconsistency – much more needs to be said about this; I shall not say it here –
we will have to make sure that the practice of those other rules and virtues
which we acknowledge in our lives is consistent with the practice of the
rules and virtues of enquiry. So engagement in the ethics of enquiry,
without which our response to systematic ongoing disagreements with
others about the human good will be less than rational, commits us to
agreement with those others, insofar as they and we are both rational,
concerning the rules and virtues of enquiry.

Thirdly, we will not however be able to do and be that which we are
thereby committed to do and be, unless we have been able to become
disinterested, that is, to distance ourselves from those particular material
and psychological interests that are always apt to find expression in those
partialities and prejudices that are nourished by our desires for pleasure,
money, and power. For those partialities and prejudices are apt to
distort our thinking and always most effectively so when we ignore or
are self-deceived about their influence.

What is necessary in order to counter that influence is a form of
intellectual and moral asceticism, both in our thinking and in the ways
in which we invite others to assent to our theses and arguments. We need
simultaneously to avoid allowing our own thinking to give expression to
and so to be guided by our preferences and aversions and to abstain from
a rhetoric that is designed to move others, not by the reasons adduced, but
by the passions to which the utterance of those reasons gives expression.
But, if we are to achieve this kind of disinterestedness our relationship to
those together with whom we are engaged in argumentative enquiry will
have to be governed by norms that afford to each participant the best
opportunity for considering the rival theses and arguments that have been
presented impersonally and impartially. What norms are these?

It is clear first of all that I will be unable to consider and to respond to
your arguments impartially and impersonally, if I have good reason to fear
present or future harm from you or from others, should I disagree with
you. And for us to be able to engage in shared enquiry, so that my
arguments and yours contribute to the common end of our enquiry,
you too must have good reason to be assured that you are secure from
harm or the threat of harm by me. It follows that a precondition of
rationality in shared enquiry is mutual commitment to precepts that
forbid us to endanger gratuitously each other's life, liberty or property.
And the scope of those precepts must extend to all those from whom we
may at any time in our enquiry – and it is a lifelong enquiry – need to

learn. So the precepts by which we will be bound, insofar as we are rational, will forbid us ever to take innocent lives, to inflict other kinds of bodily harm on the innocent, and fail in respect for the legitimate property of others. But these are not the only types of precept whose authority must be recognized as a precondition for engagement in rational shared enquiry.

If I am to engage with you in shared rational enquiry, we must both be assured that we can expect the other to speak the truth, as she or he understands it. There must be no deceptive or intentionally misleading speech. And each of us must be able to rely upon commitments made by the others. We must not make promises, unless we have good reason to believe that we will be able to keep them, and, when we have made such promises, they must be treated as binding. And even this is not all. If we are to pursue enquiry within our community through extended periods of time, we will have to make provision for the security of our communal life from both internal and external threats, by assigning authority to some fit individual or individuals to do what is required for its security. But we need go no further than this to recognize that the set of precepts conformity to which is a precondition for shared rational enquiry as to how our practical disagreements are to be resolved has the same content as those precepts that Aquinas identified as the precepts of the natural law. Yet it is not only in respect of content that the two sets of precepts are one and the same. For the precepts conformity to which is a precondition of reason-informed practical enquiry also share other characteristics that belong to the precepts of the natural law.

First, they are universal in their scope. There is no one with whom I may not find myself in the future a partner in deliberation concerned with some good or goods that we have in common. Therefore there is no one with whom my relationships can be in violation of these precepts. Secondly, those precepts are exceptionless. They state the necessary preconditions for *any* cooperative rational enquiry and to make an exception to them is *always* going to threaten the possibility of such enquiry. Thirdly, they are therefore also one and the same for everyone. And, fourthly, just because they are preconditions for rational enquiry we do not acquire our knowledge of them as a result of enquiry. They are not findings or conclusions inferred from some antecedent set of judgments. It is rather the case that in adopting the attitudes of rational enquiry we discover that we have already – implicitly, characteristically, rather than explicitly – had to accord them authority. They cannot but be presupposed and are therefore the necessary starting-point for any enquiry that pursues the truth about goods or good in order to pursue goods or good. They are, in this sense, first principles for practical reasoning. And that is to say that the precepts conformity to which is required as the precondition for practical enquiry *are* the precepts of the natural law.

Since those precepts as the first principles of practical reasoning cannot be justified by presenting them as conclusions inferred from premises, they cannot be supported by any theoretical argument, including of course the argument of this essay. What theoretical argument can aspire to show is that they *are* so presupposed and that practice which does not presuppose them fails in rationality. And the theoretical argument of this essay is designed to support this conclusion by showing that the facts of moral disagreement do not in fact afford us grounds for rejecting the authority of those precepts, understood as Aquinas understood them.

Let me recapitulate the main heads of that argument. It began by our noting that, when confronted by some immediate disagreement as to what you or I or we should do here and now, reason requires us to ask who is in the right, and the argument then proceeded by our further noting that, if we are to enquire effectively who is in the right, we must do so in the company of others and more especially of those others with whom we are in disagreement. We next remarked that what such deliberative enquiry sometimes discloses is that practical disagreement about what to do here and now derives from some underlying disagreement about the nature of the final end for human beings. So in order to answer questions posed by practice enquiry has to become theoretical and systematic. But it was then argued that it is a condition of the rationality of shared enquiry that the social relationships of those engaged in it should be structured by certain norms, norms that find their expression in the primary precepts of the natural law.

Each stage in the sequence of this argument corresponds to some point at which reason may fail in those sequences of conversation and action that are the sequels to the identification of some fundamental moral disagreement. We may first of all fail to ask who is in the right in our initial disagreement over what is to be done here and now, simply taking it for granted complacently that we are, and deploying our further arguments to support this conclusion. Or we may ask who is in the right, but suppose unthinkingly that the resources that each individual has within her or himself for answering such questions rationally are adequate and so never pause to consider the social dimensions of deliberative and other enquiry. Or we may recognize those dimensions and yet be so moved by, for example, our desire to triumph in the argumentative debate, that we violate one or more of the preconditions of effective rational enquiry.

Each of these types of failure will be apt not only to perpetuate the initial disagreement, but also to generate further disagreements. What the outcome is on particular occasions will depend in key part on the distribution of power among the particular contending parties. For insofar as the social relationships between those who disagree are not governed by the norms of reason, they will be open to the solicitations of pleasure, money, and power. And of these it is power that will decide the outcomes of social conflicts, although money and pleasure will often act as the agents of power or the masks of power.

Consider all those situations in which to hold one moral view rather than another will be psychologically more comfortable, more pleasing, or will be more acceptable to those who will determine how I am to be financially rewarded, or will render me less dangerous, less of an obstacle to those who have it in their power to determine my future in some nontrivial way. No one can of course allow to her or himself or to others that his or her present sincere moral judgments are determined not by the goodness of the reasons that there are for holding those judgments to be true, but by the influences of pleasure, money and power. But we recognize easily enough in certain others, both in the present and the past, and sometimes in our own past selves that what they now take or what we or they have in the past taken to be excellent reasons for judging such and such to be the good now to be pursued were in fact taken to be excellent reasons only because of the unacknowledged persuasions of pleasure, money, or power. The outcome of these nonrational persuasions may be the acquisition or the sustaining of beliefs that involve us in moral disagreement and conflict with others. Or they may instead bind us to others in firm, but nonrational agreement. And whether the outcome is agreement or disagreement will depend on the contingencies of the particular situation. It is disagreement that I have treated in this essay as problematic. But moral and social agreements arrived at only or primarily because of the seductions and the threats, the hopes and the fears, that are generated by pleasure, money, and power will exhibit failures in practical rationality of a sometimes more dangerous kind than disagreements generated by those same seductions and threats, hopes and fears.

What then am I claiming? That Aquinas's account of the precepts of the natural law, far from being inconsistent with the facts of moral disagreement provides the best starting-point for the explanation of these facts. It is not accidental that the treatment of the natural law in the *Summa* is immediately preceded by an Augustinian discussion of sins and vices, in which sins are characterized as "transgressions of reason" (Ia-IIae 73, 2) in the context of a complex account of human evil. The questions at once arise for the reader of Aquinas's text: in what way are sins transgressions of reason? And what are the precepts of reason that sins transgress? These are the questions, I believe, that Aquinas immediately proceeds to answer by advancing his account of law in general and of the natural law in particular.

PART II
Ethics

CHAPTER 5

Moral dilemmas

DILEMMAS AND DISAGREEMENTS ABOUT DILEMMAS

It is an oddity in recent philosophical discussions of moral dilemmas that some of the examples from an older past recurrently cited in the literature are of persons who, although confronting daunting alternatives, themselves identified no insuperable difficulty in deciding between those alternatives. They, unlike those who now write about them, did *not* experience their situation as dilemmatic. So it is for instance with Aeschylus' Agamemnon and Sophocles' Antigone.[1] Had we, so recent commentary seems to suggest, been confronted with the alternatives faced by Agamemnon or Antigone, we would have been at a loss in a way in which they were not. And this is perhaps a sign that with us it has become easier than it once was to find oneself in a moral dilemma.

Certainly there has been a striking increase in the philosophical discussion of moral dilemmas. Since E. J. Lemmon published his "Moral Dilemmas" in *The Philosophical Review* in 1962 over one hundred articles, chapters of books, and books have been published, either directly concerned with or highly relevant to the topic. If one were to publish two volumes, the first containing the entire preceding philosophical literature dealing with this topic, broadly construed, from Plato to W. D. Ross through Gregory, Aquinas, Kant, Hegel, Mill, Sidgwick, and Bradley while the second was devoted to the publications of the last thirty years, the second volume would be by far the larger. What would we be able to learn from that second volume? And how instructive would a reading of it be for those lay persons whose contemporary moral predicaments present themselves in the form of dilemmas?

---

1 On Agamemnon see the remarks of Earl Conee in "Against Moral Dilemmas" in *Moral Dilemmas*, ed. Christopher W. Gowans, Oxford: Oxford University Press, 1987, pp. 241–42. On Antigone see Karl Reinhardt, *Sophocles*, translated by H. and D. Harvey, Oxford: Basil Blackwell, 1979, pp. 64–66.

A useful preliminary to addressing these questions is to sketch three different types of situation which seem inescapably dilemmatic, when described from the standpoint of the agent. The first is of someone who having assumed or been assigned the responsibilities of more than one social role – and which of us, it may be asked, has not? – discovers that to discharge the responsibilities of one will prevent him from discharging those of the other. Qua officer in some military unit, it is his responsibility to act as leader in some life-endangering enterprise. Qua parent of a seriously disturbed child, it is his responsibility not to be away from home for extended periods and not to risk leaving his child without a parent. There is, it must seem, no way for him to act without someone being gravely wronged. No course of right action appears to be possible.

A second type of dilemma involves apparently inescapable failure by some morally serious person, not in doing what her role responsibilities require, but in doing what generally accepted norms for human beings as such, independently of their roles, require. Consider the case of someone bound to confidentiality by his own promise and by the trust reposed in him by another person to whom she is indebted. Someone, for example, has inadvertently disclosed confidential information concerning future events on the stock market and has asked for and been given a promise that the information will go no further. But it now transpires that only by passing on this information to the trustees of a charity for gravely ill children can a financial calamity for the charity be averted. Here the dilemma arises from the apparent incommensurability of the relevant norms. Actions which preserve confidentiality and trustworthiness will be in breach of those precepts which forbid bringing avoidable harm upon the innocent; actions which avoid such harm will violate the norms which enjoin trustworthiness. Once again there appears to be no course of right action open to the agent.

A third type of situation concerns alternative ideals of character. Someone is compelled by his or her realistic analysis of what is required for supreme excellence in some activity – at tennis, say, or as a painter – to which he is passionately devoted to conclude that at least for himself a ruthless singlemindedness is indispensable. But he also finds good reasons to conclude that such ruthlessness precludes the development of qualities needed in a good friend or for compassion towards the needy. The latter sensitivities are for him at least incompatible with genuine caring about excellence as a tennis-player or painter and caring about such excellence is what gives meaning to his life. One or the other must be sacrificed. So the prospect is of developing an inescapably defective life. The virtues of the one ideal of character are or bring about the vices of the other. Yet again there seems to be no right way to proceed.

What these three examples have in common differentiates them from some cases in the recent philosophical literatures which involve choices, but not genuine dilemmas, for example, that of everyday conflicts of duties: my commitment to attend my friend's concert conflicts with my duty to return my students' essays, duly corrected, by the assigned date. Such conflicts are recurrent, but there are always strategies available for managing or resolving them: I ask my students to be indulgent for one day more, I take some compensatory step by helping my friend in some other way, and I am duly apologetic. And it is morally important to become skilled in managing or resolving them. But there can be no such thing as skill in managing the types of moral dilemma described in my three examples.

A second type of case that needs to be distinguished from genuine moral dilemmas is that in which of two people about to drown I can only save one. But here there is no dilemma. Which of the two I save does not matter, unless of course one of the two is my wife, and then again there is no dilemma. As Alan Donagan has pointed out,[2] what matters morally is *only* to save one rather than none. The right course of action is plain. Another example of a choice that is not a dilemma is supplied by the case of the philanthropist who can either provide child-care for the new-born or a hospice for the dying, but not both, and can find no good reason for choosing one rather than the other. But once again nothing is morally at stake in choosing one rather than the other. There is a right way to proceed, namely to do either. It would not be in the least frivolous to toss a coin in either of these types of case except that, when someone is drowning, it would waste valuable time.

It would however be quite inappropriate to toss a coin in the case of the three examples of dilemmas that I cited earlier, if they are to be understood and described as I have understood and described them. For in each case what is taken to be morally at stake could not be more considerable. Which alternative the agent chooses determines what wrong they will have done or may do in the future and for what therefore they will have to acknowledge guilt. Wrongdoing and therefore guilt for wrongdoing in respect of one or other alternative seems inescapable. Bas C. van Fraassen[3]

---

2 See Alan Donagan, "Consistency in Rationalist Moral Systems" in Gowans, *Moral Dilemas*, pp. 271–90.
3 See Bas C. van Fraassen "Values and the Heart's Command" in Gowans, ibid., pp. 138–53.

in the course of asserting both the possibility and the actuality of moral dilemmas has argued that it is the appropriateness of *guilt* rather than *regret* which distinguishes the genuine moral dilemma from other types of case, for the genuine moral dilemma involves genuine wrongdoing. The individual entangled in a dilemma seems debarred from discovering any way of acting rightly.

This conclusion about the appropriateness of guilt has been resisted. Earl Conee,[4] who denies the possibility of moral dilemmas, also denies that in those cases which have been represented as moral dilemmas feelings of guilt and beliefs that one is guilty are "appropriate to the facts." And Walter Sinnott-Armstrong,[5] who has argued systematically in favor of the conclusion that there are moral dilemmas, and who holds that remorse is an appropriate response to the violation of significant moral requirements, distinguishes the remorse appropriate to someone who has violated what would normally be a moral requirement, while finding his way out of a dilemma, from any feeling that presuppose such beliefs as that one "deserves punishment" or "that one is or was a bad vicious person"[6] for doing what one did.

We have therefore two questions and not just one. The first is: are there moral dilemmas? The second is: if there are, in what way do those who as a result violate what would normally be a moral requirement do wrong and what response – guilt? remorse? regret? – is appropriate on their part? I turn now to the first of these questions, beginning with the answer presented by those philosophers who take the occurrences of moral dilemmas to be a central and ineliminable fact of the moral life, deniable only by those blinded by theory.

THE APPEAL TO FACTS

Bernard Williams has declared that "It seems to me a fundamental criticism of many ethical theories that their accounts of moral conflict and its resolution do not do justice to the facts of regret and related considerations."[7] And van Fraassen, whose claims concern guilt rather than regret, speaks of "the kind of fact of moral life on which ethical

---

4 Ibid., p. 243.
5 *Moral Dilemmas*, Oxford: Basil Blackwell, 1988, is a book of quite unusual value; my failure to agree with its basic contentions should not disguise my indebtedness.
6 Ibid., pp. 21 and 50.
7 "Ethical Consistency" in Gowans, *Moral Dilemmas*, p. 125.

theories founder."[8] But the conception of fact invoked in these assertions is not entirely straightforward. Sinnott-Armstrong has written that "In order to show directly that moral dilemmas actually occur, I would have to give an actual example and argue that it really is a moral dilemma. However, all actual situations are so complex that what seems to be a moral dilemma might not really be a moral dilemma . . ."[9] So what role, if any, should empirically warranted detailed descriptions of actual examples from history and biography – as contrasted with the bare outline sketches of types of example from which I began – play in our enquiries?

It is a commonplace that we need to avoid the error of supposing that there are facts of the moral life completely independent of and apart from theory-laden characterizations of those facts. But from this it does not follow, and it is not in fact the case, that a moral agent may not encounter situations which he or she experiences as radically discrepant with, or anomalous in terms of, the moral theory which he or she holds. Experience may really or apparently be discordant with a moral theory in a way that falsifies that theory, if one condition is satisfied: that the reasons for redescribing and reclassifying the experience, so that it no longer falsifies the theory, are outweighed by the reasons for treating it as a genuine counterexample to the theory. How such reasons are to be weighed will depend upon further theoretical considerations. Notice that in these respects the relationship of theory to experience in moral enquiry is no different from what it is in natural scientific enquiries. And the parallel extends at least this much further, that it is only in the light afforded by confrontation between some tolerably well-developed theory and what we have hitherto understood to be the facts of our moral experience that we can hope to discover adequate reasons for revising our characterization of those facts and our understanding of their significance.

It is therefore important to confront the claim that what I have identified as genuine moral dilemmas do in fact occur with one of those well-developed theories whose denial of their possibility, or at least of their actuality, is such that enquiry has to move towards *either* a conclusion that the occurrence of such dilemmas provides adequate grounds for rejecting the theory *or* a conclusion that the theory provides adequate ground for denying that such dilemmas occur.

8 Ibid., p. 142.   9 Ibid., p. 34.

DILEMMAS, PRACTICAL RATIONALITY, AND INCONSISTENCY

Can a theory according to which true moral judgments express precepts of reason admit the possibility of moral dilemmas? Consider as an example one particular type of such theory[10] with the following characteristics. First, its proponents understand particular moral judgments, whether expressed in action or in utterance, as following from a conjunction of some universal moral judgment, taken to be a precept of reason, and some judgment or set of judgments about what type of situation it is in which the agent finds him or herself. True moral judgment is the outcome of sound reasoning. Secondly, the universally applicable precepts employed in such reasoning are on this type of view principles of practical rationality. To fail to appeal to them or to employ them incorrectly is to fail qua rational being. Such principles together with statements concerning the types of situation to which they apply and statements identifying particular situations as being of particular types provide premises for deductive reasoning whose conclusions specify what rationality requires by way of action. Reasoning that issues in inconsistency is a sign of error on the part of the reasoner rather than of any lack of consistency in the system of beliefs, judgments, and inferences.

Thirdly, on this type of view it may indeed be the case that in order for agents to reason correctly and to act on that reasoning they must be in some particular type of dispositional state with respect to their desires and will. But, when in that state, they are sufficiently motivated to act in accordance with reason by their understanding that it is rational so to act. And, insofar as it is necessary to be in that particular type of dispositional state in order to act rationally, reason possesses the resources for instructing the agent on how to shape his or her desires and will in the requisite way. Particular agents may on occasion encounter particular obstacles to rational action which are such that nothing which they can do now and nothing which they could reasonably have been required to do in the past, in preparation for encountering their present situation, can enable or could have enabled them to overcome or circumvent such obstacles. But apart from such obstacles it is always in the agents' power to do what rationality requires; and in the face of such obstacles the agents' failure is not a failure in rationality. Reason, on this type of view, never fails.

---

10 See Donagan, "Consistency" pp. 272–73, for one source of my account. Where I have disagreed with Donagan, I am still largely indebted to him. His characterization of the relevant class of theories, although not the same as mine, is not inconsistent with it.

Hence, it must seem, as Alan Donagan argued forcefully,[11] that on this type of view there cannot be any moral dilemmas. There can be of course and there are situations in which it is extremely difficult to arrive at a conclusion about what reason requires. The claims upon an agent of two or more alternative and incompatible courses of action, when rationally evaluated, may well be such that he or she can find no good reason for preferring one to the other. But, from this theoretical standpoint, it cannot be the case that, whichever course of action the agent chooses, he will do the kind of wrong which renders guilt appropriate. For were that to be so, and were the agent to have made no mistake in his or her practical reasoning, it would be possible for the exercise of practical reason to generate an inconsistency, which is absurd. So it might seem that any such theory would have to exclude any possibility of the occurrence of moral dilemmas.

Yet against this it has been argued that to admit the possibility of dilemmas does not entail admitting the possibility of inconsistency in one's moral beliefs and judgments. Two alternative strategies that allow for the possibility of dilemmas, while still insisting upon the requirement of consistency in one's moral beliefs and judgments, have been proposed. One such strategy is to follow van Fraassen in revising the interpretation of deontic logic,[12] so that someone who concludes that X ought to do A *and* that X ought to do B *and* that doing B makes it impossible also to do A is not obliged further to conclude that it is both the case and not the case that X ought to do A. Another is to follow Ruth Barcan Marcus,[13] who has defended a conception of consistency significantly different from that which was presupposed in judging that the very statement of a moral dilemma involves inconsistency. A set of moral rules is on her view to be judged consistent "if there is some possible world in which they are all obeyable in all circumstances in *that* world."[14]

The adoption of either of these strategies would indeed furnish an adequate response to the charge that the statement of a moral dilemma necessarily involves inconsistency in the assertion. But Donagan has urged that neither strategy is available to upholders of the type of moral theory which we are discussing. The argument which he provides for this conclusion in the case of Marcus's strategy is compelling. Since the type of theory which I have sketched makes as one of its central claims that

11 Ibid., pp. 273–74.   12 Ibid., pp. 148–52.
13 "Moral Dilemmas and Consistency" in Gowans, *Moral Dilemmas*.   14 Ibid., p. 194.

there can be no actual situation in which its principles fail to provide consistent directives for right action, and since Marcus's strategy is compatible with allowing that in the actual world such failures may well occur, the incompatibility of assertion of the theory with adoption of the strategy is plain.

Donagan's argument against adopting van Fraassen's strategy is less obviously conclusive. The deontic system in which contradiction is prevented, even although dilemmas can be admitted, is one in which the rule of agglomeration does not hold and van Fraassen was able to show that such a system can be interpreted as a system of commands. Donagan argues that the moral rules of this type of theory, being rules of reason, are not to be interpreted as commands, although someone may enjoin as a command what such rules enjoin. To this it might be replied that it is only insofar as what such rules enjoin can be commanded, that is, insofar as there is a counterpart to each simple or conjoint or disjoint rule in some system of commands, that they can be taught as rules in the first instance, and that therefore van Fraassen's system of commands could provide the upholder of a rationalist theory with a constraint upon the conjoint rules to be admitted as moral rules. So inconsistency in the moral system by admitting the possibility of dilemmas would be avoided by this indirect device.

Whether this kind of reply to Donagan is worth developing further or not depends however upon whether there is a reply to a more fundamental objection to the use of either of these strategies by a defender of the type of theory that we are discussing. For both strategies are designed to enable us to admit the possibility of dilemmas, while avoiding inconsistency. And their relevance to the type of theory under discussion derives from the fact that for proponents of this type of theory inconsistency is always a sign of a failure in practical rationality. Yet, if one holds a theory of this type, there would be no inconsistency in allowing that it is a fact of the moral life that moral agents sometimes are practically irrational, that they do find themselves entangled in inconsistencies. So the fact that the expression of a moral dilemma in which someone takes him or herself to be entangled involves inconsistency on that agent's part is something which anyone holding this type of theory can allow without difficulty. And, if so, any attempt to use either the van Fraassen or the Marcus strategies would miss the point. For the fact of moral inconsistency, of the utterance of practical contradictions by some particular agent on some particular occasion might be an important symptom of something amiss in that agent's life, providing matter for further moral reasoning.

Contradictions play different roles in different types of discourse, in Hegelian philosophical investigations, for example, or as steps in *reductio ad absurdum* demonstrations by mathematicians or logicians. Their function in the moral life, as specified by this type of theory, must be by giving expression to an apparent moral dilemma to signify first that reasoning according to the standard modes prescribed by the theory has failed to provide the agent with a conclusion which either is, or directs him or her to, the right course of action now to be undertaken, and secondly that the source of this failure is neither in those modes of reasoning nor in the fundamental principles and rules, as formulated by the theory. The attention of the agent is thereby redirected towards an attempt to discover what additional factor is present in this particular situation, lack of attention to which has produced this particular outcome, and attention to which could remove the contradiction. There is of course no guarantee that this attempt will be successful; but the agent knows that he or she will in one way or another be responsible for failure.

To recognize this is to recognize that what follows from the assertion of the type of moral theory which we have been discussing is not after all a simple and unqualified denial that moral dilemmas occur. Certainly on this view moral dilemmas are not among the ultimate facts of the moral life, as van Fraassen and Bernard Williams have contended. But, because almost any moral agent may well on this view find him or herself in a situation which, on the best rational account which he or she can give of it, has all the features ascribed to genuine moral dilemmas, and furthermore will have to recognize that it remains his or her responsibility to discover what the right course of action is, the occurrence of moral dilemmas, thus understood, has to be accounted among the penultimate facts of the moral life.

To put this point in another way: for an ideally rational agent, who, if not omniscient, at least knows every practically relevant fact, there can be no moral dilemmas, but for actual human agents, insofar as they are less than ideally rational and have yet to learn, as is often the case, some of the practically relevant facts, situations can occur that not only have all the characteristics of genuine moral dilemmas which I noted initially, but also one further crucial characteristic. That is, they will find themselves in a situation in which they have arrived at a pair of conclusions, each derived from premises of a kind on the basis of which they have often constructed sound practical arguments, and each derived by modes of inference whose validity they have no reason to doubt, but which jointly are or entail a contradiction, a contradiction such that, had reason exhausted its resources in affording them this pair of conclusions, no course of right action would be open to them. The further characteristic of such situations is, generally and characteristically, a continuing conviction on the part of the agent or agents involved that there is nonetheless some right course of action to be identified which it is incumbent upon him, her, or them to discover and carry out, a conviction that the resources of reason have not yet been exhausted.

Notice that were this conviction not present, dilemmatic situations would not be painful in the way that they are. For the pain of apparently unavoidable guilt depends on the belief that feelings of guilt are appropriate. And what makes guilt appropriate is the justified belief that there is, in spite of appearances to the contrary, a right course of action which it is the agent's responsibility to identify. Notice also that, confronted by a contradiction, such agents do not respond in either of two ways open to them. They do not assert that just because this system of precepts and rules has produced a contradiction, they are entitled to abandon one of these precepts or rules. That is, they do not respond as a logician would on similarly encountering a contradiction within some formal system. And they do not behave as if they had been placed in a classical double-bind situation, oscillating between alternatives until paralyzed into inaction.[15] What prevents agents from responding in either of these two ways is just their conviction that there is a right course of action to be taken. Lacking such a conviction they would not be burdened with the responsibility that gives to dilemmas their peculiarly painful nature.

Against this thesis two objections may be made. It may be suggested that as a matter of empirical fact this is *not* in fact how dilemmas characteristically appear to moral agents. And since this thesis concerns such appearance, concerns the phenomenology of the dilemmatic situation, this objection is to the point. It could only be answered adequately by a series of empirical studies. Literary examples might be suggestive, but no more than this. Hence at the moment all that can be done is to concede the relevance of the objection and the need for such empirical support.

---

15 See G. Bateson, D. D. Jackson, J. Haley, and J. Weakland, "Towards a Theory of Schizophrenia," *Behavioral Science*, 1956, for empirical findings about the outcome of a certain type of encounter with inconsistency. See also R. D. Laing, *Self and Others*, London: Tavistock, 1961, chapter XII. On the inconsistency involved in moral dilemmas, see Terence C. McConnell, "Moral Dilemmas and Consistency in Ethics" in Gowans, *Moral Dilemmas*.

A second objection is that since the conception of a moral dilemma which I have advanced as not only compatible with, but integral to the type of moral theory under discussion is a matter of how things appear to moral agents in certain circumstances, rather than of how things ultimately are, it is a trivial thesis, irrelevant to the philosophical debate of recent years. So Sinnott-Armstrong has written that "the issue is not about appearances," because "almost everyone admits that some situations appear to be moral dilemmas."[16]

This brushing aside of appearances however itself misses the point. Any adequate moral theory must offer a cogent account of appearances as well as of realities, if only because appearances are among the realities of the moral life. In this respect the parallel with the natural sciences is once again instructive. From time to time contradictions, occasionally intractable contradictions, make an appearance within physical theory. Boltzmann and Maxwell had to confront the impossibility of conjoining the conclusions which Maxwell and others had arrived at about chemical spectra, the empirical findings about specific heat, and Boltzmann's equipartition principle without producing a contradiction.[17] Contradiction *appeared* inescapable. It was several decades before the removal of this contradiction from physics was made possible by the work of Planck and Bohr. What that work provided was not merely a contradiction-free theory, but an explanation of why such an appearance of inescapable contradiction was bound to be engendered in this area on the basis of the principles of classical mechanics, so long as the internal structure of atoms had not been deciphered in terms of quanta. Until the source of the perplexity had been identified, it would have been mistaken for physicists to abandon any one of the set of statements yielding the contradiction. Such a physicist did of course know, as Bernard Williams has put it, that his or her reasons for holding the beliefs which jointly generate the contradiction cannot in the case of every such belief "be the best possible reasons."[18] He or she had, as Maxwell said, to adopt an attitude of "thoroughly conscious ignorance."[19] But nonetheless such physicists had every reason provided by the best methods of scientific reasoning available

16 Ibid., p. 30. See on the importance of apparent dilemmas Terence C. McConnell, ibid., pp. 170–71.
17 C. W. F. Everitt James, *Clerk Maxwell: Physicist and Natural Philosopher*, New York: Charles Scribner's Sons, 1975 pp. 152–53.
18 "Consistency and Realism" in *Aristotelian Society Supplementary Volume XL*, London: Aristotelian Society, 1966, p. 13.
19 *Nature* 20, 1877, p. 242, quoted in ibid., p. 153.

to them to affirm each of these beliefs; they could not have abandoned any one of them without flouting some well-established body of theory and observation. And the contradiction produced by their conjunction had to accompany a conviction that there was a right and consistent theory to be discovered. Their conviction had to be that physics had not issued in perplexity as such, that the nature of the scientific enterprise precludes such an outcome, but only in a perplexity *secundum quid,* a perplexity deriving from their ignorance, although they could not as yet say what it was ignorance of which had generated their perplexity.

If I am right in supposing that this kind of theoretical perplexity among natural scientists is analogous in this way to the practical perplexities of moral agents in dilemmatic situations, then it is clear that the moral agent who finds him or herself involved in this type of inconsistent utterance provides thereby no more support for construing moral judgments and predicates in antirealist terms than does the natural scientist similarly involved. Bernard Williams argued against this that conflicting moral obligations, like conflicting desires, are quite unlike conflicts of belief.[20] To discover that one possesses a pair of beliefs, both of which cannot be true, is simply to have discovered that at least one of them, as it now stands, is false. To arrive at the truth I must abandon either or both beliefs as lacking the rational claim upon me which I formerly supposed them to possess. By contrast in a genuine moral dilemma in deciding between rival moral obligations I do not, so Williams asserts, reject the claim of either obligation as ungrounded, just as in deciding to implement one desire at the expense of another I do not thereby necessarily cease to feel the supplanted desire. But Williams advances this thesis in the course of developing an account of moral obligation incompatible with that given by the type of theory which I have been discussing. So that it is not after all from brute facts about dilemmas, but rather from facts understood in a way compatible with a particular theory about obligation that Williams derives his conclusion that the occurrence of dilemmas affords evidence for moral antirealism. On the account of dilemmas which I have sketched, the adequately rational agent knows that he or she does have to reject the claims of at least one of the conjoint constituents of the dilemmas as not having a well-founded claim upon him or her. The agonizing character of his or her situation arises from knowing this and also knowing both that he or she cannot as yet see any way of identifying which constituent or

---

20 See both "Consistency and Realism" and "Ethical Consistency."

constituents have to be rejected and that it is his or her responsibility nonetheless to determine and embark upon the right course of action.

Up to this point I have been discussing a type of moral theory which does indeed exclude the occurrence of genuine moral dilemmas as ultimate facts of the moral life, but which allows for their occurrence in the lives of particular agents as what I have called penultimate facts. So the question arises of the relationship between such penultimate facts to ultimate facts and I turn to consider the answer to this question by one particular moral theorist of the relevant kind, Thomas Aquinas. I begin with Donagan's interpretation of Aquinas. Aquinas, so Donagan claimed, asserted that there is a class of moral situations in which "somebody would find that there is a precept he can obey only if he violates another."[21] But this does not, on the view which Donagan imputes to Aquinas, involve damaging inconsistency in the system of moral reasoning. For this inconsistency arises for particular agents only as a result of their having already violated one or more of its precepts. Such a person is not *perplexus simpliciter*, but is said to be *perplexus secundum quid.*

The moral problem that provided the context for Donagan's discussion of Aquinas is one that has been presented as crucial in the recent philosophical literature. It is that of the person who, having made a promise the fulfillment of which would require a wrong action, seems to be in an irresolvable dilemma: either he or she breaks the promise, thereby acting wrongly, or he or she keeps the promise, thereby acting wrongly, and there is no third alternative. Donagan takes himself to be following Aquinas in holding that agents do confront such irresolvable dilemmas, that they are however always and only perplexities *secundum quid* and as such reconcilable with Aquinas's conception of moral judgments as expressive of precepts of reason.

Yet there surely remains a difficulty. A contradiction engendered within a system of reasoning remains a contradiction, no matter how engendered. And the premises from which this particular type of contradiction is derived may all on Donagan's account be true, so that the argument employed by the reasoner may well be a sound one. It would follow that the person *perplexus secundum quid* would thereafter be at a moral loss,

---

21 "Consistency," p. 285.

either committed by this assertion of a contradiction to endorsing any and every moral precept whatsoever or, on an alternative view, at least confronted with an ineliminable blank contradiction in his or her moral thought. But this, although it is a difficulty for Donagan, is not a difficulty for Aquinas, as can be seen by considering first what Aquinas actually says about the problem of promises which it would be wrong to keep and secondly what he says about perplexity *secundum quid.*

Aquinas considers the example of someone who has sworn an oath to commit adultery or homicide and enquires if it is the case, as it might seem to be, that such a person either sins by committing adultery or homicide, or else sins by violating his or her oath, so that whatever he or she does he or she sins.[22] Such a person would be indeed *perplexus.* But in fact, according to Aquinas, *this* should not be an occasion for perplexity. For an oath to commit an impermissible act does not bind and no wrong is done in violating it. We can easily generalize this solution to all cases of promising. Both someone who promises and someone to whom a promise is made have misunderstood the moral force of promise-making, if they do not realize that a promise to do that which is or turns out to be a wrong action is thereby void, something already presupposed in the giving and receiving of promises. So not to keep such a promise is to wrong nobody. No perplexity of any kind is involved.

On Aquinas's view no one is ever genuinely *perplexus simpliciter.* To seem to be *perplexus* is to seem to be in a situation in which whatever one does, one does wrong. This class of situations includes both those in which someone mistakenly takes him or herself to be *perplexus simpliciter,* that is, mistakenly takes herself to be in an irresolvable dilemma, and also those in which the agent may be aware of no dilemmatic or other perplexity, yet may seem to rational observers to have no alternative but to do wrong. So it is, for example, with the person whose erroneous conscience instructs him that it is permissible to fornicate.[23] If he or she obeys the mandate of conscience, he or she does wrong; but to act against conscience is always wrong. What then is the solution? What can make right action possible? Aquinas's answer is clear: to understand that one's conscience is in error is something possible at any moment for anyone. Aquinas never offers us an example of perplexity without also telling us how agents can resolve that perplexity.

---

22 *Summa Theologia* IIa-IIae 98, 2, 1.   23 *De Veritate* 17, 4, 8.

It might therefore seem that we ought to conclude with Edmund N. Santurri that Aquinas allows no place for the occurrence of dilemmas.[24] But this, although less misleading than Donagan's view, is still not quite right. For Aquinas in allowing that one can be *perplexus secundum quid* does recognize that one may seem to oneself to be in an irresolvable dilemma, to be *perplexus simpliciter*. What one always has to remind oneself is that this cannot really be so; what one must be is *perplexus secundum quid*, perplexed indeed but only relative to some factor, identification of which will be the key to resolving the dilemma. Knowing this is never sufficient to determine what it is neglect of or ignorance of or inadequate reflection upon which has put one in this dilemmatic situation and the pain of this type of situation for a rational agent continues until this is determined and acted upon. Hence Aquinas's position both admits the possibility of an agent finding himself entangled in contradiction and so apparently facing an irresolvable dilemma – that is, he allows for the occurrence of some dilemmas as penultimate facts of the moral life – and asserts that this situation is one from which the agent can always be rescued by right reasoning – that is, he denies that moral dilemmas are among the ultimate facts of the moral life.

DILEMMAS AND THEORIES

The three types of dilemma which I identified initially all turn out to be, if construed in accordance with a Thomistic view, examples of perplexity *secundum quid*. There is after all in each case a right action to perform. There seems not to be such only so long as a failure to recognize why no wrong is involved in one of the possible courses of action persists. So, in the first example, nobody binds himself irrevocably by a commitment potentially, even if not predictably, incompatible with some fundamental moral commitment; someone who gives others to understand that he has bound himself unconditionally commits a wrong, but not an irresolvable dilemma-engendering wrong. In the second example, only the concurrence of the person who provided the confidential information could release someone thus informed from her promise of silence, even if this

24 *Perplexity in the Moral Life: Philosophical and Theological Considerations*, Charlottesville: University of Virginia Press, 1987, pp. 91–94. To establish that my interpretation of Aquinas is correct I would have to argue at far greater length both against Santurri's view and the opposing view of William E. Mann in "Jephtha's Plight: Moral Dilemmas and Theism," in *Philosophical Perspectives*, ed. J. Tomberlin, vol. V, Atascadero, Calif.: Ridgeview, 1991.

promise is an obstacle to the bringing about of a considerable good. Lacking that concurrence, the information ought not to be disclosed, whatever the consequences. Once again the dilemma can be resolved. In the third example, if someone cannot achieve some particular type of excellence without losing qualities necessary for the virtues of friendship and generosity, then it is not permissible for them to pursue that type of excellence. And in each of these types of cases the agent involved will be *perplexus secundum quid,* unless and until he or she understands how to resolve the apparent dilemma.

That this, or something very like it, is what would have to be concluded by any upholder of a moral theory of a Thomistic kind and of its particular precepts seems clear. And it is equally clear that from any standpoint committed to the occurrence of irresolvable moral dilemmas as a brute fact these conclusions would provide sufficient reason for the rejection of any such theory and of its moral precepts. Judgments about the occurrence and nature of moral dilemmas are thus in key respects not independent of either moral or theoretical standpoints. To acknowledge this is to reinforce the suggestion that the period in moral philosophy in which it was fruitful to enquire as to the occurrence and nature of moral dilemmas as though into a set of isolable philosophical problems, soluble in relative independence of and prior to the resolution of larger theoretical and moral issues, is now over. By following out a line of enquiry initiated by Alan Donagan it has become evident that answers to questions about moral dilemmas stand or fall in systematic conjunction with answers to questions about moral theory in general. What the recent philosophical literature about moral dilemmas achieved is substantial: the statement of a set of conceptual constraints upon the ways in which the problems may be rationally resolved in the form of a number of requirements for coherence and consistency. But it is plausible to conclude that controversy now has to shift its focus.

CHAPTER 6

Truthfulness and lies: what is the problem and what can we learn from Mill?

I

When children are young, they learn that it is wrong to lie, but the rule that they learn varies from culture to culture and sometimes within cultures. For some lying as such is prohibited. For others some types of lie is permitted or even enjoined, but about which types of lie are permitted or enjoined there are also significant differences. It is not difficult to understand why. Among those types of lie that are often permitted or enjoined in different social orders are protective lies, lies designed to defend oneself or one's household or community from invasive hostility, perhaps from religious persecutors or witches or the tax-collectors of some alien power, or to shield the vulnerable, perhaps children or the dangerously ill, from knowledge thought to be harmful to them. Since who is judged to need protection from what varies from one social and cultural order to another, which of these types of lie is permitted or enjoined can be expected to vary accordingly. But these are not the only types of exception that are sometimes accorded social recognition and sanction, And, unsurprisingly, reflection upon how the rule that provides for such different types of exception should be formulated and justified commonly gives rise to controversy. Consider as one contributor to those controversies a moral tradition that belongs to the background history of our own moral culture.

One of the earlier statements of that tradition, often appealed to later on, is in Book III of the *Republic* (382c-d), where Socrates is represented as describing some lies as useful against enemies or for the prevention of evils. Some Greek patristic theologians, among them Clement of Alexandria, held similarly that on occasion untruths might be told, for example, to protect the Christian community from the invasive enquiries of persecutors. About precisely which classes of untruths are permitted they and later writers sometimes differ, and they also disagree on how to formulate the view that they share, some saying that all lying is prohibited, but that an untruth told for a just reason is not a lie, others that some lying is not prohibited. Newman in summarizing their shared standpoint emphasized that all of them agree that such a just reason "is, in fact, extreme, rare, great, or at least special" (*Apologia pro Vita Sua*, note G). Modern exponents of this view, he adds, include John Milton, Jeremy Taylor, and Alfonso di Liguorio. None of these were, of course, consequentialists. Their position was expressed succinctly by Samuel Johnson:

> The general rule is, that Truth should never be violated, because it is of the utmost importance to the comfort of life, that we should have a full security by mutual faith . . . There must, however, be some exceptions. If, for instance, a murderer should ask you which way a man is gone, you may tell him what is not true, because you are under a previous obligation not to betray a man to a murderer. But I deny the lawfulness of telling a lie to a sick man for fear of alarming him. You have no business with consequences; you are to tell the truth.
> (James Boswell, *The Life of Samuel Johnson*, June 13, 1784).

John Milton, Jeremy Taylor, and Alfonso di Liguorio would have agreed with Johnson that there is indeed an hierarchical ordering of duties and obligations and that any type of exception to an otherwise universal binding rule can be justified only as required by some other binding rule that is superior in that ordering. But Johnson's statement suggests consequentialist questions. If there is indeed an ordering of duties and obligations, what is the principle by which they are ordered, if it is not a consequentialist principle? The consequentialism of J. S. Mill, for example, was intended to provide, by means of the principle enjoining the promotion of the greatest happiness of the greatest number, a standard for just such an ordering. What an evaluation of consequences by means of that principle is to tell us is which binding rules in practice at least have no exceptions (or almost so; see the penultimate paragraph of chapter 5 of *Utilitarianism*) – the rules prescribing justice, for example, and which such rules do have a few well-defined classes of exception, such as that which generally prohibits lying. The onus seems to be on the adherents of Johnson's Christian anticonsequentialism to offer us an alternative and rationally superior principle of ordering. Moreover, if the rule prescribing truthfulness is to be defended as Johnson defends it, further consequentialist questions arise. Conformity to the rule seems for Johnson to be a means to a further end, what Johnson calls "the comfort of life," a necessary condition for which is "that we should have full security by mutual faith." But insofar as this rule is treated *only* as a means to some such further end, no matter how important, the possibility of evaluating the consequences of making a few well-defined exceptions to it has been opened up. And once again we need to know why we should not move to some more general consequentialist position, such as Mill's.

Someone may retort that I have only reached a point at which it seems difficult to reply to consequentialist claims, because I erred in my starting point. I began after all by considering the kind of rule that is taught to young children when they are first detected in a lie, perhaps at three or four years of age, and noted that often such rules allow for exceptions to the general prohibition of lying. But, it may be said, I ought to have begun with another, more fundamental exceptionless rule, one learned somewhat earlier and not by explicit instruction. This is the rule prescribing truth telling that we learned to follow by learning to speak our native language, whatever it is. That rule governs speech-acts of assertion. To assert is always and inescapably to assert as true, and learning that truth is required from us in assertions is therefore inseparable from learning what it is to assert. So two Danish philosophers of language, H. Johansen and Erik Stenius, suggested that "the utterance of a falsehood is really a breach of a semantic rule,"[1] although Stenius understood the relevant rule as one concerning what he called the language-game of reporting, while in fact it is assertion in general – acts of reporting are only one species of acts of assertion – that is governed by the semantic rule "Assert p, only if p is true." Mary Catherine Gormally has more recently characterized the relationship of lying to assertion by saying that "a lie (in language) is a cheating move in the language-game of truth telling"[2] and by further arguing that "'assertion' . . . carries moral weight, like 'property,' 'right' and 'obligation.' It is a value-laden concept" (p. 65). It is, that is to say, among those "concepts which are used to describe human actions in a way which makes it appear why our actions or omissions are bad if we act in certain ways, or fail to do so" (p. 67).

Note that the rule enjoining truth telling in speech-acts of assertion is constitutive of language use as such. It is a rule upon which therefore all interpreters of language use by others cannot but rely. And it is not merely a rule of this or that particular natural language. Hence Gormally concluded that about it "one cannot be culturally relativistic" (p. 58), in this following Peter Winch, who had argued that it would be "nonsense to call the norm of truth telling a 'social convention,' if by that were meant that

---

1 Erik Stenius, "Mood and Language Games," *Synthèse* 17, no. 3 1967, 269.
2 "The Ethical Root of Language" in *Logic and Ethics*, ed. P. Geach, Dordrecht: D. Reidel, 1991, p. 53.

there might be a human society in which it were not generally adhered to."[3] And David Lewis (who has also argued that in part our commitment to truthfulness in speech *is* a matter of convention, since "a language L is used by a population P if and only if there prevails in P a convention of truthfulness and trust in L – sustained by an interest in communication")[4] says about what he calls the "regularity of truthfulness and trust *simpliciter*" and characterizes as "the regularity of being truthful and trusting in whichever language is used by one's fellows" that it "neither is a convention nor depends on convention" (p. 184). We stand, so all these writers agree, and surely rightly, in the same relationship to speakers of other languages in respect of the semantic requirement of truthfulness in assertion as that in which we stand to other speakers of our own language, a relationship defined by the rules governing the use and interpretation of asserted sentences as such.

What then are these rules, if they are not conventional? Winch's answer was framed in terms of the distinction that Aristotle drew between natural and conventional justice, by saying of the precepts of natural justice that they "have the same power everywhere and do not depend for it on being accepted or rejected" (*Nicomachean Ethics* V, 1134b19–20). This characterization of the natural holds equally of the semantic rule requiring truthfulness in assertion, which, like the precepts of natural justice, cannot but be accorded universal recognition, and in the vast majority of cases obedience, by the users of all natural languages. In Aristotle's terms the semantic rule enjoining truth telling is to be accounted natural because recognition of it belongs to the essential nature of human beings as language users.

We notice at once that liars cannot withhold recognition from it any more than the truthful can, and this not only because even habitual liars cannot but tell the truth far more often than they lie, sustained in their truth telling by the interest in communication that, as Lewis emphasized, they share with everyone else. But liars have in addition their own distinctive interest in general conformity to that rule. For they can only hope to lie successfully insofar as it is taken for granted by others that the rule requiring truthfulness in assertion is respected more particularly by the liar herself or himself. The liar, as Kant put it, cannot consistently will

---

3 "Nature and Convention," in *Ethics and Action*, London: Routledge and Kegan Paul, 1972, pp. 62–63.
4 "Languages and Language," in *Philosophical Papers*, Oxford: Oxford University Press, vol. I, 1983, p. 169.

that the maxim upon which she or he acts in lying should be the universal rule governing truth telling and lying. What successful lies achieve for those who utter them is an advantage over those who are deceived. And successful liars necessarily deceive us not only about the subject matter about which they lie, but also about their own beliefs and their intention in asserting what they assert falsely, and indeed about their further intention to conceal this intention from us. So that even in the simplest case of lying there is a complexity in the liar that is absent from the truthful person. Truthful persons may have much to conceal, including their own intentions not to disclose what they are concealing. But they do not misrepresent themselves to others as liars do, with regard to the relationship of their beliefs and their intentions to their assertions.

The kinds of advantage to be gained by lying are of course various and so therefore are the motives for lying. Many lies, as I already noticed, are protective – motivated by a fear of harm at the hands of others. Some are acts of aggression, motivated by a wish to damage others. Some are intended to maximize advantage in competitive situations. Some are acts of flattery and some are intended to make the speaker appear more interesting than he or she in fact is. Some lies are told by office-holders from devotion to what is taken to be the public interest and some are told both to and by office-holders to subvert that interest. But in each of these cases, if a lie has been successful, it may well be that the liar will have altered the relationships of power in her or his own favor, or perhaps in favor of someone else. Yet in so doing, whether the lie is successful or not, the liar will also have altered her or his relationship to others in general, by deliberately violating the norm presupposed in all human relationships involving assertive speech-acts. She or he will have relied upon the general human regard for truth, while failing to have regard for it. "Without truth," Kant wrote, "social intercourse and conversation become value-less."[5] And the offense of the liar, thus understood, is not a matter of the harmful consequences of particular lies. To tell a lie is wrong as such, just because it is a flouting of truth, and it is an offense primarily not against those particular others to whom this particular lie has been told, but against human rationality, everyone's rationality, including the liar's own rationality. By lying she or he has failed not only to acknowledge truth as a good that is indispensable in rational relationships with others, but also

---

5 *Eine Vorlesung Kant's über Ethik*, ed. P. Menzer, p. 285, trans. L. Infield, *Lectures on Ethics*, Indianapolis: Hackett, 1980, p. 224.

to recognize that a failure to respect truth is a failure in respecting oneself as a rational being.

This conception of the wrongness of lying was elaborated within a moral tradition whose central theses were in crucial respects at odds with those of the tradition that I described earlier. For where the exponents of that tradition, from Clement to John Stuart Mill, had agreed on the need to exempt certain types of lie from the general prohibition of lying, the adherents of the tradition of which Kant was a late and distinguished exponent agreed in insisting that the rule prohibiting lying was exception-less. Instead of looking back to Plato, its protagonists look back to Aristotle's condemnation of all lying as disgraceful and to his praise of the lover of truth who is truthful whether something further is at stake or not (*Nicomachean Ethics* IV, 1127b4–8). There are trenchant restatements of this standpoint by St. Augustine, by St. Thomas Aquinas, by the Catechism of the Council of Trent, by Pascal, and by Protestant theologians both before and after Kant. Augustine declared in the *Contra Mendacium* (31C) that "it is said to God 'Your law is truth.' And for this reason what is contrary to truth cannot be just. But who doubts that every lie is contrary to truth? Therefore no lie can be just." Aquinas argued that truth itself is a virtue, since to say what is true makes a good act and a virtue is that which makes its possessor good and renders its possessor's action good (*Summa Theologiae* IIa-IIae, 109, 1). Of the vices opposed to the virtue of truth lying is the first (110, prologue). Aquinas captured a thought central to this tradition when he distinguished between the wrong done by intentionally asserting what is false and the wrong done by intentionally deceiving someone by that false assertion. Even without an intention to deceive, the intentional assertion of what is false is wrong (110, 1 resp. and 3 ad. 6). The offense is against truth.

Some adherents of these two contrasting and generally rival traditions may in fact disagree about very little of moral substance. For among some of those for whom lying is altogether prohibited, the definition of a lie is such as to exclude just those cases that some adherents of the other tradition treat as permissible or required lies. But it would be a mistake to conclude from these cases that the differences between the two traditions are unimportant, as Newman seems to have done. They extend to three kinds of issue.

First there is the question of how a lie is to be defined. Those for whom some types of lie are permissible or even required characteristically define a lie so that an intention to deceive is a defining property of a lie, and the wrongness of lies is the same as that of other acts of deception, while those for whom no lies are permissible characteristically define a lie in terms of an intention to assert what is false, sometimes, like Aquinas, denying that an intention to deceive is necessary for an assertion to be a lie. A second difference concerns the nature of the offense committed by a liar. For those for whom some types of lie are permissible or even required the wrong done by a lie is understood in terms of the harm inflicted upon those social relationships that need to be sustained by mutual truth and credibility. Because of the constitutive part played by such trust in every important human relationship, that harm is never held to be entirely negligible. But evidently there are occasions on which the utterance of a particular lie will prevent some harm greater than that which its telling will cause to the social fabric. By contrast, for those for whom no lie is permissible the wrong committed by making a false assertion is understood as a type of wrong that inescapably puts in question one's standing as a rational person in relationship to other rational persons.

A third set of issues concerns the kind of justificatory argument advanced within each tradition. Those who hold that some types of lie are permissible advance justifications that cite the effects of different types of lie, even when those who advance them are not consequentialists. Those who hold that all lies are forbidden advance justifications citing the nature of the act of lying. And at this point the self-definition of each of these two rival traditions makes something plain that has been insufficiently remarked within either tradition. There are, so I argued, two distinct grounds for our concerns about truth telling and lying: one deriving from the invariant semantic rule governing the utterance of assertions and one from our varying evaluations of the motives for and the effects of the utterance of different types of lie. Reflection upon the first of these focuses attention upon lying as an offense against truth, as an error-engendering misuse of assertion, while reflection upon the second focuses attention upon lying as an offense against credibility and trust, as having effects that tend to be destructive of relationships between persons. And each of the two rival moral traditions that I identified has developed a line of argument well designed to uphold the claims upon our allegiance of *its* formulation of what it takes to be *the* moral rule concerning truth telling and lying.

In this case at least two moral traditions seem to be one too many. In answer to such questions as "What should be our socially established rule about truth telling and lying?", "What should we teach our children?", "And how should we justify rationally what we teach them?", we are presented with two incompatible and rival types of rule and two incompatible and rival types of justificatory argument. At the same time we cannot but

recognize the compelling and insightful character of central considerations advanced from each side. The problem is therefore not so much
that of finding sufficient reasons for choosing to align ourselves with one
standpoint or the other, but rather that of finding some rationally justifiable framework within which the concerns articulated within both traditions can be integrated in such a way as to provide a single set of answers
to those questions.

This then is the problem. In what direction should we turn for an
answer? One suggestion might be first to examine the practice of one or
more other cultures with a somewhat different moral tradition concerning
truthfulness: for example, Confucianism with its conception of appropriate speech and of the virtue of *hsin*. And in the larger enquiry of which
these lectures are a part this will be a necessary undertaking. But an
important preliminary is to understand a good deal better just what it is
that we ourselves need here and now and why. What *is* the moral
condition of the culture now dominant in North America in respect of
truth telling and lying?

II

Three features of that culture are relevant and notable: the nature and
extent of disagreement about what the rule concerning lying should be,
the frequency of lying of various kinds, and the nature of the underlying
dilemmas that make that disagreement and that frequency intelligible.
Consider each of these in turn.

Discussion, sometimes in depth, with a number of different American
groups in the last ten years has convinced me that the only shared near-
universal agreement is on the form that any acceptable rule concerning
lying and truth telling should take. That form is "Never tell a lie" – this
part of the rule is generally enunciated firmly and clearly, especially to
children – "except when" – here the voice begins to drop – and there then
follows a list of types of exception, culminating with an "etc." That list
includes most often "when by lying one will save an innocent human life,"
almost as often "when by lying one will avoid offending someone," and
quite tolerably often "when by lying one will secure advantage in one's
career or to one's financial prospects." At one end of a spectrum there are
those Americans who hold that one ought *never* to tell a lie; at the other
those who regard themselves as free to misrepresent their own past or the
truth about others in trivial anecdotal gossip as readily as on occasions
when something important is at stake.

We have then a set of wide-ranging disagreements, not only about what types of exceptions should be included in the list, but also about how these should be spelled out further. To what classes of person may we avoid giving offense by telling a lie? Is untruthful gossip only permissible when it could not damage anyone, or are there people whose reputations need not matter to us? May I secure advantage to my career only by lying about what I, but not others, take to be irrelevant considerations or may I misrepresent what everyone would agree to be relevant? Different answers to questions such as these find expression not only in what people say about lying, but also by how and when they lie. That this is so makes the facts about the incidence of certain types of lying a little less surprising than they might otherwise be.

What then are those facts? Bella DePaulo, a University of Virginia psychologist who studied lying by having her subjects keep a diary recording the lies that they told, concluded from her study that "People tell about two lies a day, or at least that is how many they will admit to."[6] James Patterson and Peter Kim, whose expertise is in research for advertising, reported in 1991 on the basis of survey research that 91 percent of Americans lie regularly, that only 45 percent refrain from lying on occasion because they think it wrong, and that those who do lie lie most to friends and relatives.[7] They also found that a distinction was commonly made between more and less serious lies and that 36 percent of their sample admitted to serious lies. Dan McCabe of Rutgers University found that 57 percent of business students would admit to having cheated in an examination at least once,[8] while in an earlier *Psychology Today* study the percentage of students who admitted to being willing to cheat in examinations or other test assignments, if they judged that they could get away with it, was 67 percent.[9]

Unsurprisingly, those who lie are apt to believe that others lie to them. So Patterson and Kim found that 31 percent of their subjects believed that they had at some time been lied to by their physicians, 34 percent believed this of their accountants, and 42 percent of their lawyers. American lawyers are of course professionally divided about lying. Some have held that a defense lawyer who knows that a client is committing perjury in court has a duty to use that perjury to secure acquittal, if she or he can; others have denied that this is so. And such divisions occur in a number of

6 *New York Times*, February 12, 1985, p. 17.
7 *The Day America Told the Truth*, New York: Prentice-Hall, 1991, pp. 45–6.
8 *Harpers Index*, September 1991.   9 James Hassett, *Psychology Today*, November 1981.

professions. But the division both in private life and in the professions is not just one between different individuals. It is also one within many individuals. The extent to which it is within and not only between individuals can be gauged by the extent of the unhappiness about their own lying that significant proportions of those who nonetheless regularly lie evince. They evince that unhappiness in a variety of ways. A significant number report that they feel uncomfortable when they lie. Some betray their anxiety, when they are put to the question about their lies, by systematically failing polygraph tests, in this being quite unlike those Eastern Europeans cited by Richard Helms, "who could defeat the polygraph at any time," because they had spent their lives "lying about one thing or another and therefore become so good at it."[10] These are the same people described by Erazim Kohak as having developed under Communist regimes an inability to admit to the differences between illusion and reality. "A factory manager, seeing the collapse around him, yet reporting inflated production figures to assure premiums for his factory, could not believe, but neither could he just lie. Instead he would refuse to acknowledge the distinction." And so after Communism this refusal persists. "Though there is no one to deceive, deception has become a habit."[11] But this is not at all how contemporary Americans are.

They for the most part recognize what they are doing, while lying, and are often far from satisfied with their own justifications for lying. This unhappiness is perhaps one cause of those oscillations and inconsistencies in responding to discovered lies that mark so much of American life, directing our attention to further dimensions of those divisions about lying on which I have already remarked. Those oscillations and inconsistencies are most obvious in political life. The lies of Richard Nixon and Oliver North incurred instant and extreme obloquy, the lies of a Lyndon Johnson about Vietnam or of a James Baker about relationships with the government of China much less.[12] Arthur Schlesinger, Jr., who had proposed to the Kennedy administration that "lies should be told by subordinate officials," so that they and not the president would take the

10 *Investigation of the Assassination of President John F. Kennedy*, vol. IV, pp. 98–99, 118, cited in John Ranelagh, *The Agency: The Rise and Decline of the CIA*, New York: Simon and Schuster, 1986, pp. 568–69.

11 "Ashes, Ashes . . . Central Europe after Forty Years," *Daedalus* 121, no. 2, 1992, 203; for systematic understanding of the function of lying in the Soviet Union the indispensable works are by Alexander Zinoviev, both the novel *Yawning Heights*, New York: Random House, 1979, and *Homo Sovieticus*, London: Gollancz, 1985.

12 On Lyndon Johnson, see the *Chicago Tribune*, October 20, 1991, p. 4–1; on James Baker, see Hodding Carter III, 'Viewpoint', *Wall Street Journal*, January 25, 1990, p. A15.

blame, if discovered,[13] has since been among the most vehement denoun-
cers of lies told by subordinate officials to protect presidents. And public
blame for lying is in general unevenly and haphazardly distributed.
What does such unevenness and inconsistency reveal concerning our
disagreements about lying?

That they are of two related kinds. There is first a set of disagreements
about which types of lie are to be treated as more serious and which less
serious offenses, and within each category how different types of lie are to
be ranked. If I lie to the police about the whereabouts of my friend, who
has fled from the scene of an unreported automobile accident, is this
better or worse than lying to my friend about my part in wrecking his car?
If I lie to my wife about having lost my job, is this better or worse than
lying to my employer in order to keep that job? Yet it is not only that we
do not agree on the gravity of the offenses committed by different kinds of
liar. It is also that we do not agree upon how to respond to different kinds
of lie, when someone's lies are discovered and we are the offended party. If
a lie concerns some relatively trivial matter, should we just ignore it or is
this to treat lying as acceptable? If a lie is a serious breach of trust, should
we break off all relationships with the liar? Ought we to make the fact of
such lying public in order to warn others? Should a lie of a certain gravity
disqualify a liar from public office or from friendship? And if we ourselves
are discovered in a lie, what do we have to do to merit forgiveness? There
seems to be no consensus on how these questions are to be answered.

Not all North Americans belong to the dominant culture that is in such
a peculiar condition in respect to lying and truth telling. Orthodox Jews,
conservative Roman Catholics, some Southern Baptists, and devoted
Confucian Chinese families provide examples of minorities that advance
systematic and unambiguous answers to these and to kindred questions.
But outside such minorities – minorities that are deviant with respect to
the dominant North American culture, but nondeviant with respect to the
larger history of humankind – the lack of consensus upon these issues is a
sign of a remarkable absence. The dominant culture fails to provide any
generally accepted and agreed upon public rule about truth telling and
lying, by appeal to which we could in relevant instances call each other to
account. Why is this so? What do we need to understand about North
Americans belonging to the dominant culture, if this absence and the
divisions and disagreements that accompany it are to be intelligible?

13 Peter Wyden, *Bay of Pigs. The Untold Story*, New York: Simon and Schuster, 1979, p. 161.

A salient moral fact about such modern Americans is, so I want to suggest, this. They are brought up to give their allegiance to two distinct sets of norms. One of these enjoins each individual to pursue her or his own happiness, to learn how to be successful in competing against others for position, power, and affluence, to consume and to enjoy consumption, and to resist any invasion of her or his rights. The other set instructs individuals to have regard for the welfare of others and for the general good, to respect the rights of others, to meet the needs of those who are especially deprived, and even to be prepared on some particular occasions to sacrifice one's own immediate happiness for the sake of the happiness of particular others. On many occasions these two sets of norms are not in conflict. But on others, and among them some of the more significant in individual lives, Americans not only recognize that such norms make rival and incompatible demands for their allegiance, but also that they possess no third, higher-order set of norms that would enable them to make a rationally justifiable choice between those conflicting demands.

This moral situation is not confined to North America. It characterizes in varying degree all the cultures of advanced modernity. And it was first articulated in philosophical terms in the late nineteenth century by Henry Sidgwick in *The Methods of Ethics*, a text that in its foreshadowing of the subsequent history both of morality and of moral philosophy deserves to be accorded the status of a prophetic book. Sidgwick had taken it to be a discovery of that distinctively modern moral philosophy that first emerged in seventeenth- and eighteenth-century England that there is not one single governing authority in moral matters, the role to which "Reason" is assigned in most Greek moral philosophy, but two distinct authorities, "Universal Reason and Egoistic Reason."[14] The first of these prescribes how it is reasonable to act if the general good and happiness is to be achieved, the second how it is reasonable to act if my own good and happiness is to be achieved. Sidgwick took it to be his own philosophical discovery, after an extended study of the claims of Kantian, utilitarian, and intuitionist moral philosophy, that when the injunctions of these two kinds of practical reason conflict, there is no rational method for deciding between their claims or for reconciling them.[15]

Sidgwick's own treatment of what he called the duty to veracity consists chiefly of an examination of those convictions that belong to what he took

14 *Outlines of the History of Ethics for English Readers*, London: Macmillan, 1886, p. 198.
15 "Concluding Chapter," *The Methods of Ethics*, 7th edn, London: Macmillan, 1907.

to be "the morality of Common Sense."[16] About veracity he concluded that among persons of common sense "there is no real agreement as to how far we are bound to impart true beliefs to others" (p. 317), perhaps because such persons seem unable "to decide clearly whether truth-speaking is absolutely a duty, needing no further justification: or whether it is merely a general right of each man to have truth spoken to him by his fellows, which right however may be forfeited or suspended under certain circumstances" (p. 315). Summarizing common-sense beliefs about truthfulness, Sidgwick declares that it is commonly held that lawyers may be justified in saying what they know to be false, if so instructed by their clients, that it is held by most persons that benevolently intended lies to invalids are justifiable, and, perhaps more surprisingly, that no one "shrinks from telling fictions to children on matters upon which it is thought well that they should not know the truth" (p. 316).

Common sense offers us no principle by which we may decide systematically in these or other cases. We have no alternative to "weighing the gain of any particular deception against the imperilment of mutual confidence involved in all violation of truth" (p. 316). The metaphor of weighing invites Sidgwick's readers to ask: what are the scales? And it turns out that, for reasons that I have already cited, Sidgwick can in the end only offer us two alternative sets of scales, which will provide us with different measures of weight, that of Universal Reason, appealing impersonally to the standard of the greatest happiness of the greatest number, and that of Egoistic Reason, by whose standard my happiness outweighs that of everyone else. There is no third and higher standard of practical reason to decide on each particular occasion which of these two rivals it is to whose verdict we should attend.

Sidgwick's philosophical analysis confirms what the evidence concerning contemporary North American moral culture already suggested, that no formulation of a rule concerning truth telling and lying and no account of the virtue of truthfulness will meet our contemporary needs, unless they overcome that moral dualism that seems to debar so many from the possibility of ordering within a single rational scheme their self-regarding reasons for action and those reasons that have regard either for particular others or for the general good. So it is not just that we need to integrate the insights and concerns of the two rival moral traditions concerning truth telling and lying. We have to impose a further condition,

---

16 *The Methods of Ethics* III, chapter 7.

that this integration provide a rational ordering of the relevant types of reason for action. The satisfaction of these two major conditions requires of course more and other than the provision of a more adequate philosophical theory. What is needed is the identification of some mode of institutionalized social practice within which generally established norms and reflective habits of judgment and action could sustain a coherent and rationally justifiable allegiance to a rule concerning truth telling and lying in a way and to a degree very different from the present dominant culture. And this is a large undertaking. But a more adequate philosophical theory would be at least a first step. How then should we proceed in attempting to develop such a theory?

We might begin by asking whether there is not more for us to learn from the most distinguished modern philosophical representatives of the two rival traditions, J. S. Mill and Immanuel Kant, than Sidgwick supposed. Sidgwick after all concerned himself with lying and truth telling only incidentally and his treatment of both Kant and Mill was restricted in scope. We not only have the benefit of what can be learned from later interpreters and more adequate editions, but we are able to bring to our reading of Kant and Mill questions that go beyond Sidgwick's, in part because of what we have learned from Sidgwick. So in order to move forward, we should first turn back, noting as we do not only that truthfulness was a topic of continuing philosophical concern for both Kant and Mill, but also that both Kant and Mill cared deeply about truthfulness. I might have begun this enquiry with either thinker, but Mill is perhaps somewhat closer to us, not just chronologically but in his hopes and fears for the culture. So it is to Mill that I turn first.

III

In the second chapter of *Utilitarianism* Mill attempted to dispel misunderstandings of the Greatest Happiness principle by defending it against a variety of accusations. Against the accusation that utilitarianism reduces morality to expediency Mill set out his account of truthfulness, arguing that

inasmuch as the cultivation in ourselves of a sensitive feeling on the subject of veracity is one of the most useful, and the enfeeblement of that feeling one of the most hurtful, things to which our conduct can be instrumental; and inasmuch as any, even unintentional, deviation from truth, does that much towards weakening the trustworthiness of human assertion, which is not only the principal support of all present social well-being, but the insufficiency of which does more than any one thing that can be named to keep back civilization, virtue, everything on which human happiness on the largest scale depends; we feel that the violation, for a present advantage, of a rule of such transcendent expediency is not expedient, and that he who for the sake of a convenience to himself or to some other individual, does what depends on him to deprive mankind of the good, and inflict upon them the evil, involved in the greater or less reliance which they can place in each other's word, acts the part of one of their worst enemies. Yet that even this rule, sacred as it is, admits of possible exceptions, is acknowledged by all moralists; the chief of which is when the withholding of some fact (as of information from a malefactor, or of bad news from a person dangerously ill) would save an individual (especially an individual other than oneself) from great and unmerited evil, and when the withholding can only be effected by denial.

This is in some respects a very plain statement. Mill is evidently a rule-utilitarian, prepared to allow only a very few types of exception to the prohibition of lying. He mentions only one such and he is careful to affirm a stringent prohibition on all merely convenient lies. And certainly, if contemporary Americans were systematically to obey Mill's rule, ours would be a very different society. Mill elsewhere considered the type of case in which the cost to some individual of telling the truth on a matter in which it is important not to lie is serious, perhaps mortal danger to herself or himself, and asserted that no general rule governs such cases, independently of circumstances.[17] But the tone as well as the content of all Mill's remarks about lying place him, not too surprisingly, particularly if we remember how influenced he was by Coleridge, in the same moral tradition as Milton and Dr. Johnson.

As to the logical structure of the justification of the rule that Mill formulates, matters at first sight appear equally straightforward. The premises are: first, that lying always weakens to some greater or lesser extent trustworthiness; second, that trustworthiness is the indispensable support of that upon which "present well-being" and "civilization" and human happiness in general depend; and, third, that right action is action that promotes the general happiness, the greatest happiness of the greatest number. Therefore lying is (almost always) wrong. But questions arise about what Mill meant in affirming the second and third premises of this argument.

---

17 Letter of February 9, 1867, to Henry S. Brandreth, in *Collected Works of John Stuart Mill*, vol. XVI: *The Later Letters of John Stuart Mill 1849–1873*, ed. F. E. Mineka, Toronto: University of Toronto Press, 1972, p. 1234.

When Mill asserted in support of the second premise that both "present social well-being" and "civilization" depend on trustworthiness, he might be thought by a casual reader to be advancing no more than a strongly worded version of a commonly reiterated warning that lying undermines credibility and that credibility is needed to sustain the social fabric. Yet experience goes to show that the social fabric generally survives a good deal more lying than Mill would have allowed. As Harry Frankfurt has remarked, "The actual quantity of lying is enormous after all, and yet social life goes on. That people often lie hardly renders it impossible to benefit from being with them. It only means that we have to be careful."[18] So that if this is what Mill meant, his second premise is false and his argument fails. But this is not what Mill meant. For, when Mill used the word "civilization," he did not use it lightly. The words Mill uses when he speaks elsewhere of those whom he took to be uncivilized are "barbarians" or "savages," and barbarians, on Mill's view, need the rule of a benevolent despot, not the doctrines of *On Liberty* (*On Liberty*, chapter 1) or the moral rules that are the counterparts of those doctrines. Among those not yet civilized Mill took lying to be endemic. In the essay "On Nature" Mill considered whether it was right to think of truthfulness as natural to human beings,[19] since "in the absence of motives to the contrary, speech usually conforms to, or at least does not intentionally deviate from, fact," but against this he cites what he takes to be the case, that "savages are always liars" (p. 395). Moreover, the same holds of the inhabitants of "the whole East and the greater part of Europe" and even in England it is only a small minority – "the higher classes," as he says elsewhere – who make it a point of honor to respect truth for truth's sake.

Habitual lying is, Mill believed, a consequence of "the natural state of those who were both uneducated and subjected." It is "a vice of slaves."[20] And it was, on his view, greatly to the credit of the contemporary English working class that, although they lied, they were ashamed of it.[21] A central political and educational problem then is that of how to transform those

---

18 "The Faintest Passion," Presidential Address to the Eastern Division of the American Philosophical Association, 1991, *Proceedings and Addresses of the A.P.A.* 66, no. 3, November 1992, 6.

19 *Collected Works*, vol. X: *Essays on Ethics, Religion and Society*, ed. J. M. Robson, Toronto: University of Toronto Press, 1969.

20 For one source of Mill's beliefs on this matter, see James Mill, *The History of British India*, 4th edn, London: J. Madden, 1848, Book II, chapter 7, p. 467: "The Hindus are full of dissimulation and falsehood, the universal concomitants of oppression."

21 Speech of July 8, 1865, during the Westminster Election, in *Collected Works*, vol. XXVIII: *Public and Parliamentary Speeches*, ed. J. M. Robson and B. L. Kinzer, Toronto: University of Toronto Press, 1988, pp. 35–36.

hitherto uneducated and subjected into the condition of that minority that does already respect truth for truth's sake. For a repudiation of lying is, on this view, an inseparable part of the rise of any social group from a condition of subjection and lack of education to one of liberty and a cultivated intelligence, both of them necessary for happiness. When Mill speaks approvingly of those who respect truth for truth's sake, he is of course not contrasting them with those who respect truth for the sake of their own or the general happiness. It is true that only happiness is, on Mill's view, desired for its own sake, but virtue is desired for *its* own sake precisely because it is, or rather has become, a part of happiness (*Utilitarianism*, chapter 4). Virtue is originally valued only as a means, but then, as a result of experience of the life of virtue, it comes to be valued also as an end. We may therefore safely infer that truthfulness as a virtue, is itself, on Mill's view, originally valued only as a means, but then also as an end, and the life of civilization is a life in which truthfulness has come to be so valued. So that when Mill, in the second premise of his argument in *Utilitarianism*, claims that a trustworthiness uncorrupted by lying is indispensable not just for happiness and well-being, but for those conjoined with civilization, his use of the word "civilization" should convey to us a conception of the general happiness to be aimed at in England in the middle of the nineteenth century, one that is not adequately communicated by the philosophical treatment of happiness in *Utilitarianism*.

What then is an adequate conception of happiness – I mean not in the abstract and general terms of *Utilitarianism*, but in terms of those political, social, and personal goals that Mill set for himself and for others in his own time and place? And how, on Mill's view, can we come to have such a conception and communicate it effectively to others? Mill's answer to this second question was that such a conception could be acquired only by extended intellectual, moral, and emotional enquiry and education. Such enquiry and education involves continuous conversation and debate with others, debate of a kind in which Mill himself had participated, both within utilitarian circles and in controversies between utilitarians and their critics. Exclusion from such debate is deeply injurious to moral education and "participation in political business" is "one of the means of national education," helping to draw human beings out of "the narrow bounds of individual and family selfishness" that otherwise make them stupid, ill-informed, and selfish.[22]

---

22 "Thoughts on Parliamentary Reform," 1859, in *Collected Works*, vol. XIX: *Essays on Politics and Society*, ed. J. M. Robson, Toronto: University of Toronto Press, 1977, p. 322.

How is that education to be contrived? Mill took himself to have learned from Coleridge the importance of providing state support for an educated class, one that would in each locality provide moral and intellectual leadership and instruction.[23] Such an educated class, so Mill argued, had to have a special place in and influence upon both public debate and the activities of government, for "one person is *not* as good as another" ("Thoughts on Parliamentary Reform," p. 323). But our constitutional and electoral arrangements, while securing the influence of the better educated, ought to be such that they become a means for general moral education, in order to remedy "the mental and moral condition of the English working classes" (p. 327). Hence Mill's disapproval of the secret ballot, which he took to promote a cowardly concealment of one's true views, and which he thought able to produce its intended effect "only at the cost of much lying" (p. 337). It is then one of the tasks of moral education to construct forms of institutional debate in and through which, among other things, those who participate in them can be sustained in their truth telling and transformed, if need be, from liars into truthful persons. Exclusion of those not yet thus educated from processes of political debate and decision debars them damagingly – damagingly for others as well as for themselves – from such education, but inclusion in those processes of debate must be such that they learn from those better educated. And the better educated themselves still need to learn from such debate. For those who do not participate in debate can only have untested opinions, whether about happiness or anything else, and not genuine knowledge.

This contention is central to Mill's *On Liberty*, where he asserts that "no opinion deserves the name of knowledge" that has not emerged from "an active controversy with opponents" and where he treats the Socratic mode of dialectic and even the medieval disputation as models for a type of institutionalized controversy much needed in his own time, but no longer provided. Without such controversy there can therefore be no knowledge concerning that happiness that is the end of right action. Infringements of liberty of thought and discussion are to be condemned precisely because liberty is necessary, if such forms of debate are to arrive at truth. But debate will also presumably require protection from violation by those types of act that Mill takes to be "fit objects of moral reprobation, and in grave cases, of moral retribution and punishment," a

---

23 "Coleridge," *London and Westminster Review*, 1840.

class that includes acts of "falsehood or duplicity" in dealing with others. So the rule requiring truthfulness will be among those rules to which conformity is necessary as a means for securing the kind of controversy in debate and enquiry from which there can emerge a true and adequate account of human happiness as an end and of the part to be played by truthfulness in any life answering to that account. What Mill called the "trustworthiness of human assertion" will have to be, on his view, if I have construed it rightly, first recognized as a necessary means to, and then as an essential constituent both of my own happiness and of the general happiness.

What I have identified as the second premise in Mill's argument for the justification of lying is then something more and other than a general claim that the social fabric is somehow endangered by lying. It is the much stronger, and also the much more interesting claim that what Mill meant by civilization, a type of social order constituted as a project of moral education through political and moral conversation and debate, requires a stringent and very widely respected rule prohibiting (almost all) lying. A civilized social order is one collectively and cooperatively concerned to understand the truth about human beings and nature, and the violation of truthfulness is injurious to the project of such a social order for the same reason and in the same way that a violation of truthfulness in reporting data is injurious to the sciences. Truthfulness in both cases is not just a useful and necessary means to, but is constitutive of the ends pursued.

In saying this I may have gone a little, although only a little, beyond what Mill himself actually asserts. But, if this is the direction in which *Mill's* argument points us, we need to go even further. Mill in his statement of the rule about lying in *Utilitarianism* identified lying as an offense against trustworthiness. But the argument that I have developed out of his writings requires us not only to identify it also as an offense against truth, but also to understand the relationship between these two aspects of truthfulness in a particular way. It is not trustworthiness in general that is crucial to our well-being as actual or aspiring members of a civilized social order, characterized as Mill characterized it, but the peculiar kind of trustworthiness that is required of those who are participants in a particular kind of social enterprise, who are collectively and cooperatively engaged in seeking through shared enquiry the truth about their present condition and their future good, as an essential part of the project of moving from their present condition towards the achievement of that good. Truth is *the* good internal to rational enquiry and the kind of trustworthiness required from each other by those who participate in enquiry includes an unfailing regard for truth and for truthfulness. So it is with those who are engaged cooperatively in the investigations of the natural sciences or the researches of historians or anthropologists. And insofar as the moral life is a life of communal enquiry – to say this is not to deny that it is also a number of other things – the kind of trust that those who engage in it have to repose in each other must therefore include mutual trust in respect of a shared regard for a norm of truth that has to be exceptionless for the same reasons that the norm governing truth telling in science and other research communities has to be exceptionless. But in reaching this conclusion I have, by following a line of argument developed by Mill, arrived at conclusions that are obviously at odds with Mill's own.

In the passage from *Utilitarianism* from which *I* began Mill identified at least two kinds of exception to the rule prohibiting lying, and he justified those exceptions by suggesting that on certain types of occasions the consequences of telling particular lies for the happiness or unhappiness of particular individuals were such as to outweigh any detriment to the general good. But how can this be reconciled with the claims that I have just made for an exceptionless rule, one necessary for us to arrive at an adequate conception of happiness? A first response may well be that it cannot be so reconciled, and that, if the line of argument that I have developed out of certain of Mill's texts is really there, then there are to be found in Mill strains of thought that are in serious tension with each other, something that a number of commentators have discerned. But a second response might run as follows.

Of the two kinds of exception allowed by Mill in *Utilitarianism* one is a matter of the withholding of information from those who would be harmed by it, the other of the prevention of serious harm intended by malefactors. About the former we should note that there are ways of withholding information other than lying and that, if we take systematic precautions in advance, as it is our duty to do, lying generally becomes unnecessary. If it does seem to have become necessary, this is perhaps to be taken as evidence of our own or someone else's lack of wit, ingenuity, and foresight, itself an important kind of moral failure. So we can perhaps agree with Mill about the need on rare types of occasions to withhold information, without agreeing that this of itself provides any good reason for rejecting the authority of an exceptionless rule. Moreover we thereby signify that those whom we are thus protecting, whoever they may be, still remain our partners in the enterprises of the moral life and therefore persons to whom we may not tell lies. The symbolic importance of upholding this rule universally without exceptions as to persons is not to be underestimated.

What then are we to say about the other class of exception, the type of lie told in order to avert grave harm intended by malefactors? The exceptionless rule requiring truthfulness, just because the moral life is one for which truth is a supreme value, binds the members of the moral community as rational persons just as the analogous rule binds the members of the scientific community. It is a norm defining the relationship of the members of those types of community to each other. But what if someone constitutes herself or himself a deliberate enemy of the moral community and not just of particular persons, as someone, for example, bent on murder does? In such situations does the same rule bind us? If so, why? If not, why not? These questions were already raised for us by Samuel Johnson. But the most important discussion of how to answer them is of course by Kant.

CHAPTER 7

Truthfulness and lies: what can we learn from Kant?

I

At first sight and on a conventional reading no two moral philosophers are more sharply at odds concerning truth telling and lying than are Mill and Kant. Mill held that some lies are not only morally permitted, but morally required, while Kant held that all lying is prohibited. In *Utilitarianism* at least Mill's justifications, both of his formulation of the rule generally prohibiting lying and of his statement of the types of exception to that rule, are consequentialist, while Kant rejects consequentialist justifications and grounds the rule prohibiting lying in the rational nature of human beings. But perhaps this opposition is not as unqualified as conventional readings have made it. I have already suggested that, when Mill reflected on the requirements that must be met, if political and social relationships were to become rational, he moved much closer to an unqualified condemnation of untruthfulness than, on a conventional reading, we might have expected. And, since Mill's concerns about rationality bring him very close to what were also central concerns of Kant, it is worth asking whether there may not be respects in which their undeniably incompatible views may nonetheless be understood as contributing to a common enterprise. Yet if we are to do so in a way that also does justice to their disagreements, we should begin our discussion of Kant in those areas in which that difference is most evident.

I have distinguished two rival moral traditions with respect to truth telling and lying, one for which a lie is primarily an offense against trust and one for which it is primarily an offense against truth. For adherents of the former tradition unjustified deception is what offends against trust and unjustified lies are a species of unjustified deception. For such persons it therefore generally makes no significant moral difference whether or not a deception is carried out by means of a lie or otherwise. If it is a justified deception, then that it was carried out by lying will not make it any less justified. If it was an unjustified deception, it will be none the worse for having been carried out by a lie. But for adherents of the rival tradition no lie can ever be justified, although some deceptions may be.

Hence the importance within this rival tradition of anecdotal teaching about the moral praiseworthiness of the ingenuity of those who succeed in some justified act of deception without committing the wrong of lying. A signal example is that of St. Athanasius, whose persecutors, dispatched by the emperor Julian, were pursuing him up the Nile. They came on him traveling downstream, failed to recognize him, and enquired of him: "Is Athanasius close at hand?" He replied: "He is not far from here." The persecutors hurried on and Athanasius successfully evaded them without telling a lie.[1] Whether one thinks this a pointless anecdote or not reveals something fundamental about one's attitude to lying. Kant's attitude is revealed in an anecdote that he told about himself.

When in 1794 Kant was required by King Friedrich Wilhelm II, shortly before the latter's death, to refrain from any distortion or depreciation of Christianity, he knew that if he made public anything further of his thoughts on religion, as he had hoped to do, he would be held guilty of just such distortion or depreciation, perhaps with baneful consequences. He therefore responded by making a declaration "as your Majesty's faithful subject, that I shall in future completely desist from all public lectures or essays concerning religion, be it natural or revealed." The Prussian censors and, if it was reported to him, the king himself would have understood Kant to be saying that he would never so publish. But that is not of course what Kant had in fact declared. As he later pointed out, his pledge to desist was made only "as your Majesty's faithful subject," a status that Kant would lose when this particular king died. "This phrase," wrote Kant in recounting the story (in the preface to *The Quarrel between the Faculties*) after the king's death in 1797, ". . . was chosen by me most carefully, so that I should not be deprived of my freedom . . . *forever*, but only so long as His Majesty was alive" and Kant knew that the death of Friedrich Wilhelm II was expected imminently. So Kant succeeded in misleading the Prussian censors without lying, something that he thought it morally important to do.

Kant therefore places himself among those who hold that my duty is to assert only what is true and that the mistaken inferences that others may draw from what I say or what I do are, in some cases at least, not my responsibility, but theirs. Those others, if they discover that, in such cases,

---

1 See F. A. M. Forbes, *St. Athanasius*, London: R. and T. Washbourne, 1919, p. 102.

what I said or did was well designed to mislead, as it was in Kant's own case, will probably in the future treat me, and possibly others, as less trustworthy. But it is not this possible consequence of injury to trust that matters; what matters is the avoidance of the assertion of falsity.

In what then does the wrongness of the intentional assertion of what is false consist? I have claimed that what is fundamental for those who understand lying as an offense against truth is the semantic rule requiring the assertion only of what is true, a rule learned by everyone who learns a natural language. The fact that language-users in the vast majority of instances cannot but conform to this universal rule, and cannot but interpret others as conforming to it, is what makes effective lying possible. A liar therefore deliberately violates that rule, while at the same time willing that others should unsuspiciously adhere to it. And so no liar can coherently will that the maxim upon which she or he acts should be universally acted upon by others. It is thus at first sight a short step – almost no step at all – from the semantic rule to Kant's first formulation of the categorical imperative: "Act only according to that maxim whereby you can at the same time will that it should become a universal law."

We may easily be tempted by this to suppose that it is because universalizability of the maxim determining the liar's action, thus under-stood, leads the liar on towards self-contradiction that lying is prohibited for any rational person. But this would be a mistake. It cannot be universalizability as such or by itself that is sufficient for the prohibition of lying. Why not? Consider two important types of case. The first is that of someone who has judged on empirical grounds that social life is, one way or another, a war of each against all, who takes pride in her or his own craft in using force and fraud and whose determining maxim for many actions is "Let everyone exert themselves to overcome others, by whatever means are available, including lying, and may the strongest win!" The second is of a person whose empirical judgments about social life and about her or his own capacities are the same, but whose determining maxim is "Let all who are strong take pride in refusing to do anything as mean-spirited as lying in their war against others, let the weak do as they wish, and, if those who are both strong and truthful go down to defeat, so be it!"

The first of these two persons – and I have known both of them – is on occasion a liar, the second always truthful, and both are able to act according to maxims that they are prepared to universalize and are able to universalize without any incoherence. But we would of course be in error if we were to suppose that they provide counterexamples to Kant's thesis. For their maxims fail to be genuinely Kantian maxims in at least two respects. First, their maxims presuppose what their authors take to be lessons, both about social life and about themselves, that had to be learned empirically. But Kant held that the prohibition on lying could not be such. In the "Fragments of a Moral Catechism" Kant put into the mouth of the teacher the words: "The rule and direction for knowing how you go about sharing happiness, without also becoming unworthy of it, lies entirely in your reason. This amounts to saying that you do not have to learn this rule of conduct by experience or from other people's instruction; your own reason teaches and even tells you what you have to do."[2] Kant then chooses as his illustration for this point the prohibition against lying in a situation "in which you can get yourself or a friend a great advantage by an artfully thought out lie (and without hurting anybody else either)" and he speaks of the unconditional constraint of this prohibition as "this necessity, laid upon a human being directly by her or his reason." The two nonKantian maxims that I have described, by reason of their empirical presuppositions, have no such necessity.

Secondly – a closely related point – these two nonKantian maxims are willed qua strong, cunning, resourceful, or proud person, whereas authentically Kantian maxims have to be willed qua rational person. As such, they have to be imposed, or rather on Kant's view impose themselves independently not only of consequences, but of the agent's contingent circumstances. Hence these two nonKantian maxims, although certainly universalizable without inconsistency, cannot play the part that maxims have to play for Kant. And this makes it clear that the first formula of the categorical imperative, as presented in the *Grundlegung*, cannot stand by itself. What is needed by way of further interpretation is provided by the second and third formulas. It is for this reason that the question of the rational justification of the derivation of maxims with particular content from Kant's first formula for the categorical imperative by itself may not have quite the significance that both some critics of Kant, including myself on previous occasions, and some Kantian, NeoKantian, and QuasiKantian defenders of Kant have sometimes supposed.

It has indeed been a commonplace, ever since Hegel's critique of Kant, that there are problems about precisely how action-guiding maxims with particular content are to be derived from the categorical imperative in its first formulation. Onora O'Neill (in one way in *Acting on Principle*, New York: Columbia University Press, 1975, and in another in "Consistency in

2 *Metaphysic of Morals*, "Methodology of Ethics," section 1, 481.

Action," in *Constructions of Reason*, Cambridge: Cambridge University Press, 1989) and Christine Korsgaard ("Kant's Formula of Universal Law," *Pacific Philosophical Quarterly* 66 1985) have made a number of different compelling suggestions here. And more recently Barbara Herman has concluded that, although on one interpretation of the first formulation of the categorical imperative – in terms of what Onora O'Neill has called contradiction in the will (*Acting on Principle*, chapter 5, pp. 82–93) – it excludes maxims that ought not to be excluded, and on another – in terms of what O'Neill has called contradiction in conception (chapter 5, pp. 63–81) – it fails to exclude what ought to be excluded, a joint use of these two formulations, supplemented by subsequent deliberation of a highly specific kind, *can* generate in a rationally justifiable way the needed kind of practical conclusion.[3] It should be noted that O'Neill's own view both of the relationship between the different formulas of the categorical imperative and of how principles relate to particular types of case is not the same as either Herman's or Korsgaard's.

Each of these detailed and elegant reconstructions of Kant's forms of argument is instructive and insightful in bringing out the richness of Kant's resources. Each inevitably goes beyond the letter of the text in its interpretation – and even at points in ways that are incompatible with Kant's own positions since he held the three formulas of the categorical imperative to be equivalent – but none of them illegitimately. Yet before they can be evaluated as adequate or inadequate what needs to be remarked is the striking contrast between their detailed interpretative subtleties and disputed questions and Kant's representation of the straightforward apprehension of the necessity of true moral judgments by plain moral persons. This was of course a problem for Kant himself before it was a problem for Kantians, the problem of how to capture what Kant called "the happy simplicity" of "the ordinary understanding" of plain persons (*Grundlegung*, first section, 405) in adequate philosophical terms without distortion. So that it might after all be best to begin not with the necessarily problematic and philosophically sophisticated issues about derivation raised by Kant's recent interpreters, but with the relatively straightforward moral conclusions, which, on Kant's view, plain persons are able to reach from their own inner rational resources, and to enquire what light those conclusions throw upon the premises from which they are taken to be derived rather than vice versa.

---

3 Barbara Herman, *The Practice of Moral Judgment*, Cambridge, Mass., Harvard University Press, 1993, chapter 7.

In the case of lying it will turn out, so I shall argue, that Kant's moral conclusions – or rather what Kant takes to be the moral conclusions of "the ordinary understanding" – bring out the importance for the Kantian moral standpoint of the fact that the first formulation of the categorical imperative cannot stand by itself, but needs to be interpreted and supplemented by the second and third formulations – and in this at least I follow Christine Korsgaard – and that there is therefore a more complex relationship between the categorical imperative prohibiting lying and the semantic rule prohibiting false assertions than at first appeared. What then are the important features of Kant's conclusions about lying? They turn out to be just those features that outraged Benjamin Constant. Constant had argued that obedience to a moral principle unconditionally enjoining everyone to speak the truth and unmodified by other principles would make all social life impossible. "We have the proof of this," he said, "in the consequences drawn from this principle by a German philosopher who goes so far as to assert that it would be a crime to lie to a murderer who enquired whether our friend, whom he was pursuing, had not taken refuge in our house."[4]

This example may have been a commonplace in eighteenth-century discussions of lying. Samuel Johnson, as I noted in the first of these lectures, had already discussed it and Johann David Michaelis, professor of theology at Gottingen until his death in 1791, anticipated Kant's conclusions with regard to it. Later on, Newman was to make use of it. Kant's response to Constant's report of his position was at once to acknowledge that he really had said this, although he could not remember where.[5] But he focused his attention upon Constant's statement of Constant's own rival view.

Constant's view was that "to tell the truth is a duty only towards a person who has a right to truth" and that therefore to someone who by reason of her or his malevolent intentions has no such right it is not wrong to lie (as quoted by Kant in *On a Pretended Right to Lie from Benevolent Motives*, in Abbott, *Kant's Critique*). Against Constant, Kant contended that "truthfulness in assertions that cannot be avoided is a human being's formal duty to everybody, whatever the disadvantage that may ensue to oneself or to another." Someone who has unjustly compelled me to make

4 *Reactions politiques*, Paris, 1797, chapter 8, quoted in *Un droit de mentir? Constant ou Kant*, by F. Boituzat, Paris: PUF, 1993.
5 *Kant's Critique of Practical Reason and Other Works on the Theory of Ethics*, trans. T. K. Abbott, London: Longmans Green, 1873, p. 361.

a statement is not, on Kant's view, the one wronged by my lie. So the question of whether or not such a one has or has not the right to truth is irrelevant. If I lie, "I do wrong to humanity in general in the most essential point of duty." There need be no injury to any particular person but rather humanity itself is wronged. And, as becomes clear if we turn to Kant's other writings, it is important that veracity is something that we owe to ourselves quite as much as to others. By lying the liar in wronging humanity wrongs herself or himself.

"The greatest violation of a duty to oneself considered only as a moral being (the humanity in one's person) is the opposite of veracity: lying . . ." And Kant proceeds to define lying by quoting Sallust and then makes a distinction between external and internal lying. "The former," he says, "renders a man despicable in the eyes of others, the latter" – Kant means by an internal lie a lie told to oneself, a piece of self-deception – "in his own eyes which is much worse and violates human dignity in his own person."

Someone who does not believe what he says to another (even if it be a person existing only in idea) has even less worth than if he were a mere thing; a thing has utility, another can make some use of it, since it is really a thing. But to communicate one's thoughts to someone by words which (intentionally) contain the opposite of what one thinks is an end directly contrary to the natural purposiveness of one's capacity to communicate one's thoughts. In so doing one renounces one's personality and, as a liar, manifests oneself as a mere deceptive appearance of a human being, not as a genuine human being."

(*Metaphysic of Morals*, Part II, first part of the Elements of Ethics, 9)

On Kant's view then no injury other than the lie itself need have been brought about, either to oneself or to another, for a lie to be a wrong and a wrong of this magnitude. From what fundamental positions do these striking, and to some affronting conclusions flow? To answer this question we need to remind ourselves of some of Kant's basic theses. One is that to lead a life in accordance with the maxims of morality, moved by a prudent understanding that conformity to the moral law can serve "the incentive of self-love and its inclinations," is to have a bad moral character. So, if we were to refrain from lying only or even in part because "truthfulness, if adopted as a basic principle, delivers us from the anxiety of making our lies agree with one another and of not being entangled by their serpent coils" (*Religion within the Limits of Reason Alone*, Book I), we would no more have genuinely obeyed the categorical imperative that prohibits lying than if we had lied. But now what of that categorical imperative? If it is to provide a premise that affords sufficient reason for the conclusion that no one ought ever under any circumstances to lie, it cannot be understood only as the categorical imperative of the first formulation. It must, for reasons that I have already indicated, be understood so that the second and third of Kant's formulations supplement and interpret the first. This conclusion, as I noticed earlier, agrees with that reached by Christine Korsgaard.[6]

She has argued that the different formulations give different answers to the question of whether if, by lying, someone may prevent a would-be murderer from implementing her or his intentions, that person may do so. The Formula of Universal Law "seems to say that this lie is permissible" but the Formula of Humanity "says that coercion and deception are the most fundamental forms of wrongdoing. In a Kingdom of Ends coercive and deceptive methods can never be used" (p. 337). We must then, it seems, understand the Formula of Humanity and the conception of the Kingdom of Ends as narrowing the restrictions imposed by the universalizability requirement so that Kant's rigorist conclusion is indeed warranted by the premises from which he derives it. But, of course, if this is so, then a problem arises for all those who stand with Benjamin Constant or with the John Stuart Mill of *Utilitarianism* or who for other reasons reject that conclusion. For if that conclusion is warranted by the premises then those who reject the conclusion are committed to rejecting at least one of the premises. So we need to enquire further about both conclusion and premises.

To this way of going about things it may be objected that Kant did not in fact hold with any great seriousness the conclusion that lies ought *never* under any circumstances to be told, except as what H. J. Paton called a "temporary indiscretion," which Paton ascribed to "bad temper in his old age."[7] Sallie Sedgwick, who repudiates Paton's characterization of what he took to be Kant's lapse, has argued nonetheless that Kant is misunderstood if we suppose that Kant's rigorist conclusion really follows from his premises. She points out that earlier in the *Vorlesung* Kant had held that, if I am compelled to make a statement of which improper use will then be made, I can be justified in telling a white lie.[8] And she contends that there was in fact no change after the *Vorlesung* in the spirit of Kant's views, but only in the letter.[9] She is, however, surely mistaken about the spirit of

6 "The Right to Lie: Kant on Dealing with Evil," *Philosophy and Public Affairs* 15, no. 4, 1986.
7 "An Alleged Right to Lie: A Problem in Kantian Ethics," *Kant-Studien* 15, 1954.
8 See on this *Eine Vorlesung Kant's über Ethik*, ed. P. Menzer, pp. 288–89, trans. L. Infield, *Lectures on Ethics*, Indianapolis: Hackett, 1980, p. 228.
9 See "On Lying and the Role of Content in Kant's Ethics," *Kant-Studien* 82, no. 1, 1991.

Kant's later views. Kant took care to reject in explicit terms the thesis, which has been defended as in the spirit of Kant's view not only by Sedgwick but also by some earlier commentators, that he should have treated the prohibition on lying only as a fundamental principle and not as one immediately determining action, but rather one that needs to be interpreted and qualified through mediating principles in its application to particular cases. When in his response to Constant Kant addressed this very issue, he concluded that "all practical principles of justice – such as the prohibition of lying – must contain strict truths, and the principles here called middle principles can only contain the closer definition of their application to actual cases . . . and never exceptions from them. . ." For this reason as well as in the light of the texts cited earlier I cannot agree with Sedgwick and I also conclude that the *Vorlesung* should not be used as reliable evidence for Kant's developed views.

Sedgwick has, however, by the insightful way in which she has pressed her case brought out features of Kant's position that it would be wrong to ignore, features that suggest possible underlying unresolved tensions within Kant's thought. But the significance of those tensions will only appear once we have a more adequate view of Kant's position and therefore of the possible grounds for rejecting it. Consider another of Kant's basic theses, that "it is our common duty as human beings to elevate ourselves" to an ideal of moral perfection, the idea of a human being whose life would in every way satisfy the requirements of a wholly good God, and that for the achievement of "this archetype of the moral disposition in all its purity" "the idea itself, which reason presents to us for our zealous emulation, can give us power" (*Religion within the Limits of Reason Alone*, Book II, section 1, A).

What these two basic theses of Kant's make evident is that, on his view, morality requires a systematic disciplining of and freeing ourselves from responsiveness to our own inclinations. It is not that we shall not as moral beings continue to have inclinations and to be recurrently responsive to them. It is that we have to become the kind of person for whom the incentive to action supplied by inclinations is always subordinated to the incentive of rational willing in the pursuit of moral perfection. Kantian rationality therefore involves a particular and radical kind of asceticism in respect of the passions, an asceticism directed towards the perfecting of the self. This is an extraordinary task, one that, as Kant understood, confronts even greater obstacles than those recognized by his predecessors in this moral asceticism, the Stoics (*Religion within the Limits of Reason Alone*, Book II). And the recognition of this task and those obstacles is one of the distinctive features of Kant's standpoint. What should that recognition involve in our relationships with others?

II

Kant's answer is illuminated by his discussion of friendship in the *Metaphysic of Morals*. Kant takes it that friendship of a certain kind "is an ideal in which a morally good will unites both parties in sympathy and shared well-being" and that aiming at such friendship is an honorable duty proposed by reason. We do need friends, but it is important that there are limitations upon the possibilities of friendship and some of them are imposed by the constraints of a morally good will. Kant distinguishes at least two kinds of friendship. He praises what he calls moral friendship, a relationship in which each friend is able to reveal her or his otherwise unspoken thoughts and opinions to the other without fear that her or his secrets will be revealed. He defines moral friendship as "the complete confidence of two persons in the mutual openness of their private judgments and sensations, as far as such openness can subsist with mutual respect for one another" (*Metaphysic of Morals*, Part II, second part of the Elements of Ethics, 47). But this of course differs in key respects from friendship as it had been traditionally understood from a variety of standpoints.

Such friendship characteristically involved not just moral, but also what Kant calls pragmatic friendship, of which he says that it burdens itself with the aims and purposes of other human beings. Because it is "a great burden to feel oneself tied to the destiny of others and laden with alien responsibilities," pragmatic friendship is a moral liability. "Friendship therefore cannot be a bond aimed at mutual advantage, but must be purely moral" (46), a friendship of equal respect as well as of mutual confidence. And equal respect is actually incompatible with a friendship based on advantage. For "if one accepts a benefit from the other, then he can probably count on an equality in their love, but not in their respect; for he sees himself as plainly a step lower, inasmuch as he is obligated and yet not reciprocally able to obligate."

This is the point at which it is salutary to recall that in the example that elicited Constant's attack upon Kant the murderer's intended victim whom one may not protect by lying is a friend. That the life to be saved is that of one's friend gives one no reason at all, according to Kant, to lie. A friend with a morally good will would not of course will it otherwise, both because she or he would herself or himself do no other in a like situation and also presumably because it would be a burden to accept the benefit conferred by this lie from the other. We should be grateful to Kant for making so clear to us what is entailed by his fundamental theses, but, as I noted earlier, not every follower of Kant has been grateful. Because, like so many nonKantians, they have found Kant's conclusion on this particular issue morally repugnant, they have hoped to show that it does not follow from Kant's premises. But I have already suggested reasons for holding that on this point they are mistaken. All that has now been added is an acknowledgment that what Kant takes to be the universally binding principles of reason can of course provide no grounds for an exception in favor of one's friends.

Someone might respond by suggesting that, since Kant unhesitatingly recognizes a duty to help those in dire need, any difficulty in accepting Kant's conclusions can be met by carefully qualified statements, first of the duty not to tell lies and second of that to help those in dire need, so that questions of which duty is to have priority in particular types of situations can be answered by making it permissible to lie in some types of situations. But this notion of priority is quite alien to Kant himself where matters of perfect duties are concerned. Kant does indeed recognize that "two grounds of obligation can be conjoined in a subject," so that a conflict may *seem* to arise, but if so, one of the grounds is not in fact a duty (*Metaphysic of Morals*, Introduction, 224). Where perfect duties such as that of truthfulness are concerned, each can give way to no other ground of obligation. And about this there seems to be something importantly right, both from a Kantian and from some nonKantian points of view, including my own.[10]

It is indeed difficult to make sense of the notion of weighing the value of refraining from lying by reason of truthfulness against that of saving an innocent human life. Within Kant's own moral and philosophical scheme there is evidently no room for any conception of the scales on which such weighing might take place. But, quite apart from Kant's scheme, it is difficult to translate the metaphor of weighing in any appropriate and relevant way into an account of a rationally justifiable criterion for deciding between the claims of what are taken to be rival values. And if there is no such criterion, then what the metaphor of weighing would disguise would be arbitrary choices between values and between duties,

---

10 See Alan Donagan, "Consistency in Rationalist Moral Systems," in *Moral Dilemmas*, ed. C. W. Gowans, Oxford: Oxford University Press, 1987, and my own "Moral dilemmas," essay no. 5 in this volume.

notions equally unacceptable to Kant. It seems to follow that no revision of Kant's moral scheme of the kind suggested is possible without abandoning too much that is crucial to Kant, so that there is further confirmation of the thesis that anyone who holds to the substance of Kant's view in general is committed to Kant's particular conclusions respecting that remarkable triad, the pursuing murderer, the pursued friend, and the intervening person of rational principle.

It is important to emphasize that although, on Kant's view, the intervening person of rational principle may not lie to the pursuing murderer, there are on Kant's and indeed on any reasonable view a number of other things for her or him to do, or at least to attempt. She or he may and presumably must attempt to distract the would-be murderer's attention, to trip up, knock down, or otherwise hinder the murderer, to remain silent, so that the murderer is deprived of needed information, to irritate the murderer into turning his aggression against her or him instead, and so on. But, if these all prove ineffective, that ineffectiveness, on Kant's view, furnishes no reason for violating fundamental principles. In this of course Kant is reiterating, as I noticed earlier, a long-held Christian view, not the only Christian view certainly, but the view *of,* among others, Augustine, Aquinas, and Pascal. Moreover, his moral standpoint agrees in its conclusions with those of a number of twentieth-century practitioners of nonviolence whose admirable moral intransigence has earned them hard-won respect. So is there after all good reason to dissent from Kant's conclusions?

I intend to assert that there is, but, before I do so, I want to accept from Kant a constraint upon any acceptable answer to this question. It is this: any principle that warrants us in lying in certain circumstances, as to a would-be murderer, must be either one and the same principle that forbids us to lie in every other case or at the very least a principle that cannot generate possible inconsistency with that primary principle. The permitted or required lie must not be understood as an ad hoc exception, since, for reasons that Kant makes admirably clear, there cannot be such exceptions to genuine moral rules. And the principle that permits or requires a lie must not be some independent principle, potentially in conflict with the principle forbidding lying, since, for reasons that Kant also makes clear, our moral principles must be a consistent set, consistent to this degree that they do not, in any situation that has occurred or will occur or may occur, prescribe incompatible actions, so that one or the other has to be modified in an ad hoc way. The best way of excluding both of these inadmissible modes of permitting or requiring a lie is to have sufficient grounds for holding that one and the same principle *both* generally and indeed almost always prohibits lying *and* yet requires it on certain normally rare types of occasion. Is there any such principle and what might it be?

I begin by considering two objections that may be made to Kant's position, objections with which, on the view that I shall be proposing, any acceptable account of lying and truth telling must come to terms. Both are objections directed not only against Kant's position, but more generally against any position that entails the same conclusions about the legitimacy and justifiability of only nonviolent and nonlying resistance to the evil of intended murder. The first of these objections is that, willingly or unwillingly, the consistent Kantian can rarely escape being a moral free-rider. The social and civic orders within which the vast majority of human beings live out their lives are sustained by systematic uses of coercion and lying that Kantians, pacifists, and others may disown and condemn, but the benefits of which they cannot escape. Indeed, if such Kantians or pacifists are to discharge adequately certain responsibilities within their own society, they may find themselves forced to recognize this. One notable example concerns the government of Pennsylvania by members of the Society of Friends in the early eighteenth century. Themselves morally committed to nonviolence and to the abhorrence of all violence, they could not protect those for whose safety they were responsible without providing a military defense against American Indian incursions. And so they hired others to fight in their place. Failure to do so would have been a dereliction of political duty, but by doing so they became moral free-riders, relying upon others to do what they themselves could thereby avoid doing. I use this example not at all to stigmatize eighteenth-century Pennsylvanian members of the Society of Friends. My point is rather that, if they, among the most conscientious and admirable of human beings by any reasonable standards, could not evade this outcome, no one else espousing such principles is likely to be able to do so.

A second objection is of a very different kind. It is that there are some particular cases – I speak here of particular cases and not of types of case, although to present the particular cannot but be to present it as being of a certain type – about which your judgment or mine may be such that, if those judgments are incompatible with the universal and general principles that you or I have hitherto held, then it is the universal and general principles, as up to now formulated, that we shall have to reject or at least revise. We have very few philosophical discussions of the status of such particular judgments[11] and here I shall put questions about that status on one side. But I take it that the experience of being constrained in one's moral judgment by the features of a particular case, prior to and independently of any subsequent universalizability, is not that uncommon. Which then are the two particular cases to which I appeal?

The first is of a Dutch housewife in the period in which the Netherlands were ruled by the military police power of Nazi Germany. Just before her Jewish neighbor was arrested and sent to a death camp, she had taken that neighbor's child into her own home and promised to take parental responsibility for that child. Confronted by a Nazi official who asked her whether or not all the children living in her home were her own she lied. The second example is of a somewhat different kind and does not concern a lie, although I hope that its relevance to the issue of lying will become clear. It is that of a Massachusetts single mother not so long ago, the life of whose infant child was immediately threatened by a violent and estranged man, a former lover, physically much stronger than she, whose threats to the life of her child were without doubt seriously intended. Her response was to snatch up a gun and kill him. A question that became of focal importance at her trial was: what else could and should she have done? The two examples are importantly different. But in both cases I find, as do at least some others, that I cannot withhold the judgment that, had either of these women done other than she in fact did, she would have failed in her duty to the child whose maternal protector she was.

Is this inability perhaps no more than evidence that those of us who exhibit it are in the grip of moral superstition? Among the ways in which this accusation might be rebutted would be the identification of some well-founded principle or set of principles that is able to provide justification for those particular judgments. The formulation of such principles has to begin from a very different starting point from that from which Kant set out. Instead of first asking "By what principles am I, as a rational person, bound?" we have first to ask "By what principles are we, as actually or potentially rational persons, bound in our relationships?" We begin, that is, from within the social relationships in which we find ourselves, the institutionalized relationships of established social practices,

---

11 There is one in *Den Etiske Fordring* by K. E. Løgstrup, Copenhagen: Gyldendal, 1956; see also more recently Michael DePaul, *Balance and Refinement*, London: Routledge and Kegan Paul, 1993.

through which we discover, and through which alone we can achieve, the goods internal to those practices, the goods that give point and purpose to those relationships. But we also begin as rational persons within those relationships, understanding them as always open to criticism, to possible modification or revision in the light of criticism, and even in the end to possible rejection, if they turn out not to be open to worthwhile modification or revision. Yet that ability to criticize is itself something characteristically acquired in and developed out of the experience of such relationships. It too, when it is rationally effective, appeals to already recognized or recognizable norms of criticism. Moreover, we cannot but acknowledge in those relationships a variety of types of inescapable dependence upon some of those others to whom we are related; we have to rely on some of these types of dependence to foster our initial autonomy and to sustain it later on. Autonomy thus achieved does not then consist in total independence from and of the sentiments, judgments, and actions of others, but in an ability to distinguish those areas in which one ought to be independent and those where one ought to acknowledge dependence. To be in this way autonomous in one's relationships is a necessary condition for achieving many, although not perhaps all, of those key goods without which our relationships no longer have point and purpose.

Why within our relationships, if they are thus understood, is truthfulness important and why ought lying to be prohibited? For at least three mutually reinforcing kinds of reason. First, without consistent truthfulness by others and by ourselves we cannot hope to learn what we need to learn. We need to be told truthfully about our own intellectual and moral deficiencies. We also need to be able to speak truthfully to others about that in them and that for which they are responsible that is or may be damaging to our relationship with them. A lack of *ressentiment* and the possession of tact, patience, and charity are of course also required, if this kind of truthfulness is to be effective. And if it is not effective, it loses its point. So the exercise of truthfulness in this area is not independent of the exercise of other virtues. But of course our own character and that of others is not the only subject matter about which we need to learn and about which therefore truthfulness is required. What does single out the subject matter of character is that it is here that we generally find the strongest motives for lying, so that it is here that truthfulness as an ingrained and not to be overcome habit is most needed.

Secondly, we also need truthfulness, if we are to be able to put our social relationships to the question in the ways and to the degree that rationality requires of us, and this for two different reasons. If we are to have integrity as critics of the established patterns of relationship in which we are involved, then our criticisms of those patterns will have to be truthful. And if we are to deserve the trust of others and to be able to trust those others, during periods in which we or they or both are engaged in sometimes painful and disturbing criticism of our ongoing relationships and of the social practices that provide their context, then we shall have to be able to rely on a shared prohibition against lying and all other relevant forms of deceitfulness.

Thirdly, truthfulness is a virtue without which the corrupting power of phantasy cannot be held in check. Phantasy is of course indispensable and ubiquitous in human life. We are only able to be a good deal of what we are and to do a good deal of what we do because we are able to imagine ourselves as thus being and thus doing. Myths, dramas, and novels, and also such peculiarly modern works of fiction as the annual reports of corporations, the programs of political parties, and the confessional disclosures of televisual interviews can only function as they do because of the modes in which we all in different degrees and different ways imagine both our own lives and the lives of others. And myths, dramas, and novels are of course sometimes powerful in conveying truths. But the same power of phantasy can be and often is used to disguise and to distort our activities and our relationships and has the effect of deforming them, and psychoanalysis should by now have taught us the extent of this power. What psychoanalysis itself, at least in some versions, has also attempted to instruct us in is one particular discipline of truth telling. And we need a corresponding discipline in our everyday lives and relationships, if we are to see those lives and relationships as they are rather than as they are misrepresented as being under the influence of a range of often unacknowledged hopes and fears.

I remarked in my discussion of Mill and Sidgwick (essay no. 6 in this volume) that the successful liar exercises a certain kind of illegitimate power over those who are deceived. That illegitimate power deprives those who are deceived of their autonomy in their relationships with the liar. And so the relationship itself is deformed, becoming one of sometimes multiplying illusions. It is therefore evident that in any relationship in which the goods of rational persons are to be achieved, the truthfulness of those participating in that relationship will be of crucial importance. And this will have to be a truthfulness that extends beyond the persons involved in that particular or any other particular relationship, and this for a good, almost Kantian reason. The truthfulness required has to embody a respect for the rationality of all persons who are or could be involved in all actual or potential relationships. It is a truthfulness that is as necessary for integrity in our relationships with strangers as much as with friends and, if this integrity is lacking in our relationships with strangers, it will as a matter of fact also be at least endangered and often enough corrupted in our relationships with friends.

From this moral point of view that I have been sketching the evil of lying then consists in its capacity for corrupting and destroying the integrity of rational relationships. To understand this is to be able to relate the evil of lying to other evils. For it is a salient characteristic of moral evils in general that they are destructive of rational relationships. Those persons who are outside our particular set of relationships constitute no threat to those relationships simply by their being outside, by their being strangers. And to suppose that they are is always itself a corrupting phantasy. But, if and when they aggress against those who are bound to each other in some particular relationship, then it is always someone's responsibility to do whatever is necessary, so far as they can, to defend that relationship against that aggression. Whose responsibility this is will depend upon the character of the relationship. What their responsibility requires them to do will depend upon the nature of the aggression. Consider in this light the cases of the Massachusetts mother and of the Dutch housewife that introduced my statement of this point of view.

I remarked earlier that moral development within institutionalized relationship involves growth from an acknowledged dependence towards rational autonomy. Part of what rational autonomy requires is a recognition of the dependence of others upon us, especially of the dependence of children and most of all of our own children. That recognition is a recognition of duties and both the Massachusetts mother and the Dutch housewife are, on the view that I am taking, examples of those who did what duty required of them. Theirs were relationships in which each had assumed responsibility for the life and well-being of the dependent child, and in each of which therefore that child was entitled to trust the mother to do what was necessary for its effective protection. In the case of the Massachusetts mother this clearly required disabling the aggressor and, if the only way open to her of disabling the aggressor was by killing him, as it seems in fact to have been, killing him. Had she failed to do this, she would have failed in her duty to her child. And if, by killing the Nazi official, the Dutch housewife could have taken the only effective course of action open to her to protect the child in her care, then it would have been her duty to kill that official. But for anyone in such a situation two questions always have to be answered and will in fact have been answered by whatever action is taken. Will this proposed action effectively protect whoever or whatever needs to be protected? And does this proposed action go beyond what is needed in harming the aggressor? The latter question matters because, insofar as I become a doer of harm beyond what is needed, I pass from being a defender of those unjustly attacked to being myself an unjust aggressor.

To the Dutch housewife it must have been evident that, even were she able to kill the Nazi official, the consequence would have been a reign of murderous terror directed against the entire community, including the children whom she was pledged to protect. Moreover, killing the Nazi official would have done unnecessary harm, provided only that she was able instead to lie convincingly. In this type of case the normally illegitimate power exercised by the successful liar becomes legitimate, first because and insofar as it provides a defense against the prior illegitimate exercise of power by the aggressor, and second because by lying she avoids other more harmful uses of power. I take it therefore that the Dutch housewife's lie and all other lies of just the same kind were and are justified. But what is this kind and how is the rule that justifies them to be formulated?

It would be misleading to state it as though its form was "Never tell a lie, except when . . ." For this would suggest that we were first formulating a rule and only later, as a second thought, introducing an exception. But this is a mistake. The rule that we need is one designed to protect truthfulness in relationships, and the justified lies told to frustrate aggressors serve one and the same purpose and are justified in one and the same way as that part of the rule that enjoins truthfulness in relationships. The Massachusetts mother and the Dutch housewife upheld in their exceptional circumstances just what the normal rational truthful person upholds in her or his everyday life. The rule is therefore better stated as "Uphold truthfulness in all your actions by being unqualifiedly truthful in all your relationships and by lying to aggressors only in order to protect those truthful relationships against aggressors, and even then only when lying is the least harm that can afford an effective defense against aggression." This rule is one to be followed, whatever the consequences, and it is a rule for all rational persons, as persons in relationships.

About this rule two things need to be said. First, although it is evidently inconsistent with Kant's fundamental principles, and moreover is justified by arguments that Kant could not but have rejected, it is nonetheless deeply indebted to Kantian insights and arguments. Its justification by appeal to particular examples, its teleological perspective, and its conception of persons-in-social-relationship as the fundamental units of the moral life do all put it at odds with Kant's standpoint, But in its acknowledgment of the fundamental character of respect for rationality, in its rejection of consequentialism, and in some features at least of its conception of autonomy it recognizably draws upon Kantian resources.

Secondly, it is a rule that is not merely consistent with but supportive of Mill's conception of truthfulness as crucial to social and moral enquiry and therefore to any social order whose relationships are systematically open to such enquiry. And it is indeed in some of its aspects a rule whose formulation is as clearly indebted to Mill as it is to Kant. It is one of the strengths of this rule that it integrates central features of Mill's view with central features of Kant's. One outcome of my examination of Mill's views in the first of these lectures was a suggestion that Mill over large areas of social life upheld what was in effect a rule requiring unqualified truth telling. Yet it is also evident that Mill was deeply committed to the view that certain kinds of threat to human welfare not only permit but may require the telling of lies. My account of what those kinds of threat are does not entirely coincide with Mill's account, but it is in agreement with all or almost all of Mill's social and political concerns, so far as those involve lying and truth telling. Most importantly, it enables us to understand better just why the moral and political life must be, just as Mill held, a life of practical enquiry. For if it is in and through our social relationships that we achieve goods and recognize the authority of rules, and if that achievement and recognition requires, as it does, shared activities of criticism, in which we ask how the goods of this and that relationship can be better ordered, so that they can become the goods of a whole human life and the goods directing communal activity, then systematic enquiry becomes one central thread of the moral life. And one ground for our concerns about truthfulness is the need for truthfulness in enquiry, just as it was for Mill. Nonetheless – it scarcely needs saying – this account that I have given remains deeply at odds with Mill's consequentialism.

At the outset I identified two distinct sources for the universal human concern over the harms and dangers of lying, one a concern primarily with truth and one a concern primarily with trust. What reflection upon Mill and Kant has led me towards is a conception of truthfulness as informing and required by rational human relationships, a conception that integrates concerns about truth and concerns about trust. For to understand the rules prescribing unqualified truthfulness as governing relationships, rather than individuals apart from their relationships, is also to understand how the concern for truth and the concern for trust can become complementary. Central to my trust in you as spouse or friend or colleague, as someone to whom I stand in a relationship of commitments, including commitment to moral enquiry, is my confidence that on any matter relevant either to our relationship or to those other relationships to which each of us is committed I will never be told by you anything other than what you believe to be true. And you know that I know that you know that what I will have discovered if I discover you in an untruth, or vice versa, is that you have to a greater or lesser degree defected from our relationship. Lies then become understood, as they should be, as small or large betrayals and the virtues of integrity and fidelity are understood to be at stake in all those situations in which the virtue of truthfulness is at stake. The disturbance characteristically caused by the discovery of such a lie is well described by Frankfurt as due to its also being a discovery that one "cannot rely upon" one's "own settled feelings of trust" ("The Faintest Passion," p. 7). But where Frankfurt is specifically concerned with lies told to one by those whom one had taken to be one's friends, I am suggesting that all violations of well-founded rules concerning truth telling in established social relationships deserve very much the same response.

It remains true of course that this account will be unacceptable to anyone who is either, unlike Mill, a consistent utilitarian or, like Kant, a consistent Kantian. And moral philosophers in general these days tend to be either utilitarian or Kantian. How then should further conversation proceed?

IV

Enquiry needs to go in more than one direction. The first is that at which we have already made a beginning by considering and evaluating rival answers to questions about the permissibility of lying. And here of course we need further consideration and further evaluation. A step beyond this would be to set those questions in a somewhat wider context, that of the ethics of conversation and discourse in general. For medieval writers and for their modern heirs up to and including Kant, lying was after all only one species of forbidden speech. Aquinas analyzed and condemned a whole range of types of malicious and abusive speech. And Kant wrote in the same tradition, when in the *Vorlesung* he discussed not only the wrongs done by liars, but also the wrongs done by those who slander, scoff, and mock.

I suggested earlier that we may be able to identify in Kant's thought certain underlying, unresolved tensions. One of these is that between his general suspicion of teleology in ethics and his occasional appeals to teleology, as when he speaks of the liar in a passage from *The Metaphysic of Morals* which I quoted earlier as doing wrong by pursuing "an end directly contrary to the natural purposiveness of one's capacity to communicate one's thoughts." One hypothesis that needs to be investigated is that the principles presupposed by Kant's contributions to an ethics of conversation and discourse are inescapably teleological and are so in a way that the framework of Kantian ethics cannot accommodate except by ad hoc patchwork. Were this hypothesis to be vindicated, we should have found in Kant, as we have found in Mill, some degree of inconsistency. And a further interesting question would then be that of whether a framework of thought and practice afforded by a conception of the moral life as that of rational persons in relationship, pursuing the goods of their relationships, in activity and in conversation – developed much more fully than I have been able to develop it here – might not more adequately accommodate both what we have to learn about truthfulness from Mill and also what we have to learn from Kant than either Mill's own utilitarianism or Kant's own apriorism can.

These then are some directions in which I would want to move. But we also need to become self-conscious about the moral requirements of enquiry itself. When Kantians, utilitarians, their various critics, and the proponents of a range of alternative and rival positions, such as my own, have completed the task of stating their reasons for holding their own views and for rejecting those of their opponents, we all confront the question of what moral basis it is on which enquiry can best be carried further, in a way that will ensure a reasonable outcome and that will not be question-begging. Any adequate answer will have to specify both what the functions are of truthfulness, trust, and truth in the work of cooperative enquiry itself and what the relevance of the conception of truthfulness, trust, and truth required by such enquiry is to the moral life in general.

Here my initial hypothesis would be that it is only in terms of a developed conception of the moral life as itself a life of practical enquiry that the relevance of moral enquiry to the moral life can be adequately understood. But for the present this too can only be presented as a hypothesis. I end therefore with questions rather than an answer, not with an ending, but somewhere still in the middle of the way. Yet that after all is not an uncharacteristic place for a philosopher to end up.

PART III

The politics of ethics

CHAPTER 8

Three perspectives on Marxism: 1953, 1968, 1995

1953 FROM THE STANDPOINT OF 1995

When in 1953 I published *Marxism: An Interpretation*,[1] later to become with some revisions *Marxism and Christianity*,[2] Stalin was not yet dead and the Cold War had already taken determinate form. In February 1953 NATO created a unified military command. In June the Soviet suppression of a workers' rising in East Berlin exemplified the ruthless subordination of the whole of Eastern Europe to Soviet interests. It had already long been part of the stock-in-trade of many Western apologists to accept at its face-value the Soviet Union's claim that its social, political, and economic practice embodied Marxist theory, in order to justify their own root-and-branch rejection of Marxism. And it was generally, if not universally, taken for granted among both theologians and ordinary church-goers that, because Marxism was an atheistic materialism, and because persecution by Soviet power was designed to deny, so far as it could, any independence to the lives of the churches, Christianity had to identify itself with the cause of the anticommunist West. It was of course true that some parts of Marxist theory and some Marxist predictions had genuinely been discredited. It was also true that Christian orthodoxy could not but oppose that in Marxism which was either a ground for or a consequence of its atheism. But the simple-minded wholesale anticommunist rejection of Marxism and the equally simple-minded understanding of the relationship between Marxism and Christianity as one of unqualified antagonism exaggerated and distorted these truths in the interests of the then dominant Western ideology.

It was against what I took in 1953 and still take in 1995 to be these distortions that I asserted the central thesis of this book: that Marxism does not stand to Christianity in any relationship of straightforward

1 London: SCM Press.
2 New York: Schocken Books, and London: Duckworth, 1968.

antagonism, but rather, just because it is a transformation of Hegel's secularized version of Christian theology, has many of the characteristics of a Christian heresy rather than of non-Christian unbelief. Marxism is in consequence a doctrine with the same metaphysical and moral scope as Christianity and it is the only secular postEnlightenment doctrine to have such a scope. It proposes a mode of understanding nature and human nature, an account of the direction and meaning of history and of the standards by which right action is to be judged, and an explanation of error and of evil, each of these integrated into an overall worldview, a worldview that can only be made fully intelligible by understanding it as a transform-ation of Christianity. More than that, Marxism was and is a transformation of Christianity which, like some other heresies, provided grounds for reasserting elements in Christianity which had been ignored and obscured by many Christians. What elements are these? They are most aptly and relevantly identified by asking what attitude Christians ought to take to capitalism and then noting how that attitude relates to the Marxist analysis of capitalism.

What, on a Christian understanding of human and social relationships, does God require of us in those relationships? That we love our neigh-bours and that we recognize that charity towards them goes beyond, but always includes justice. An adequate regard for justice always involves not only a concern that justice be done and injustice prevented or remedied on any particular occasion, but also resistance to and, where possible, the abolition of institutions that systematically generate injustice. Christians have far too often behaved badly – thereby confirming what Christianity teaches about sinfulness – in failing to recognize soon enough and to respond to the evils of such institutions. Long after the evils of North American and Latin American slavery and the possibility of abolishing it should have been plain to them, too many Christians remained blind to those evils. And when the wickedness of Fascism and that of National Socialism were all too apparent, too many Christians refused to acknow-ledge them, let alone to engage in resistance. We therefore do well to honour those who did understand what charity and justice required: such Christians as the Dominican, Bartolomé de Las Casas, the evangel-ical Anglicans, John Newton and William Wilberforce, the Lutheran, Dietrich Bonhoeffer, the Catholics, Edith Stein and Maximilian Kolbe and Franz Jägerstetter.

For the same reasons we ought also to honour those Christian laity and clergy, a very small minority, who recognized relatively early the systematic injustices generated by nascent and developed commercial and industrial capitalism. Those evils were and are of two kinds. There is on the one hand the large range of particular injustices perpetrated against individuals and groups on this or that particular occasion, where those other individuals who committed the injustices could have done otherwise consistently with conformity to the standards of profit and loss, of commercial and industrial success and failure, enforced by and in a capitalist economic and social order. The immediate cause of such injustices lies in the character of those individuals who commit them. But there is on the other hand a type of injustice which is not the work of a particular person on a particular occasion, but is instead perpetrated institutionally.

Such injustice has a number of distinct, if closely related, aspects. There is the source of injustice that confronts every individual or group at the point at which they first encountered the capitalist system, usually by entering the labor market, from the period of nascent capitalism onwards. This source of injustice arises from the gross inequalities in the initial appropriation of capital whatever point in time is taken to be the initial point – an appropriation that was in significant part the outcome of acts of force and fraud by the appropriators. This inequality in the relationship of those with capital to those without it is much more than the inequality between rich and poor that is to be found in the vast majority of societies. In many premodern social orders, just because the poor provide products and services that the rich need, there is still something of a reciprocal relationship between rich and poor, governed by customary standards. And in such societies characteristically the poor will have, and be recognized as entitled to, their own resources: a share of the product of the land they work, customary rights over common land, and the like. But the relationship of capital to labor is such that it inescapably involves an entirely one-sided dependence, except insofar as labor rebels against its conditions of work. The more effective the employment of capital, the more labor becomes no more than an instrument of capital's purposes, and an instrument whose treatment is a function of the needs of long-term profit maximization and capital formation.

The relationships which result are the impersonal relationships imposed by capitalist markets upon all those who participate in them. What is necessarily absent in such markets is any justice of desert. Concepts of a just wage and a just price necessarily have no application to transactions within those markets. Hard, skilled, and conscientious work, if it does not generate sufficient profit, something that it is not in the power of the worker to determine, will always be apt to be rewarded by unemployment. It becomes impossible for workers to understand their work as a contribution to the common good of a society which at the economic level no longer has a common good, because of the different and conflicting interests of different classes. The needs of capital formation impose upon capitalists and upon those who manage their enterprises a need to extract from the work of their employees a surplus which is at the future disposal of capital and not of labor. It is of course true that the fact that the profitability of an enterprise in the longer run requires a relatively stable and, so far as possible, satisfied labor force means that such exploitation must sometimes, to be effective over time, be tempered and assume a relatively benign face. And it is clearly much, much better that capitalism should provide a rising standard of living for large numbers of people than that it should not. But no amount of a rise in the standard of living by itself alters the injustice of exploitation. And the same is true of two other aspects of injustice.

Relationships of justice between individuals and groups require that the terms of their relationship be such that it is reasonable for those individuals and groups to consent to those terms. Contractual relationships imposed by duress are not genuinely contractual. So freedom to accept or reject particular terms of employment and freedom to accept or reject particular terms of exchange in free markets are crucial elements in those markets being in fact free. When in premodern societies markets are auxiliary to production that is not primarily for the market, but for local need, so that markets provide a useful means of exchange for what is surplus to local need, a means whereby all those who participate in them benefit, then the conditions of such freedom may be satisfied. And in a society of small productive units, in which everyone has an opportunity to own (and not indirectly through shareholdings) the means of production – the type of economy envisaged by Chesterton and other distributists – free markets will be a necessary counterpart to freedom of ownership and freedom of labor. (This is a type of economy which does in fact give expression to the understanding of human freedom of the encyclical *Centesimus Annus*, an encyclical whose exaggerated optimism about the actualities of contemporary capitalism, both in Eastern Europe and in the United States, has led to unfortunate misconstruals of its doctrine.) But in the markets of modern capitalism prices are often imposed by factors external to a particular market: those, for example, whose livelihood has been made subject to international market forces by their having become exclusively producers for some product for which later on there is no longer sufficient demand, will find themselves compelled to accept imposed low prices or even the bankruptcy of their economy. Market relationships in contemporary capitalism are for the most part relations imposed both on labor and on small producers, rather than in any sense freely chosen.

I have tried so far in this account of the injustice characteristic of capitalism to make it clear that, when apologists for capitalism point out quite correctly that capitalism has been able to generate material prosperity at a higher level and for more people than any other economic system in human history, what they say is irrelevant as a rebuttal of these charges of injustice. But the rising standard of material prosperity in capitalist economies is itself closely related to another aspect of their failure in respect of justice. It is not only that individuals and groups do not receive what they deserve, it is also that they are educated or rather miseducated to believe that what they should aim at and hope for is not what they deserve, but whatever they may happen to want. The attempt is to get them to regard themselves primarily as consumers whose practical and productive activities are no more than a means to consumption. What constitutes success in life becomes a matter of the successful acquisition of consumer goods, and thereby that acquisitiveness which is so often a character trait necessary for success in capital accumulation is further sanctioned. Unsurprisingly *pleonexia*, the drive to have more and more, becomes treated as a central virtue. But Christian theologians in the Middle Ages had learned from Aristotle as well as from Scripture that *pleonexia* is the vice that is the counterpart to the virtue of justice. And they had understood, as later theologians have failed to do, the close connection between developing capitalism and the sin of usury. So it is not after all just general human sinfulness that generates particular individual acts of injustice over and above the institutional injustice of capitalism itself. Capitalism also provides systematic incentives to develop a type of character that has a propensity to injustice.

Finally we do well to note that, although Christian indictments of capitalism have rightly focused attention upon the wrongs done to the poor and the exploited, Christianity has to view any social and economic order that treats being or becoming rich as highly desirable as doing wrong even to those who having accepted that goal succeed in achieving it. Riches are, from a biblical point of view, an affliction, an almost insuperable obstacle to entering the kingdom of heaven. Capitalism is bad for those who succeed by its standards as well as for those who fail by them, something that many preachers and theologians have failed to recognize. And those Christians who have recognized it have often enough been at odds with ecclesiastical as well as political and economic authorities.

Notice that this Christian critique of capitalism relied and relies in key part, even if only in part, upon concepts and theses drawn from Marxist theory. Just as Marxism learned certain truths from Christianity, so Christianity in turn needed and needs to learn certain truths from Marxism. But what does this mean for practice in general and for political practice in particular?

When I posed this question in 1953, I was able to find no satisfactory answer. Partly this was because I then aspired to an impossible condition, that of being genuinely and systematically a Christian, who was also genuinely and systematically a Marxist. I therefore tried to integrate elements of Christianity with elements of Marxism in the wrong way. But in so doing I was also in error in another respect. Among my as yet unquestioned assumptions was a belief that the only possible politics that could effectively respond to the injustices of a capitalist economic and social order was a politics that took for granted the institutional forms of the modern state and that had as its goal the conquest of state power, whether by electoral or by other means, so that I could not as yet recognize that those who make the conquest of state power their aim are always in the end conquered by it and, in becoming the instruments of the state, themselves become in time the instruments of one of the several versions of modern capitalism.

1968 FROM THE STANDPOINT OF 1995

Large as these errors were, they were not the matters on which I was in 1953 most fundamentally at a loss. In the first version of this book there was a chapter on philosophy and practice that was omitted when I revised it in 1968. That chapter was originally included because it attempted to pose what I had rightly recognized as the fundamental problem. It was later omitted because I had by then learnt that I did not know how to pose that problem adequately, let alone how to resolve it. So in 1968 I mistakenly attempted to bypass it. But it cannot be avoided. What is that problem?

Any adequate account of the relationship between Marxism and Christianity would have to embody and be justified in terms of some systematic standpoint on the major issues of moral and political philosophy and of related philosophical disciplines. By 1953 I had acquired not only from my

Marxist teachers, both in and outside the Communist Party, but also from the writings of R. G. Collingwood, a conception of philosophy as a form of social practice embedded in and reflective upon other forms of social practice. What I did not then fully understand was that philosophy needs to be conceived as having at least a fourfold subject matter and a fourfold task. There is first of all that which has to be learned empirically: the rules and standards, concepts, judgments, and modes of argumentative justification, actually embodied in or presupposed by the modes of activity which constitute the life of the social order in which one is participating. Secondly, there are the dominant ways of understanding or misunderstanding those activities and the relevant rules and standards, concepts, judgments, and modes of argumentative justification. Thirdly, there is the relationship between these two in respect of how far the second is an adequate, and how far an inadequate and distorting representation of the first. And finally there is that of which a philosopher must give an account, if she or he is to vindicate the claim to have been able to transcend whatever limitations may have been imposed by her or his historical and social circumstances, at least to a sufficient extent to represent truly the first three and so to show not just how things appear to be from this or that historical and social point of view, but how things are.

Philosophy thus understood includes, but also extends a good deal beyond, what is taken to be philosophy on a conventional academic view of the disciplines. It is crucial to the whole philosophical enterprise, on any view of it, that its enquiries should be designed to yield a rationally justifiable set of theses concerning such familiar and central philosophical topics as perception and identity, essence and existence, the nature of goods, what is involved in rule-following and the like. But, from the standpoint towards which Marx and Collingwood had directed me, the discovery of such theses was valuable not only for its own sake, but also because it enables us to understand about particular forms of social life what it is that, in some cases, enables those who participate in them to understand their own activities, so that the goods which they pursue are genuine goods, and, in others, generates systematic types of misunderstanding, so that those who participate in them by and large misconceive their good and are frustrated in its achievement.

Marx, for example, in his analysis of *bürgerlich* society, had shown how the characteristic forms of thought of that society at once articulate and disguise its underlying structure, and some of his heirs both within and outside Marxism – I think especially of both Karl Mannheim and Karl Polanyi – have since developed his insights further. But Marx and Engels were both blind to the extent to which their own thought not only has the marks characteristic of *bürgerlich* theorizing, but was distorted in a characteristically *bürgerlich* manner, notably in their treatment of the economic, the political, and the ideological as distinct and separate, albeit causally interrelated areas of human activity, a treatment whose effect was to transform contingent characteristics of mid and late-nineteenth-century capitalist societies into analytical categories purporting to provide the key to human history and social structure in general.

By 1968 my reading of Lukács had taught me to recognize this fact and with it the general form of a central problem for any philosophical enquiry conceived as I was beginning to conceive it: how is it possible to identify in the case of other and rival theses and arguments a variety of distortions and limitations deriving from their authors' historical and social context, while at the same time being able to exhibit one's own theses and arguments, including one's theses and arguments about their theses and arguments, as exempt from such distortion and limitation? This was a question that had of course already been asked and answered by Hegel, by Marx, and by numerous others. But by 1968 I knew that not only their answers, but also their detailed formulations of the questions were vulnerable to insuperable objections.

Because I did not as yet know how to formulate this question adequately enough even to know where to look for an answer to it, I found myself distanced from identification with any substantive point of view. Whereas in 1953 I had, doubtless naively, supposed it possible to be in some significant way both a Christian and a Marxist, I was by 1968 able to be neither, while acknowledging in both standpoints a set of truths with which I did not know how to come to terms. In the case of Marxism, my reaction to recurrent attempts to reinstate Marxism as both economic and political theory and as *weltanschauung* had led me for a considerable time to reject more than I should have done; for redirecting my thought I am much indebted to conversations with George Lichtheim, Heinz Lubasz, Linda Nicholson, Marx Wartofsky, and Cheney Ryan, who provided a variety of illuminating perspectives on the problems of Marxism. One result is that I would not now endorse what I wrote dismissively about the labor theory of value in 1953 and I would want to say considerably more on a number of topics, including the theory of value, than I did in 1968.

Christianity had become problematic for me as a consequence of my having supposed that the theology in terms of which its claims had to be understood was that of Karl Barth. But what Barth's theology proved unable to provide was any practically adequate account of the moral life, and, although I should have known better, I mistakenly took what is a defect in Barth's theology to be a defect of Christianity as such. This judgment seemed to be confirmed by the platitudinous emptiness of liberal Christian moralizing, whether Protestant or Catholic, a type of moralizing in which the positions of secular liberalism reappeared in various religious guises. And this liberalism, the moral and political counterpart and expression of developing capitalism, I rejected just as I had done in 1953 and for the same reasons.

Why is political liberalism to be rejected? The self-image of the liberal is after all that of a protagonist of human rights and liberties. Those liberals who are social democrats aspire to construct institutions in the trade union movement and the welfare state that will enable workers to participate in capitalist prosperity. And it would be absurd to deny that the achievement of pensions, health services, and unemployment benefits for workers under capitalism has always been a great and incontrovertible good. Why then did and do I reject liberal social democracy? For at least three reasons. First, Marxist theorists had predicted that, if trade unions made it their only goal to work for betterment within the confines imposed by capitalism and parliamentary democracy, the outcome would be a movement towards first the domestication and then the destruction of effective trade union power. Workers would so far as possible be returned to the condition of mere instruments of capital formation. In both 1953 and 1968 I took this prediction to be warranted, although it was then treated with great contempt by the theorists of liberal social democracy. Since then it has of course turned out to be true.

Secondly, liberalism is the politics of a set of elites, whose members through their control of party machines and of the media, predetermine for the most part the range of political choices open to the vast mass of ordinary voters. Of those voters, apart from the making of electoral choices, passivity is required. Politics and its cultural ambiance have become areas of professionalized life, and among the most important of the relevant professionals are the professional manipulators of mass opinion. Moreover entry into and success in the arenas of liberal politics has increasingly required financial resources that only corporate capitalism can supply, resources that secure in return privileged access to those able to influence political decisions. Liberalism thus ensures the exclusion of most people from any possibility of active and rational participation in determining the form of community in which they live.

Thirdly, the moral individualism of liberalism is itself a solvent of participatory community. For liberalism in its practice as well as in much of its theory promotes a vision of the social world as an arena in which each individual, in pursuit of the achievement of whatever she or he takes to be her or his good, needs to be protected from other such individuals by the enforcement of individual rights. Moral argument within liberalism cannot therefore begin from some conception of a genuinely common good that is more and other than the sum of the preferences of individuals. But argument to, from, and about such a conception of the common good is integral to the practice of participatory community. Hence if one holds that both justice as understood by St. Paul and that justice which aspires to move from the maxim "From each according to her or his ability, to each according to her or his contribution" to "From each according to her or his ability, to each according to her or his need" can be embodied only in the internal and external relationships of participatory community, then liberalism will be incompatible with justice thus understood and will have to invent its own conceptions of justice, as it has indeed done.

When my grounds for rejecting liberalism are expressed in this way, it is evident that they presuppose a commitment to some set of positive affirmations. But these I did not in 1968 know how to formulate, in part because I did not know how to come to terms with either Marxism or Christianity and in part because I still lacked an adequate philosophical idiom for the statement, let alone the resolution of the relevant issues. So it was natural that for a considerable period I found it relatively easy to say what I was against, rather than what, if anything, I was for. Perceptive critics recognized some of my underlying commitments – hostile critics saw them as underlying credulities – better than I myself did.

Marxism and Christianity were themselves in continuing and striking transformation. The debates and the documents of the Second Vatican Council, which had met from 1962 to 1965, had by their definitive restatement of Christian doctrine provided resources for identifying both the negative legalism of theological conservatives and the vacuous moralism of theological liberals as twin distortions of faith and practice. But since the discussion and evaluation of the Council was all too often framed in terms of a set of conservative-liberal antitheses and so distorted by the very errors from which the Council should have delivered us and will perhaps in time deliver us, the immediate effect was one of apparent theological confusion. For Marxists many events of the late 1960s – the beginning of the Brezhnev era in the Soviet Union, the crushing by Soviet troops of the Czech project for socialism with a human face, the student uprisings, and the variously ineffective responses to those events of communist parties in France and Italy and of small sectarian Marxist groups – should have given further evidence of the systematic failure of Marxism as politics. Where Marxists were to continue to be politically effective – as in the Communist Party of South Africa – it was always because they had adopted programmes and forms of action only connected with Marxism in the loosest and most indirect ways.

1995

As I write, capitalism, taking a variety of forms that range from the corporate capitalism of the United States to the state capitalism of China, seems to be almost unchallenged worldwide – except of course by its own self-destructive and disillusioning tendencies. In the United States during a decade in which productivity has continually risen, the real wages of many types of worker have failed to rise. The gap between richer and poorer has widened. When unemployment falls, this is treated as bad news on the stock market. Larger sections of the work force have become aware of their job insecurity, since profitability and capital formation require an ability to fire and to hire at will. In service industries many employees face continuing low-wage drudgery. Growth in technological expertise and in productive power have as their outcome societies of recurrently disappointed expectations, in which electorates, not knowing where to turn, exchange one set of political charlatans for another. In the world at large the crucial gap is that between the wealthy capitalist nations and their immediate satellites on the one hand and those now condemned to the poverty of exclusion and marginality in respect of international markets on the other.

In this situation what is most urgently needed is a politics of self-defense for all those local societies that aspire to achieve some relatively self-sufficient and independent form of participatory practice-based community and that therefore need to protect themselves from the corrosive effects of capitalism and the depredations of state power. And in the end the relevance of theorizing to practice is to be tested by what theorizing can contribute, indirectly or directly, to such a politics. At the very least we can hope for this from sound theoretical enquiry: that we become able to approach the political tasks of the present freed in some significant measure from some of the major errors that so often undermined anticapitalist politics in the past, in the hope that reopening enquiry and debate on issues and questions whose final resolution is widely supposed to have been achieved long since may turn out to be of a good deal more than academic interest. And so I have found it.

As early as the 1970s I had begun to formulate positions that would enable me to understand somewhat better not only what it was that had to be rejected in the moral, social, and economic theory and practice of liberalism and individualism, but also how to evaluate in a more searching way the claims of Christian orthodoxy and the critique of Marxism. I came to recognize that the competing moral idioms in which contemporary ideological claims, whether liberal or conservative, are framed – the praise of Victorian values, various theories of natural rights, Kantian universalism, contractarianism, utilitarianism – were the result of a fragmentation of practical and evaluative discourse. Those competing moral idioms were to be understood as the outcome of a history in which different aspects of the life of practice had first been abstracted from the practical and theoretical contexts in which they were at home and then transformed into a set of rival theories, available for ideological deployment. What needed to be recovered, in order both to understand this and to correct it, was some reconstructed version of Aristotle's view of social and moral theory and practice. I also understood better what type of community it was by contrast with which I had rightly found the social relationships of both capitalist individualism and Soviet command economies, very different as they were, deformed and inadequate. The modes of social practice in some relatively small-scale and local communities – examples range from some kinds of ancient city and some kinds of medieval commune to some kinds of modern cooperative farming and fishing enterprises – in which social relationships are informed by a shared allegiance to the goods internal to communal practices, so that the uses of power and wealth are subordinated to the achievement of those goods, make possible a form of life in which participants pursue their own goods rationally and critically, rather than having continually to struggle, with greater or lesser success, against being reduced to the status of instruments of this or that type of capital formation.

These were not two discoveries, but one, since what Aristotelian theory articulates are in fact the concepts embodied in and presupposed by such modes of practice, and such concepts themselves need to be understood in terms of their functioning within just those same modes of practice. Aristotle's statement of his own positions is of course at some points in need of greater or less revision and at others – in, for example, his treatment of women, productive workers, and slavery – requires outright rejection. But the fruitful correction of these inadequacies and mistakes turned out to be best achieved by a better understanding of Aristotelian theory and practice. My realization that this was so was only one of several large consequences of my finally adopting what was a basically Aristotelian standpoint and then developing it in relation to contemporary issues inside and outside philosophy.

Having done so, I discovered that I had thereby discarded philosophical assumptions that had been at the root of my difficulties with Christian orthodoxy. And the removal of these barriers was one, even if only one, necessary stage in my coming to acknowledge the truth of the biblical Christianity of the Catholic church. But I also understood better than I had done earlier not only what had been right in official Catholic condemnations of Marxism, but also how much had been mistaken and rooted in obfuscating and reactionary social attitudes. Part of what Catholic theologians – and more generally Christian theologians – had failed to focus upon sufficiently was the insistence by both Marx and Marxists on the close relationships of theory to practice, on how all theory, including all theology, is the theory of some mode or modes of practice. Just as the propositions of scientific theorizing are not to be either understood or evaluated in abstraction from their relationships to the practices of scientific enquiry within which they are proposed, revised, and accepted or rejected, so it is too with other bodies of propositions. Detach any type of theorizing from the practical contexts in which it is legitimately at home, whether scientific, theological, or political, and let it become a free-floating body of thought and it will be all too apt to be transformed into an ideology. So when Catholic theology is in good order, its peculiar work is to assist in making intelligible in a variety of contexts of practice what the church teaches authoritatively as the Word of God revealed to it and to the world. When and insofar as theology does not subordinate itself to that teaching, but claims independence of it, it becomes no more than one more set of competing religious opinions, sometimes perhaps opinions of great interest, but functioning very differently from theology in the service of the teaching and practicing church.

Marxism was proposed by its founders as a body of theory designed to inform, direct, and provide self-understanding in the practice of working-class and intellectual struggle against capitalism. It too has recurrently become detached from such contexts of practice. When and insofar as it does so, it too becomes no more than a set of competing political, economic, and social opinions. And of course its tendency towards degeneration into this condition is one of the marks of its failure. The errors and distortions that have afflicted Marxism are of course various and have a range of different causes, some of them deriving from the vicissitudes of its later history. But if we are now to learn how to criticize

Marxism, not in order to separate ourselves from its errors and distortions – that phase should be long over – but in order once again to become able to learn from it, then we shall need once more to re-examine Marx's thought of the 1840s and above all the changes in his conception of the relationship of theory to practice. If we do so, we will have to recognize that Marxism was not so much defeated by criticisms from external standpoints, important as these certainly were, so much as it was self-defeated, defeated that is by the failures of both Marx and his successors to provide a resolution of key difficulties internal to Marxism.

Central among these was Marx's refusal or inability to press further some of the questions posed in and by the *Theses on Feuerbach*.[3] And we need answers to these questions, if we are to be able to construct and sustain practice-based forms of local participatory community that will be able to survive the insidious and destructive pressures of contemporary capitalism and of the modern state. The politics of such communities and of the struggles to construct and sustain them will be much more effective, if it is conducted by those able to understand and to learn from both Christianity and Marxism and to understand their relationship.

3 For a first attempt to reopen such questions, even if only in a preliminary way, see my "The *Theses on Feuerbach:* A Road Not Taken" in *Artifacts, Representations and Social Practice: Essays for Marx Wartofsky,* ed. R. S. Cohen and C. C. Gould, Dordrecht: Kluwer, 1994.

CHAPTER 9

Poetry as political philosophy: notes on Burke and Yeats

To write about Yeats in a volume honoring Donald Davie is an act not of courage but of foolhardiness. For during the years in which he directed the Yeats School in Sligo, Donald Davie must have heard, let alone read, more words uttered about Yeats than any other human being has ever been subjected to. There can be almost no conceivable view to be taken about any poem of which Davie has not had to hear the case for and the case against elaborated at a length that would seem excessive anywhere but in Sligo. So to write about Yeats in partial disagreement with Davie, as I am about to do, is perhaps more than foolhardiness. Yet it has been part of Davie's *magisterium* as teacher and critic that he has often educated by inciting to disagreement. So that those who disagree with him are in their very disagreement indebted. As I shall be in writing about Yeats.

In the poetry that W. B. Yeats wrote in the decade between 1927 and 1937 one recurrent concern is the shedding of political illusions. Any life that embodies truth requires, so Yeats asserted in his poetry, a recognition that a coherent political imagination is no longer available. Yeats was himself concerned to make a particular poetic claim: that politics as understood by Edmund Burke could no longer achieve imagined and embodied reality in the Ireland of that period. But I shall suggest that the poetry which says this to us, and which said it to his contemporaries, uses the local Irish condition as a symbol to assert more generally that no coherent political imagination is any longer possible for those condemned to inhabit, and to think and act in terms of, the modernity of the twentieth-century nation-state. The question to which, in the end, although not in this essay, I want to find an answer is: is what Yeats says on this subject in this poetry true?

Questions about the truth or falsity of poetry are not often posed nowadays. For in the compartmentalizations of modern culture, questions about truth and falsity, rational justification, and the like are allocated to philosophy and the sciences and more generally to theoretical enquiry, while poetry is conceived of as an exercise of quite a different order. Theorizing about poetry is of course admissible; but that a poem qua poem might itself *be* a theory, let alone that a poem qua poem might provide for some particular subject matter the most adequate expression for some particular theoretical claim, these are thoughts excluded by our culture's dominant ethos.

I say "poem qua poem," because the notion that a poem may incidentally express a thought whose prose version makes a theoretical claim is acceptable and familiar. So those who write about Yeats's political theory and attitudes commonly supplement reference to his prose utterances by a use of quotation from the poetry which treats that quotation as if it were prose. I by contrast aim to discuss what the poetry shows us about politics qua poetry; such reference as I make to the prose will be only to elucidate the poetry, and Yeats's own political attitudinizing I shall exclude from attention almost altogether.

The poet who philosophizes qua poet – as Lucretius, Dante, Pope, Wallace Stevens, and Marianne Moore did – presents us with structures in which, although concepts and propositions may appear, they are subordinated to, and in key part derive sense and significance from, images of greater or lesser complexity. It is in and through the image that poetic form and philosophical content are unified. The poetic claim for the primacy and necessary contribution of the image to understanding involves of course a view of the relationship of images to concepts that is itself philosophically controversial; and it cannot be argued for here. But some aspects of it need to be stated in outline.

Images are true or false, but not in the same way that statements are. Statements say or fail to say how things are; images show or fail to show how things are. Images are true insofar as they are revelatory, false insofar as they obscure, disguise, or distort. But the reality that an image represents more or less adequately is not one to which we have access independently of any exercise of imagination. Our perceptions are partly organized in and through images, and a more adequate imagination is one that enables us to see or envisage what we could not otherwise see or envisage.

A true statement remains true when conjoined with other statements, whether true or false. But an image conjoined with others may thereby either acquire new revelatory power or lose what it previously had. Images may be on occasion composed of statements, and statements may be true or false of realities constituted in key part by the imagination. For there are both human relationships and objects of attention in nature that could not exist without the constitutive work of imagination. So a landscape or a sunset may be constituted as a structured object of attention; and so the community of a monastery or the society of a café or the complex relationships of a nation required imagination's work. One cannot be a monk or a member of café society without being able to imagine oneself as such; living the role of either is a form of imaginative acting out. And so too with the community of a nation: to be Irish or English, I must be able to imagine myself as Irish or as English, something achievable in part by participating in the shared poetic utterance of the nation. Take away shared songs and poetry, shared monuments and architecture, shared imaginative conceptions of what is for *this* nation sacred ground and you at the very least weaken the bonds of nationality.

So nations to be real must first be imagined. And so too the loss of a coherent imagination can transform the kind of society that a nation is into something else. The poet and only the poet may be able to represent absolutely to us the incoherence or the sterility or both of the substitute images, the *ersatz* images, by which such a deprived form of political society may try to conceal from itself its condition. The poet may achieve a disclosure of this failed political imagination by putting the relevant images to the test, by using them in a poem and showing that when they are used with integrity what they disclose is imaginative incoherence or sterility or both. And it is just this, so I shall want to claim, that Yeats achieved for Ireland in some of his mature poetry. Those images that provided Yeats at once with part of his vocabulary and with part of his subject matter were, some of them at least, drawn from Burke and from Yeats's extended reflections on Burke. So that it is with Burke that we have to begin.

Burke was a thinker a large part of whose stock-in-trade, at least in his political philosophy, was images. Arguments and concepts do their work in his writings only with the aid of images. When he identifies what his images represent, he sometimes moves from speaking of "the state" or of "the commonwealth and its laws" to speaking of "society" as though the differences between these were insignificant. And his images were well-designed to obscure those differences. The habits of mind and action that the British state of his day, as he imagined it, prescribed exemplified for him the fundamental principles of social order itself. But this Burke could not have argued systematically without himself becoming just the kind of *theorist* (a term of condemnation for Burke) whose false abstractions (*abstract* is another such term) had on his view misled the French revolutionaries.

So in the self-imposed predicament of one who is a theorist against theorists Burke drew on the resources of the image-maker: British liberties are "an entailed inheritance," "a sort of family settlement."[1] In relying on established prejudices and the experience underlying them we avail our-selves "of the general bank and capital of nations and of ages" rather than each individual's "private stock of reason";[2] and in so doing we respect that "great primeval" contract "between those who are living and those who are dead and those who are to be born," which ordains for society and the state – Burke in a single paragraph slides from speaking of the one to speaking of the other – the same divinely appointed order as that prescribed for nature.[3]

Images of inheritance, accumulated capital, and timeless contract and of these as reproducing the order of nature are juxtaposed to some very different types of image, which nonetheless reinforce Burke's overall thesis. One of these is of weight. The holders of a certain kind of extreme position are guilty of "levity" and "think lightly of all public principle"; governments are contrived so as not to "be blown down"; and the large property-users provide "the ballast in the vessel of the commonwealth."[4] Another set are images of natural growth. What "the British constitution" affords is "firm ground,"[5] the ground presumably on which grows "the British oak" in whose shadow silently repose "thousands of great cattle," while "half a dozen grasshoppers," those who agitate against the established order, mislead by the noise they make.

Burke's images are thus designed to secure the allegiance of the im-agination to certain conceptions of stable continuity and hierarchical order, as well as an antipathy to any kind of theoretical reflection apt to produce skepticism about the credentials of the established order. By these means Burke invited the English to imagine or reimagine themselves as members of an order in which the hierarchies of authority embodied the wisdom of continuity and for whom any radical disruption of the rela-tionships of power and property would be an unprecedented calamity. The English were thus invited to join with Burke in an act of collec-tive self-deception. For what Burke's images masked and concealed were the radical discontinuities and disruptions, of both political and pro-perty relationships, which marked English history: the thefts by the large

---

1 *Reflections on the Revolution in France*, ed. C. C. O'Brien (Harmondsworth, 1968), pp. 119–20.
2 Ibid., p. 183.   3 Ibid., pp. 194–95.
4 Ibid., pp. 155, 112, 141.   5 Ibid., p. 376.

proprietors, both of the lands owned by the church and of the common lands stolen by enclosure; the new invasive and destructive power of markets and of banks; the use of legalized terror to enforce new property relationships in the Black Act of 1723; the changed and increased polarization of power and property, described and condemned with gentle bitterness by Burke's fellow-Irishman, Goldsmith. Burke was not the first maker of myths about the continuities of English history. The fabrications whereby the College of Heralds in the sixteenth and seventeenth centuries endowed the newly rich and powerful with fictitious ancient genealogies had the same function. But Burke was the greatest of these myth-makers.

He had his own immediate purposes in so writing, but the importance of his image-making transcends those purposes. Burke's imaginary England was a prototype in and for the modern world in the way in which it seemed to provide a much-needed mask to be worn by the modern state. The modern state and those who inhabit and seek to uphold it confront a dilemma. It has to present itself in two prima facie incompatible ways. It is, and has to be understood as, an institutionalized set of devices whereby individuals may more or less effectively pursue their own goals, that is, it is essentially a *means* whose efficiency is to be evaluated by individuals in cost-benefit terms. Yet at the same time it claims, and cannot but claim, the kind of allegiance claimed by those traditional political communities – the best type of Greek *polis* or of medieval commune – membership in which provided their citizens with a meaningful identity, so that caring for the common good, even to the point of being willing to die for it, was no other than caring for what was good about oneself. The citizen of the modern state is thus invited to view the state intellectually in one way, as a self-interested calculator, but imaginatively in quite another. The modern state presented only in the former light could never inspire adequate devotion. Being asked to die for it would be like being asked to die for the telephone company. And yet the modern state does need to ask its citizens to die for it, a need that requires it to find some quite other set of images for its self-presentation.

The attempt to resolve or dissolve this incoherence by a more adequate conceptualization of the state is the conjuring-trick demanded of modern political theory: there is Rousseau's version of the conjuring-trick, there is Kant's, there is Hegel's, there is Mill's. But the conjuring-tricks all break down. It was the great insight informing Burke's work – one he himself could not have formulated, since he had to deceive himself as well as others – that where the conceptual resources of theory were bound to fail, since what was in fact incoherence could not be transformed into coherence, the image-making resources of rhetoric might succeed. What could not be transformed might be disguised. So Burke's work has had an importance other than and more general than he intended. But the political effectiveness of his rhetoric as a performance (and all rhetoric is performance) owed much to the fact that in it he reimagined not only the English, but also himself, so that among the images effectively authored by Burke there appear not only those of the British oak and the ballast in the ship of state but also that of Edmund Burke.

Burke, the spokesman for inherited property, himself inherited nothing, but near the start of his political career he purchased an English estate as one of the properties for his masquerade as a British, even an English, gentleman. The education he had received first in an Irish hedge-school, when still living among his mother's Catholic kin, and then from Irish members of the Society of Friends, had led on to the Anglican conformism of Trinity College, Dublin, and then at the age of twenty-one in 1750 to a quick exit to the larger stage of London. Here in *A Philosophical Enquiry into the Origin of Our Ideas of the Sublime and Beautiful* he argued that it is not the intellectual content of language, but the psychological force of the use of words that produces responses in action: "not clear, but strong expressions are effective" (V, 7). And Burke put this thesis into practice when he entered the House of Commons in 1766 as the political and financial dependent of the class that, by purchase of his estate, he aspired to join. Conor Cruise O'Brien has emphasized the ways in which Burke exhibited "Irishness."[6] But even he notes that Burke wrote "in the *persona* of an Englishman." And it was as an Englishman that for the most part he behaved and spoke. "Do you, or does any Irish gentleman," he asked a correspondent in a letter in 1773, in which he opposed the imposition of a tax on absentee landlords, "think it a mean privilege that, the moment he sets foot upon this ground, he is, to all intents and purposes, an Englishman?"

Burke's close friends were such Englishmen as Johnson and Reynolds. He planned to obtain a peerage for himself as an English, not an Irish, peer. Even on Irish matters he spoke as the English gentleman he had imagined himself into being. Arthur Young put him on his list of absentee landlords. And Burke argued in a speech in the Commons of 1785 that "independence of legislature had been granted Ireland; but no other

6 Ibid., pp. 23–41.

independence could Great Britain give her without reversing the order of nature. Ireland could not be separated from England; she could not exist without her; she must ever remain under the protection of England, her guardian angel."[7]

So Burke deliberately discarded his Irishness, flouting both his Catholic and his Quaker teachers. He invented new images of England as a country in which his new image of himself could be at home. And in so doing he separated himself not only from the Irish, but also from the Anglo-Irish, whose Protestant ascendancy in Ireland he constantly, and to his credit, condemned. When Yeats reimagined Burke as an Anglo-Irishman, Yeats's Burke was, at least in that respect, a work of dramatic and distorting fiction. But so after all was Burke's English Burke.

Yeats read Burke copiously, if not carefully. He underlined passages as he read, and he drew upon Burke as a key source in his political speeches. But in so doing he reinvented Burke. Burke is spoken of in conjunction with Berkeley and less often with Swift and Goldsmith, but never with Johnson or Reynolds. Swift too, of course, became at Yeats's hands more emblematically Irish than he in fact was (*The Words Upon the Window-Pane*). But it was not just that Burke was added to a roll-call of the great Anglo-Irish dead. Yeats also denied Burke any place in English thought: "We have in Berkeley and Burke a philosophy on which it is possible to base the whole life of a nation. That is something which England, great as she is in modern scientific thought and in every kind of literature has not" (*Speech on the Child and the State*, 1925).

Moreover in the same speech Burke was converted from image-making rhetorician to theorist, by way of a comparison with Berkeley: "Berkeley proved that the world was a vision, and Burke that the State was a tree, no mechanism to be pulled to pieces and put up again, but an oak tree that had grown through centuries." So Burke's image has become a generalization, the conclusion of a proof. And when Yeats uses Burke's images, he alters them by the way he selects from them. Images of inheritance remain; those of contract disappear; levity remains, but not the ballast in the ship of state. The tree becomes other than and more than the merely British oak. And Burke himself is added to the list as an image: "Burke with his conviction that all states not grown slowly like a forest tree are tyrannies." But to these reordered Burkean images Yeats gave genuine poetic allegiance.

7 Quoted by John Mitchel, *The History of Ireland* (Glasgow, 1869), p. 164.

I speak of poetic rather than of political allegiance, since what Yeats said about politics in his poetry by means of these images was not necessarily what he took himself to be saying, let alone what he actually said, thought, and felt in the realm of politics, as conventionally understood. It is particularly important not to read into the poetry of 1925 to 1937 the tatterdemalion fascism that Yeats came to embrace during that period. For whatever Fascist states were, they were not "states grown slowly." Donald Davie, generally the most perceptive of readers, has seen Yeats's later fascism in "Blood and the Moon," a poem of 1928;[8] but the presence of Burke in that poem signals an antipolitics, not a politics, a rejection of the modern state as a possible work of the imagination. Davie is right of course in emphasizing that in "Blood and the Moon," as indeed elsewhere, Yeats rewrote and to a significant degree falsified Irish history; but this falsification does nothing to discredit Yeats's claim that whereas in the past the power that is expressed in blood and its spilling could be allied with wisdom, now they are split apart. And the towers of the past, including the Anglo-Norman Thoor Ballylee, have become what the modern nation is: "Half dead at the top."

Goldsmith, aesthetically honey-sipping, Swift, "in sybilline frenzy blind," and Berkeley, as an alleged witness to the power of mind to dissolve the world, are three of Burke's companions in "Blood and the Moon." But Shelley too is numbered among his predecessors. The list is a catalogue of types of insightful mind, culminating with

> . . . haughtier-headed Burke that proved the State a tree,
> That this unconquerable labyrinth of the birds, century after century
> Cast but dead leaves to mathematical equality.

Haughtier-headed? Perhaps the reference is to Thomas Hickey's portrait of Burke now in the National Gallery in Dublin. Certainly the adjective is intended to accentuate Burke's contribution of wisdom to "The strength that gives our blood and state / Magnanimity of its own desire," a magnanimity now lost. For in the third section "we," gathered where our blood-shedding ancestors were, "clamour in drunken frenzy for the moon." The politics that seeks to revive this past in the present is, as Davie recognizes, the politics of lunatics.[9] So in the final section of the poem the tower that was at the poem's opening "blessed" has become "Half dead at the top."

8 *Trying to Explain* (Ann Arbor, 1979), pp. 165–73.
9 Ibid., p. 171.

> For wisdom is the property of the dead
> A something incompatible with life; and power,
> Like everything that has the stain of blood,
> A property of the living . . .

"Blood and the Moon" is not, by the standards of Yeats's mature achievement, a successful poem. Too many disparate images are laid side by side, and there is no poetic intention clearly manifest in their conjunction. So the Burkean image of the state as a tree coexists with Yeats's comparison of the state to a tower, but the two images are brought into no particular relationship. The lack of coherence is a limitation of the poem and not itself a product of imaginative insight. Nonetheless the poem does give effective expression to Yeats's negative verdict on the politics of the Irish Free State.

What was the Irish reality that evoked from Yeats this type of negative response? It was the contrast between that in the movement for the making of Irish independence with which he had identified and that which the movement turned out to have made. On the one hand, there was the imaginary and imagined Cathleen Ni Houlihan and the real, but equally imagined Padraic Pearse and Maud Gonne. Few potentially revolutionary movements have been as easily hospitable to poetry and to theatre as the Irish; fewer still have been as fortunate in the poetry and theatre which accepted that hospitality. At certain moments Irish politics had become transparently in key part a work of constitutive imagination, promising to restore traditional forms of communal order. Yet, on the other hand, the end result of that work was a modern bureaucratic parliamentary state, the outcome of negotiated and calculated sets of accommodations in which the skills of bargaining had displaced the virtues of heroism. The Irish Free State had provided an arena for individuals to make whatever way they will and can in the world, an arena for individual calculation, ambition, and aggrandisement, in which success and failure have a measure that has remarkably little to do with the common good.

The predicament of the Irish Free State was that it had to present itself as meriting the allegiance of those whose political imagination had been formed in the movement that led towards Easter 1916, while at the same time functioning effectively as a form of imposed bureaucratic order. It confronted the problem of all modern postrevolutionary states, that of how to betray the revolution while appearing as its heir and guardian. And, that is to say, what it confronted was not in any way a problem peculiar to Ireland. It was indeed just one more version of that incoherence for the masking and disguising of which Burke's images were especially well designed, the incoherence involved in the relationship of *the state as bureaucratic mechanism* to *the state as object of imaginative allegiance*.

The first great classic statement of these two aspects of the modern state was that by Marx in *The Eighteenth Brumaire of Louis Bonaparte*, who saw in the English Revolution of the seventeenth century and in the French Revolution of the eighteenth a sequence in which a stage of imaginative heroism, in which the historical actors were able to "sustain their passion at the poetic level appropriate to a great historic tragedy," was followed by one of "sober reality," the prosaic reality of bourgeois society. The politics of poetic imagination gave way to a quite other politics. Marx, however, misled his readers in two ways. He thought that he was describing the genesis of the peculiarly bourgeois state, when in fact it is the modern state as such that clashes with any politics of the imagination. And he failed to see that the "sober reality" of the modern state in good working order still requires an appeal to imagination, if only by way of disguise, an appeal which claims for the modern state that it is entitled to the same kind of imagination-informed allegiance appropriate for some at least of its antecedents and predecessors. Of course the continuing need for that appeal generates the incoherence that Burke disguised and Yeats diagnosed. What Yeats succeeded in showing, in the poetry in which he put Burke's images to work in specifically modern terms, was in part the failure of those and kindred images to mask or disguise (let alone remove) that incoherence in its modern Irish version, but also Yeats succeeded more generally in the course of exhibiting that particular Irish failure in revealing the incoherence of *any* specifically modern political imagination. The state can no longer be adequately imagined; and it can no longer function, therefore, as an object of allegiance to anyone educated into imaginative integrity.

"Blood and the Moon" is a significant part of Yeats's statement of this thesis, in spite of its flaws. It is effectively supplemented by and ought to be read in conjunction with two other poems or sets of poems. The first is the relatively simple proclamation of what Burkean thought cannot be accommodated to, but is necessarily opposed to, in "The Seven Sages." Goldsmith, Berkeley, and Swift are once again Burke's companions, but what unites them now is not that they are Irish, but that they are "four great minds that hated Whiggery." Goldsmith for once receives part of his political due as one who "sang what he had seen / Roads full of beggars, cattle in the field," although there is of course no reference to Goldsmith's corresponding indictment in "The Deserted Village" of the landed proprietors whom Burke had served and loved so well. Yet in this falsifying assimilation of Goldsmith, as of Swift and Berkeley, to Burke, Yeats is careful to note that their hatred of Whiggery was an attitude that Yeats recognizes in them, whether they themselves did so or not. What was this Whiggery?

> A leveling rancorous, rational sort of mind
> That never looked out of the eye of a saint
> Or out of a drunkard's eye.

And Yeats added immediately that "All's Whiggery now. . ." So that he asserts a deep incompatibility between the dominant contemporary Whiggism of liberal individualist modernity and the Burkean view of things. That incompatibility Yeats ascribed to and saw as embodied in the one-sided personalities of the participants in the politics of the Free State. In "Parnell's Funeral" Yeats ascribed to Cosgrave and to de Valera the same lack – Parnell's heart. "Had Cosgrave eaten Parnell's heart, the land's / Imagination had been satisfied. . ." O'Higgins is dead, and O'Duffy too has failed. Yeats at this time sees no leaders. And a fore-knowledge of the political failure that lay ahead was later to be ascribed to Parnell:

> Parnell came down the road, he said to a cheering man:
> Ireland shall get her freedom and you still break stone.

Yeats's image of Parnell was of course yet another falsification, but once again this does not discredit the use to which he put it in commentary upon what had made it the case that "All's Whiggery now. . ." Yeats in his political life never quite despaired of the possibility of finding leaders to replace the contemporary Whigs. But what he said in his poetry had a finality that is lacking in the attitudinizing of some of his later speeches. That finality is evident in the transition from the earliest version of what were at first entitled "Three Songs to the Same Tune," published in 1933, to the second version "Three Marching Songs," published in *Last Poems* (both sets to be sung to the same tune by Arthur Duff and so constrained to the same musical structure).

Most obviously the order of the three songs is changed. The opening song of the later version corresponds to the second in the earlier; the opening song of the earlier version is the final song of the later. These changes are related to a transformation of content. In the earlier version the second song declares a central theme of the whole: "Justify all those renowned generations" who made Ireland's past, "Defending Ireland's soul." The present generation are being summoned to complete the work of the past and so rescue it from failure:

> Fail, and that history turns into rubbish,
> All that great past to a trouble of fools. . .

Yeats has not yet come to assert the resourcelessness of the Irish political present.

This is emphasized by the way in which in the earlier version the second song is linked to the first. That first song recounts the hanging of the singer's grandfather in a culture in which it has been the peculiar function of our grandparents to mediate the past to us. In the chorus the blame for trying to undo that in our present achievement which could justify the past is put upon fanatics, and the song of those who fight against such fanaticism is "The Tune of O'Donnell Abu," a song summoning the people of Donegal to victory over their enemies. Thus Yeats still looks for a reversal, for a possible victory. But in the later version it is quite otherwise.

The tune of O'Donnell Abu has disappeared from the poem. The chorus to the grandfather's song is about turning away from worldly resources to magical devices and not about any fight against fanaticism, and the theme of the poem in what has now become the first of the three songs is not the justification of the work of the dead, but the memory of that work: "Remember all those renowned generations. . ." Consequently the line "Fail, and that history turns into rubbish" is changed from a warning to a prediction. In both versions the grandfather dies on the gallows for a cause. But in the later version it is a cause that is already lost.

What has any of this to do with Yeats's use of Burkean images? It is in what becomes the second section in the later version that these reappear, and the rewriting of the songs has prepared the way for and provided the necessary context for their use. It is Burke's tree, as an image of the state, that reappears and so does the levity that cannot resist the wind and so does that wind, which in Burke's version cannot blow down the firmly established state. But in this poem what there is at the top of the tree is emptiness. "Great nations blossom above," but "What tears down a tree that has nothing within it?"

There is a deliberate reference back to "Blood and the Moon" where Yeats had asked: "Is every modern nation like the tower, / Half dead at the top?" But the lack of solidity is now ascribed to tree rather than to tower.

So the modern nation-state can be conceived in Burkean terms only as a tree dead from half-way up and liable to be blown down by the winds of change. Yeats, having committed himself to the use of Burke's political image, has been compelled by his perception of Irish political reality to invert its use, so that the state is now to be imagined only as what has failed to flourish as a tree. The imagination either of the life of more traditional forms of community and social order or of the movement towards independence and a new restoration of those forms of community has given way to the Irish state of the twenties and thirties in which nothing coherent can be found for the imagination to represent, to express, or to constitute as an object of allegiance.

I suggested earlier that those features of the Irish state that allow Yeats to find only a negative and condemnatory use of Burkean images belong to it not as Irish, but as state. They are features of the modern state as such. And hence derives my thesis that Yeats reveals to us in the images of his mature poetry the imaginative poverty not of a particular regime, but of the structure of every modern state. About this thesis, however, two final caveats need to be entered.

The first is about the political implication of the poetic claim that I have taken Yeats to be making. The imaginative sterility of the modern state certainly puts constraints on the possibilities of creative political action. But there are forms of institutionalized community in the modern world other than those of the state, and the preservation of and enhancement of certain at least of such forms of community may set tasks for a less barren politics, one very different from the conventional politics of the contemporary state.

A second caveat concerns the justification of my own claims: about what Yeats is saying, as a poet who is qua poet *a* political philosopher, about the problems confronting the modern state, and about the relationship between these. All that I have been able to do is to state a case in bare outline and to gesture towards the arguments required to support it. Those arguments would have to supply answers to questions that give expression to very different types of objection. There are those who would ask whether Yeats was not in fact blind to what they take to be the merits of the modern Irish state because of his aristocratic prejudices. And there are those who would ask whether Yeats failed to evaluate Irish realities correctly, because the language of his poetry was English and not Gaelic. That I do not answer these questions here does not mean that I do not recognize their relevance. This is an essay that sets an agenda for work yet to be done.

CHAPTER 10

Some Enlightenment projects reconsidered

The Enlightenment is of course an historian's construction. There were several of them, French, Scottish, and German, each complex and hetero-geneous. Nonetheless we can identify some major shared themes and projects, each of which claimed and still claims the badge of Enlightenment. There is, first of all, the attempt to define *enlightenment* by drawing a distinction between the unenlightened and the enlightened, unenlightened them and enlightened us. Here the canonical text was and is Kant's *Beant-wortung der Frage: Was ist Aufklärung?* of 1784. And Kant's text has of course had its heirs and successors, most recently Foucault's of 1984, whose title repeats Kant's *Was ist Aufklärung?* ("What is Enlightenment?")[1]

Both Kant and Foucault defined Enlightenment as primarily a task, the task of achieving a condition in which human beings think for themselves rather than in accordance with the prescriptions of some authority. For Kant in 1784 such reasoning in the sphere of morality requires the adoption of the standpoint of what he took to be universal reason, a standpoint independent of the particularities of kinship and political ties, of one's culture and one's religion. But how is this standpoint to be characterized? About this widespread disagreement had already been generated by a second major Enlightenment project, that of specifying in detail the nature and content of the moral rules that universal reason requires, a project embodied in what were to become canonical Enlight-enment texts by authors as various as Locke, Hume, Smith, Diderot, Bentham, Robespierre, Jefferson, and Kant himself, each of these affirming positions incompatible in some respects with those of most or all of the others. And these disagreements have proved irresoluble. Does this outcome of the second project damage the first?

---

1 In *The Foucault Reader*, ed. P. Rabinow, New York: Pantheon Books, 1984.

Foucault's answer was: not too much. In his 1984 essay he asserted that the task set by Kant embodies attitudes towards the relationship of past to present and towards practical enquiry into how we are "constituted as moral subjects of our own actions" (*Was ist Aufklärung*, p. 49) that we still need to make our own, but we must now do so without the hope of being able to "identify the universal structures . . . of all possible moral action" (p. 46). It is, instead through investigating our contingency and our particularity that we will become able to test those limits that we must transcend, if we are to become free. Foucault's hope was that such investigation would enable us to disconnect "the growth of autonomy" from that intensification of power relations "which had resulted from the technologies of economic production, social regulation and communication" (p. 48). And he thus raised sharp questions about the relationship of the first project of the Enlightenment, that of becoming enlightened, not only to what I have called its second project, that of providing a single set of universal moral prescriptions, compelling to all rational individuals, but also to yet a third major Enlightenment project, that of bringing into being and sustaining a set of social, economic and technological institutions designed to achieve the Enlightenment's moral and political goals. It has of course been a central belief of the Enlightenment's modern heirs that such institutions have by now been brought into being in so-called advanced countries and that they do, substantially even if imperfectly, embody the Enlightenment's aspirations, so that those actual institutions – apart from their imperfections – have a claim to the allegiance of rational individuals, analogous to that which rationally founded moral principles have.

The roll-call of those institutions is a familiar one: representative democracy through which potentially autonomous individuals are portrayed as expressing their political preferences; a legal system purporting to safeguard the rights which individuals need, if they are to be treated as autonomous, including rights to freedom of expression and enquiry; a free-market economy through which individuals are to express their preferences as consumers and investors; an expansion of those technologies which supply the material and organizational means for the gratification of preferences; and a system of public education designed to prepare the young for participation in these institutions. Were it to be the case that the conjoint workings of these institutions systematically achieved and achieves very different outcomes from those expected by the Enlightenment, by in fact frustrating or undermining the autonomy and choices of individuals, how much would *this* matter to the ultimate fate of the Enlightenment's projects?

I

On this reading of the Enlightenment, its first project is presupposed by the other two. So I begin by examining Kant's claims about thinking for oneself. *Aufklärung*, enlightenment, so Kant asserted, is the casting off of an immaturity which is self-caused insofar as its cause is not lack of intelligence. That immaturity consists in thinking as directed by some other. Casting it off requires courage, the courage to think for oneself, and Kant quotes Horace: *Sapere aude!* He goes on to assert that if I have a book which takes the place of my understanding, if I have a spiritual director who takes the place of my conscience, or if I have a physician whose judgment about my dietary regime displaces my own, then, according to Kant, I have not yet shown this courage. Thinking for oneself is thus contrasted with thinking in accordance with the dictates of any authority. But this is not the only relevant contrast. Statutory rules (*Satzungen*; the term is used principally of articles of association) and formulas, useful aids as they may be, often instead act as a substitute for thinking for oneself. So unenlightened thinking is characterized by the indiscriminate and unintelligent use of and appeal to rules and formulas. How then is the courageous individual to free her or himself from bondage either to alien direction or to rules and formulas? Such freedom may not, Kant held, be possible when one is acting or speaking in some official civic or ecclesiastical role in which obedience and conformity can be justly required, if that role-playing is to be effective. But it is possible for someone to achieve the requisite independence, when that individual instead makes what Kant calls "public use" of her or his reason, that use "which the scholar makes before the whole reading public." What does Kant mean by this?

Foucault points out that the verb Kant uses here – "*räsionieren*" – is characteristically used by him to refer to reasoning which pursues the goals internal to reasoning: truth, theoretical and practical adequacy and the like. Those to whom such reasoning is presented are invited to evaluate it, not instrumentally from the standpoint of their own particular purposes or interests, but simply qua reasoners, in accordance with standards which are genuinely impersonal, just because they are the standards of reason as such. I hold myself accountable to other such reasoners in the light of those standards. I expose my reasoning to their objections, as they expose theirs to mine. And who, we may ask, could object to this and still claim the title of "reasonable" for her or his objection?

The force of this question has seemed to be such that it has been turned into an argument. Suppose that someone were to advance an objection to this Enlightenment ideal of public reason. Then in order for this objection to be evaluated as a better or worse reason for asserting its conclusion, it would have to be framed in accordance with these very same standards of public reason, and its author would thus have implicitly conceded just what she or he had intended to dispute. So the adherents of Enlightenment can know, in advance of any particular objections, that this fundamental position of theirs is immune from refutation.

Yet what this argument ignores is the fact that such public reasoning always occurs in a local context as part of a set of conversations that have their own peculiar history. We reason not just in the company of others, but in the company of particular others, with whom at any given time we will share some set of background presuppositions. What makes your theses or my objections to those theses relevant to our shared enquiries always depends upon the specifications of the social and intellectual context of our enquiries and debates. And here the example of Kant's practice is instructive. For in his essay on Enlightenment Kant was himself a scholar making use of reason "before the whole reading public." What was that reading public? It was of course one particular, highly specific, reading public.

The journal in which Kant's essay appeared in November 1784 was the *Berlinische Monatsschrift*, edited by J. E. Biester, a librarian in Prussia's Royal Library. In December, 1783, the Berlin pastor and educator J. F. Zöllner had raised the question to which Kant was now supplying an answer – not the first of such answers, since in September 1784 Moses Mendelssohn had contributed his response. The *Berlinische Monatsschrift* was one of a number of such journals in various European countries with overlapping circulation, so that there had come into being a collective readership, not only for those periodicals but for books reviewed or otherwise noticed in them. In some cities local societies brought such readers together. And individual readers engaged in often prolonged intellectual correspondence with those at a distance. So the public which Kant addressed was a network of periodical subscribers, club members, and letter-writers, to whose collective conversation he was a major contributor.

What this suggests is twofold: first that *the* reading public at any particular time and place is always some particular, highly specific, reading public with its own stock of shared assumptions, expectations, and focus of attention. What is regarded as obvious or taken for granted, what is treated as problematic, which considerations have more weight and which less, which rhetorical modes are acceptable and which not, vary from reading public to reading public. Indeed in some times and places there may be more than one reading public. So that it is not so much humanity in general as some socially particularized "anyone" whom a scholar making public use of her or his reason addresses, when she or he addresses what she or he takes to be "the whole reading public."

Secondly, reading publics have to be distinguished from other types of public, such as the public that is composed of every member of some particular political society or the public constituted by some other shared interest. How do reading publics relate to such other publics? Kant avoids this question, for he equates considering oneself "as a member of the whole commonwealth, in fact even of world society," with considering oneself "in the quality of a scholar who is addressing the true public through his writing." And at the end of his essay he envisages a spreading of Enlightenment from the cultures of the arts and the sciences to religion and thereafter to politics, the framing of legislation. "This free thought gradually acts upon the mind of the people and they gradually become more capable of acting in freedom. Eventually, the government is also influenced by this free thought and thereby it treats the human being, who is now more than a machine, according to his dignity."[2] Kant's conclusion provokes questions: is he right in asserting that it is through one's relationship to this kind of reading public that one comes to think for oneself? What is the relationship between thinking for oneself, however that is understood, and effective action on the basis of such thought? And what is the relationship between thinking for oneself in any one particular sphere – that, say, in which one addresses a particular *reading* public – and thinking and acting for oneself in other spheres of activity? These are questions that Kant did not pursue. Perhaps they were among those whose answers seemed to him and his readers unproblematic. For that reason alone they are worth pursuing.

II

Kant is unquestionably right in this: that thinking for oneself always does require thinking in cooperation with others. Some episodes of thought do

2 Immanuel Kant, "An Answer to the Question: What is Enlightenment?" in *Perpetual Peace and Other Essays on Politics, History, and Morals*, trans. Ted Humphrey, Indianapolis, Ind.: Hackett, 1983, pp. 41–48.

of course consist in solitary monologues. But even solitary monologues have to begin from what others have provided, and their conclusions have to be matched against rival conclusions, have to be stated in such a way as to be open to critical and constructive objections advanced by others, and have to be thereby made available for reflective interpretation and reinterpretation by others, so that sometimes one comes to understand only from those others what one means or must have meant. We learn to think better or worse from others, much that is matter for our thought is presented to us by others, and we find ourselves contributing to a complex history of thought in which our debts to our predecessors are payable only to our successors. What distinguishes my thought from my meditative fantasy is in key part the relationship in which that thought stands to the thought of others, a very different relationship from that which holds between my fantasies and the fantasies of others. For, in the case of thought, what I say both to myself and to others and what they say both to themselves and to me has to involve recognition, almost always implicit rather than explicit, of shared standards of truth, of rationality, of logic, standards that are not mine rather than yours or vice versa. This kind of relationship to others is an essential and not an accidental characteristic of thought.

We can always enquire therefore about any public, reading or otherwise, how well its practices embody the kinds of relationship that genuine thought requires. And all reading publics have this in common, that they depend upon the art of writing and the dissemination of writing. In the *Phaedrus* Plato warned us about – perhaps not unqualifiedly against – those whose relationships depend upon writing. There is of course a well-established interpretation of the *Phaedrus* according to which we are to ascribe the unqualified condemnation of writing as such, which Plato puts in the mouth of the Egyptian King Thamus, to Plato himself. And from this interpretation it is the shortest of steps to Derrida's claim that there is something inherently paradoxical and deconstructive in what he takes to be Plato's use of writing to issue an unqualified condemnation of writing, one endorsed by Socrates who never taught by writing.[3] Yet perhaps the condemnation implied by the argument of the *Phaedrus* is more qualified than the condemnation by Thamus. Perhaps what the *Phaedrus* in fact condemns is one particular kind of writing and all writing only insofar as it approaches the condition of that particular kind, so raising the question of whether and how far the *Phaedrus* itself falls under that condemnation,

3 Jacques Derrida, *Dissemination*, trans. Barbara Johnson, London: The Athlone Press, 1981.

but not answering it. What *is* condemned is all writing that has become detached from the author who speaks in and through it, so that the author as author cannot be put to the question along with her or his text. Yet must not this be the case with *all* writing when the author is dead? Perhaps not, if someone else is able to stand in the author's place, to supply the needed authorial voice, and to respond to interrogation by others.

The thesis that I am ascribing to Plato, as conveyed by the dialogue rather than by what Thamus or Socrates says in it, is that, if writing is to escape condemnation, it must function as subordinated to and only within the context of spoken dialogue. Texts, on this Platonic view, can play no part in the dialectical and dialogical development of genuine thought except when they are part of the matter of spoken conversation. But, if this view is correct, then the whole notion of a reading public as the type of public required for thought, required for thinking for oneself, is a little more complex than it at first appeared.

Consider the difference between the relationship of Plato's pupils at the Academy, who were able to put Plato to the question about the doctrines of the *Phaedrus*, to Plato, and the relationship of Kant's readers, many of them far distant from Koenigsberg and therefore unable to question Kant, to Kant. Texts such as Kant's serve as matter for genuine thought for their readers only insofar as their reading and the ideas drawn from that reading become part of the dialectical conversation of some group, in which imagination enables someone – perhaps more than one person – to speak on Kant's behalf and others – or on occasion perhaps the same person – to raise objections. So the kind of reading public which provides the context for genuine thought will be a network, not of individuals but of small face-to-face conversational groups who pursue their enquiries systematic-ally and make their reading part of those enquiries. And there certainly were places and periods during the eighteenth and the early nineteenth century in which the Enlightenment's reading public did to greater or lesser degree approximate to that condition – I am thinking here of various societies ranging from those meeting under the auspices of the great Academies in Paris or Berlin or St. Petersburg to such bodies as Berlin's *Mittwochsgesellschaft*, a group closely associated with the *Berlinische Monatsschrift*, the Oyster Club in Glasgow, the Rankenian Club in Edinburgh, and the Philosophical Society in Aberdeen.[4]

4 For a discussion of this type of public see J. Habermas, *The Structural Transformation of the Public Sphere*, Cambridge, Mass.: The MIT Press, 1989.

Thinking then is indeed an essentially social activity. But when he wrote of the public use of reason Kant was not engaged in characterizing thinking as such, but rather thinking for oneself, contrasting an immature reliance upon authorities and formulas with mature intellectual activity. What are we to make of *this* contrast? Thinking for oneself is in the first instance a condition for one's being able genuinely to contribute to and to benefit from those exchanges with others through which thinking is carried on. And this precludes the substitution of appeals to authority or to formulas for one's own conclusions, just as Kant contended. But is it the case that any kind of appeal to authority is thereby precluded? What about – to return to Kant's example – my reliance upon my physician's judgment in respect of my diet? She or he after all has the relevant expertise, while I do not. It cannot be a mark of maturity for me to substitute my untrained judgment for her or his trained judgment. (Kant, it is true, did pride himself on having restored himself to health without medical aid, after he became ill at the time of writing the first *Critique*.) But presumably it is not *any* reliance on the superior knowledge of others which is to be condemned, but only a reliance that exempts authority from rational scrutiny and criticism.

All representatives of rationally unfounded authority need of course to inculcate just such an uncritical reliance, attempting to ensure that others argue and enquire only within limits prescribed by them. When they succeed, the result is indeed that those others think not for themselves, but only as the representatives of authority prescribe. And even legitimate authority will have the same bad effect if it is relied upon uncritically, since such reliance will set the same kind of arbitrary limits to thinking. Note that in both types of case the failure to think for oneself is also a failure in thinking as such. And because all thinking is social, such failures are generally more than failures of individual thinkers, and the only effective remedies for such failures may always involve some change in the social condition of thought, in those social and institutional frameworks within which rational enquiry is carried on and by which it is sustained.

To recognize this involves acknowledging both the truth of Kant's central claim in *Beantwortung der Frage: Was ist Aufklärung?*, and the need to go beyond Kant. Thinking, in any particular time and place, let alone thinking for oneself, always involves thinking with certain particular others, thinking in the context of some particular and specific public, with its own institutional structure. Every such public has its own limitations and failure to recognize such limitations and to examine them critically may well involve a reliance upon them quite as damaging to enquiry as the reliance upon unscrutinized authority. The key question at any particular time and place is then: within what kind of public with what kind of institutionalized structures will we be able to identify the limitations imposed on our particular enquiries as a prelude to transcending those limitations in pursuit of the goods of reason?

The theorists of the European Enlightenment were brilliantly successful for their own time and place in identifying certain types of social institution which could not but frustrate that pursuit, and they did so by their negative critique of the intellectual justifications advanced by the representatives of the established powers of eighteenth-century Europe. It was for them, and it remains for us, crucially important to recognize that the centralizing state powers that had reduced local communities to administered dependence, the landed powers that had systematically encroached upon or abolished customary peasant rights, the imperialist hegemonies that had wiped out the original inhabitants of Prussia, enslaved large parts of the Americas, and conquered Ireland and India, all of these had rested on what was in fact arbitrary power disguised by a set of false legitimating theories and histories: the sixteenth-century French invention of the doctrine of the divine right of kings, the mythologizing genealogies devised for *nouveau riche* landowners by imaginative English heralds, the ad hoc theories of property which purported to justify the enclosure by the rich and powerful of hitherto common land, the defenses of slave-owning which elicited Vittoria's refutation, the doctrines of ethnic inferiority attacked by Las Casas. Insofar as it was the Enlightenment's project to expose the groundlessness of these pretensions of the ruling and owning classes of the seventeenth and eighteenth centuries, its theorists succeeded both argumentatively and imaginatively, and we are all of us the better for it.

Yet if the institutions of the *ancien régime* and of the post-1688 British oligarchy fail the tests of the Enlightenment, indeed the tests of rationality on any adequate view of it, what about the institutions characteristic of postEnlightenment modernity? How do those institutions fare, if judged by the same standards?

III

Within what kinds of institutional structure have the moral and political concepts and theories of the Enlightenment been at home? Within what types of discourse in what types of social context have they been able to find effective expression? A salient fact is that for some considerable time now in postEnlightenment culture moral and political concepts and theories have led a double life, functioning in two distinct and very different ways. They are afforded one kind of expression and exposed to one kind of attention in the contexts of academic life, in university and college teaching and enquiry, and in the professional journals of philosophers and theorists, but receive very different expression in the contexts of modern corporate life, whether governmental or private, contexts constituted by a web of political, legal, economic, and social relationships.

Each of these two contexts is constituted by a public or set of publics very different from those to which the concepts and theories of the Enlightenment were first announced and among which they were initially elaborated, as well as from each other. Reading has had a different part to play in each; discussion and debate, too, play very different parts; and the relationship of power and money to argument is not at all in each case the same. Yet both in contemporary academic milieus and in contemporary political, legal, and economic life, Enlightenment and postEnlightenment concepts of utility, of right, of moral rules, of presupposed contractual agreements and shared understandings, are very much at home. And in each they are put to use in formulating and answering such questions as: how is the maximization of my utility to be related to the maximization of the utility of particular sets of others and to the general utility? When the maximization of either my or the general utility requires the infringement of somebody's rights, how are rights to be weighed against utility? Is each right to be weighed in the same way? How more generally is utility to be conceived and how are rights to be understood? When may I legitimately mislead, deceive, or lie to others? When may or should I keep silent when I know that others are lying? By what tacit agreements am I bound? What generally and in such and such types of particular case is required of me, when I have encouraged and relied upon reciprocal relationships with others? When such questions are posed in academic contexts at the level of philosophy and theory, they receive not only incompatible and rival answers, but incompatible and rival answers each of which has by now been developed in systematic detail. I noted earlier how the great Enlightenment theorists had themselves disagreed both morally and philosophically. Their heirs have, through brilliant and sophisticated feats of argumentation, made it evident that if these disagreements are not interminable, they are such at least that after two hundred years no prospect of termination is in sight. Succeeding generations of Kantians, utilitarians, natural rights' theorists, and contractarians show no signs of genuine convergence.

It is not of course that the partisans of each view do not arrive at conclusions which they themselves are prepared to treat as decisive. It is rather that they have provided us with too many sets of conclusions. And each has been subjected to the most stringent tests that can be administered by a reading public in which face-to-face discussion provides a basis for and reinforces the effects of publication in books and journals. The modern academic philosophical community constitutes a reading public and a conversational public of a high order, in which each participant tests what is proposed to him by others and in turn subjects her or his own proposals to criticism by those others. So what we get is not at all what the early protagonists of the Enlightenment expected; what we get is a combination of exactly the right kind of intellectual public with a large absence of decisive outcomes and conclusions.

The contrast in this respect with the areas of political, legal, economic, and social life is striking. For within the corporate institutions that dominate government and the economy the needs of practice are such that decisive outcomes and conclusions cannot be avoided, and philosophical or other disagreement cannot be allowed to stand in the way of effective decision-making. All those questions about utility, rights, and contract that remain matters for debate in the academic sphere receive decisive answers every day from the ways in which those who engage in the transactions of political, legal, economic and social life act or fail to act. But in those areas the fact that there is no rationally established and agreed argumentative procedure for evaluating the claims of utility against rights or vice versa – or, if you like, that there are too many such procedures, but each rationally established and agreed only among its own protagonists – has a quite different significance. For what is unsettlable by argument is settlable by power and money; and, in the social order at large, how rights are assigned and implemented, what weight is accorded to this or that class of rights and what to the maximization of the utility of this individual or this group or people in general, what the consequences of following or failing to follow certain rules are, are questions answered by those who have the power and money to make their answers effective.

One peculiar set of features of distinctively modern social structures will bring out one aspect of this use of power. It is that compartmentalization of social life as a result of which each sphere has its own set of established norms and values as a counterpart to the specialization of its tasks and the professionalization of its occupations. So the activities and experiences of domestic life are understood in terms of one set of norms and values, those of various types of private corporate workplace in terms of somewhat different sets, the arenas of politics and of governmental bureaucracies in terms of yet others, and so on. It is not of course that there is not some degree of overlap. But the differences between these compartmentalized areas are striking, and in each of them there are procedures for arriving at decisions, procedures generally insulated from criticism from any external standpoint.

Consider as an example how the deaths of individuals are valued in different sectors of social life. Premodern societies characteristically have a shared view of the significance of death, and their public rituals express shared beliefs. Modern societies generally have no such shared public view, but teach their members to respond to individual deaths differently in different contexts. (There are of course some widely shared attitudes, one of them expressed in the attempt by the medical profession in the United States to use its technologies to postpone death for as long as possible, an attempt which is a counterpart to the general loss of any conception of what it would be to have completed one's life successfully and so to have reached a point at which it would be the right time for someone to die. But this is the expression of something absent, something negative.) So – all the examples that I use are North American – in the private life of the family or household it is taken to be appropriate to treat the death of a young adult as the kind of loss for which *nothing* can compensate. And this is what is commonly said to and by the recently bereaved. Yet in the world of the automobile industry and the automobile user things are very different. Over quite a number of years the society of the United States has tolerated without strain the deaths of many thousand persons – about 17 in every 100,000 persons die on the roads each year, a significant proportion of them young adults. (The only class of such deaths about which there is any public concern is that due to drunk-driving.) Such deaths were and are treated as an acceptable and unavoidable trade-off for the benefits conferred by the use of automobiles and the flourishing of the automobile industry. The benefits are taken, without any soul-searching, to outweigh the costs. Yet generally if a parent were asked, immediately before or after the death of an adolescent child, what degree of social benefit would outweigh the cost of that child's life and make that death an acceptable occurrence, the question would be thought shocking.

Contrast with both of these two other areas in which questions of compensation for death *are* systematically answered. One socially established measure for the loss incurred by families as a result of accidental deaths for which someone can be held liable is that established by juries. When the victim is a married woman, the sum awarded in recent years may be over a million dollars.[5] But the socially established measure for the loss incurred by the families of police officers killed in the line of duty is very different. What is awarded is a very modest pension and some act of ceremonial recognition. And the same is true of the deaths of soldiers in action. So in each of these social contexts the value assigned to a life and the measure of that value are determined by norms specific to each particular context. There is indeed evidence from time to time of pressure to make measures and judgments more consistent within each particular context, but there seems to be little or no evidence of pressure towards consistency *between* contexts. And so, in each particular context in which different possible courses of action which have potentially fatal consequences for some person or set of persons are evaluated, practical reasoning and decision-making will be guided by different norms.[6] Note that in 1981 an Executive Order by President Reagan resulted in the assignment by various government agencies during the next ten years of a monetary value to a human life. The differences between them are notable, with the values varying from, for example, $8.3 million by the Environmental Protection Agency to $650,083 by the Federal Aviation Administration.

These and similar facts support a crucial generalization: that the dominant culture of postEnlightenment modernity lacks any overall agreement, let alone any rationally founded or even rationally debatable agreement, on what it is that would make it rational for an individual to sacrifice her or is life for some other or others or what it is that would make it rational to allow an individual's life to be sacrificed for the sake of some other individual or some group or institution. But this does not mean that within that culture there is no way of arriving at practically effective agreements on the basis of shared norms and values. It is rather that what shared norms and values there are vary from one compartmentalized context to another, within each of which the relationships between rights, duties, utility, and presupposed contract are understood in a way that is the outcome of the power relationships which dominate that particular context. Hence practically effective agreements embody conclusions that also vary from one context to another. And, given that there are no generally agreed rational standards available for deciding how

5 "Compiling Data, and Giving Odds, on Jury Awards," *New York Times*, 21 January 1994.
6 See also E. J. Mishan, *Cost Benefit Analysis*, Amsterdam: North Holland, 1969, chapters 22 and 23; and J. Broome, "Trying to Value a Life," *Journal of Public Economics* 9, 1, 1978 pp. 791–100.

competing claims concerning rights, duties, utility, and contract are to be adjudicated, it could scarcely be otherwise. (Hence failure to reach agreement in academic moral and political enquiry is not without practical significance. It renders the academic community generally politically impotent except in its provision of services to private and public corporations.) In this type of social situation reason has no effective way of confronting the contingencies of power and money.

Notice then that it is not just in its inability to provide rationally justifiable and agreed moral values and principles that the Enlightenment and its heirs have failed. The failure of those modern institutions that have been the embodiment of the best social and political hopes of the Enlightenment is quite as striking. And those institutions fail by Enlightenment standards. For they do not provide – in fact they render impossible – the kinds of institutionalized reading, talking and arguing public necessary for effective practical rational thought about just those principles and decisions involved in answering such questions as: "How is a human life to be valued?" or "What does accountability in our social relationships require of us?" or "Whom, if anyone, may I legitimately deceive?" – questions to which we need shared answers. And there is no type of institutional arena in our society in which plain persons – not academic philosophers or academic political theorists – are able to engage together in systematic reasoned debate designed to arrive at a rationally well-founded common mind on these matters, a common mind which might then be given political expression. Indeed the dominant forms of organization of contemporary social life militate against the coming into existence of this type of institutional arena. And so do the dominant modes of what passes for political discourse. We do not have the kinds of reading public necessary to sustain practically effective social thought.

What we have instead in contemporary society are a set of small-scale academic publics within each of which rational discourse *is* carried on, but whose discourse is of such a kind as to have no practical effect on the conduct of social life; and, by contrast, forms of organization in the larger areas of our public life in which effective decisions are taken and policies implemented, but within which for the most part systematic rational discourse cannot be systematically carried on, and within which therefore decisions and policies are by and large outcomes of the distributions of power and money and not of the quality of argument. Within these contexts of academic and public life the same central moral and political concepts of the Enlightenment are at home, but the divorce between them is such that the original projects of the Enlightenment have been frustrated.

CHAPTER II

Social structures and their threats to moral agency

THE CASE OF J

Imagine first the case of J (who might be anybody, *jemand*). J used to inhabit a social order, or rather an area within a social order, where socially approved roles were unusually well defined. Responsibilities were allocated to each such role and each sphere of role-structured activity was clearly demarcated. These allocations and demarcations were embodied in and partly constituted by the expectations that others had learned to have of those who occupied each such role. For those who occupied those roles to disappoint those expectations by failing to discharge their assigned responsibilities was to invite severe disapproval and other sanctions. To refuse to find one's place within the hierarchies of approved roles, or to have been refused a place, because judged unfit for any such role, was to be classified as socially deviant and irresponsible.

The key moral concepts that education had inculcated into J were concepts of duty and responsibility. His fundamental moral beliefs were that each of us owes it to others to perform her or his assigned duties and to discharge her or his assigned responsibilities. A good human being performs those duties, discharges those responsibilities, and does not trespass into areas that are not her or his concern. A philosopher who comes across the likes of J will understand his attitudes as cultural parodies, in part of Plato (conceiving of justice as requiring "that each do her or his own work and not meddle with many things," *Republic* 433a) and in part of Kant (doing one's duty just because it is one's duty and not for the sake of any further end), authors who had influenced J's schoolteachers. A sociologist will entertain the suspicion that in certain types of social order it may be only in the form of parodies that some types of concept can continue to find expression. But for the moment let us put this thought on one side and return to J.

J, like everyone else, occupied a number of roles. He was a father, the treasurer of his sports club, and in wartime had been a noncommissioned officer. Afterwards he spent his working career in the service of the railways, rising to a position in which he was responsible for scheduling passenger and freight trains, monitoring their drivers' performance, and coping with break-downs. Early in that career he had been mildly curious about what "his" trains carried: commuters or vacationers, pig-iron or cattle. But he was instructed firmly by his superiors to take *no* interest in such questions, but to attend *only* to what belonged to his role, so as not to be irresponsibly distracted. Hence he acquired the habit of taking no cognizance of what his trains carried, a habit that endured through a later period, when the freight consisted in munitions and the passengers were Jews on their way to extermination camps. When still later J was questioned about this, he said sincerely: "I did not know. It was not for someone in my position to know. I did my duty. I did not fail in my responsibilities. You cannot charge me with moral failure." Was J's defence adequate?

MORAL AGENCY

To many the answer will be obvious and that answer is "No." Their answer presupposes a widely shared conception of moral agency. On this view to be a moral agent is to be justifiably held responsible. Responsible for what? For one's actions, certainly, but for one's actions in at least three respects. First moral agents so conceived are justifiably and uncontroversially held responsible for that in their actions which is intentional. Secondly, they may be justifiably held responsible for incidental aspects of those actions of which they should have been aware. And, thirdly, they may be justifiably held responsible for at least some of the reasonably predictable effects of their actions.

It is in spelling out the second and third of these that we encounter complexities. Consider two examples. I intentionally in my role as examiner award the prize to the competitor with highest marks, incidentally awarding the prize to the most arrogant competitor, and having reasonable grounds for predicting that the effect of the award will be to make him even more objectionable. But in this case it is my responsibility, because of my role, to ignore these latter considerations. Contrast a second example. I intentionally return a handgun to its owner, as my role in the lost property office requires, incidentally and, as it happens, knowingly returning it to someone dangerously paranoid, and having reasonable grounds for predicting that in consequence someone innocent will be harmed. In this case, because I am aware of these latter aspects of my action, I am justifiably held responsible for them, and, even if I had not known what I did, I might, at least in certain circumstances, be justifiably held responsible for not having found out what I should have found out. What the first example makes clear is that we may indeed sometimes be able to rebut charges that we were responsible for not taking cognizance of certain facts by citing a role that required us not to take account of them. And what the second example makes clear is that sometimes we are justifiably held responsible for not having made ourselves aware of certain facts about our actions, whatever the requirements of our role may have been.

How is the one type of case to be discriminated from the other? Two remarks are sufficient, not to answer this question, but to return us to the case of J. The first is that it is part of the responsibility of moral agents, on this view of moral agency, to know how at the level of practice to discriminate between such cases, and to give reasons for so discriminating, in the light of the best standards available. One reason, although only one, why children, the mentally retarded, and those suffering from some kinds of brain damage are denied the status of moral agent, or at least of fully fledged moral agent, is that they are unable to do this. And, if we hold J responsible for knowing what he was doing, whatever the requirements of his role might have been, we are ascribing to J just such a power of reasonable discrimination. Yet we are entitled to hold J responsible only if the best standards available to J would have warranted him in making those reasonable discriminations that we judge that he ought to have made. So what were the best standards available to J?

Here a second remark is to the point. J had been taught that the unquestionably best standards were the standards defining and governing the role requirements of his social order. His habits of mind and action had been formed in a culture in which the truth of this claim was generally taken for granted, so that those whose expectations were that J would do what his role required, and who held him accountable, shared his view that the established standards were the unquestionably best standards. If we condemn J, we are treating him as justifiably responsible, not only for his actions and for his knowledge of them, and not only also for his practical reasoning, but in addition for having failed to question the hitherto unquestioned. We are taking the view that responsible deliberation requires that on occasion one puts established standards in question, whatever verdict about them one may arrive at in the end.

Moral agents, that is to say, are on this view justifiably held responsible for the standards governing the reasoning from which their actions flow and they have to understand themselves as thus responsible. When J attempted to rebut the accusations advanced against him by saying that he had discharged all his responsibilities, he laid himself open to the questions of what reason he had for taking his socially assigned responsibilities to be his only responsibilities and what reason he had for continuing to believe that the established standards governing his deliberations were the best standards. By having failed to ask, let alone to answer these questions, J's defense of his deliberate setting of limits to his knowledge also fails, or rather it fails, provided that we are justified in ascribing to J the full powers of moral agency. But is it possible that we are not so justified?

That human beings have by their specific nature a capacity for recognizing that they have good reason to acknowledge the authority of evaluative and normative standards that are independent of those embodied in their own particular social and cultural order, and so share equally in a capacity to be able to transcend in thought the limitations of those established standards, has been a widely held doctrine. Disagreements about what such evaluative and normative standards prescribe and what awareness of their authority consists in have not precluded widespread agreement in ascribing to normal adult human beings a capacity that makes them responsible as individuals for not putting their established social and cultural order to the question, if and when they have occasion to do so. So it would seem that it can be justifiably asserted of J that as a normal human being he must have had the powers of moral agency and therefore had the responsibility for doing what he failed to do.

Yet questions arise. If we were to spell out further what it is to be a moral agent, it would be crucial to note that one cannot be a moral agent without understanding oneself as a moral agent at the level of one's everyday practice and that one cannot exercise the powers of a moral agent, unless one is able to understand oneself as justifiably held responsible in virtue of one's ability to exercise those powers. But how human beings are able to understand themselves depends in key part upon and is always in some ways limited by the nature of the social and cultural order they inhabit. The question therefore is: are there or might there be types of social structure that would prevent those who inhabited them from understanding themselves as moral agents? Or if this seems to envisage too extreme a state of affairs, are there or might there be types of social structure that seriously threaten the possibility of understanding oneself as a moral agent and so of acting as a moral agent?

WHAT IS IT TO UNDERSTAND ONESELF AS A MORAL AGENT?

What then is it to understand oneself as a moral agent at the level of everyday practice? Three characteristics of such self-understanding are relevant. First, I have to understand myself as and to present myself to others as someone with an identity other than the identities of role and office that I assume in each of the roles that I occupy. I have to understand myself as someone who brings to each role qualities of mind and character that belong to her or him qua individual and not qua role-player. It is a mistake to think of the relationship of individuals to roles as being the same as or closely similar to that of stage actors to the dramatic parts that they play. For the lives of individuals are constituted in large part by the various roles that they play, although they are generally able to reflect upon their role-playing in ways not dictated by those roles. It is characteristically, even if not only, in how they play out their roles that individuals exhibit their individual character. What more there is to individuals than their role-playing also includes the continuities of each individual's history, as they move from role to role, from one sphere of social activity to another. My awareness of and understanding of myself as an individual is exhibited in and partly constituted by the various acknowledgments of that individuality by others and my ability to respond to those others as individuals and not just as role-players. This mutual acknowledgment of our individuality characterizes some of our social relationships rather than others and some of our social relationships more markedly than others. And central among such acknowledgments are those judgments in which we evaluate individuals as individuals, in respect of their virtues and the goodness of their lives. But initially such judgments, we should note, just as much as our judgments about individuals as role-players, are generally governed by socially established standards. We all begin unquestioningly with the unquestioned.

Secondly, moral agents have to understand themselves not just as individuals, but as practically rational individuals. If moral agents are to be able to put in question those socially established standards, both standards defining and governing their roles and standards to which they appeal in evaluating individuals, they are going to have to understand themselves as entitled to rationally justifiable confidence in the critical judgments about those standards at which they arrive. Confidence is necessary, because these are practical judgments that are to provide them with reasons for action. Rationally justifiable confidence is necessary, because the critical response of the moral agent has to be distinguished from, and to present itself to others as distinguished from, mindless deviance and revolt. So the moral agent has to be entitled to confidence in her or his own moral judgments, when they are of the form "Even although it is almost universally agreed in this social order that in these circumstances someone in my role should act thus, I judge that I should act otherwise." What entitles someone to confidence in such judgments?

We are always liable to error in making particular moral judgments, sometimes intellectual errors such as going beyond the evidence or relying upon some unsubstantiated generalization, sometimes moral errors such as being over-influenced by our liking and disliking of particular individuals or projecting on to a situation some unrecognized phantasy or exhibiting either insensitivity to or sentimentality about suffering. And our intellectual errors are often rooted in moral errors. We need therefore to have tested our capacity for moral deliberation and judgment in this and that type of situation by subjecting our arguments and judgments systematically to the critical scrutiny of reliable others, of co-workers, family, friends. Such others, of course, are not themselves always reliable and some may influence us in ways that strengthen the propensity to error. So to have confidence in our deliberations and judgments we need social relationships of a certain kind, forms of social association in and through which our deliberations and practical judgments are subjected to extended and systematic critical questioning. But this is not all.

Moral agents have to understand themselves as accountable, not only in their roles, but also as rational individuals. The responsibilities that are socially assigned to roles are defined in part by the types of accountability that attach to them. For each role there is a range of particular others, to whom, if they fail in their responsibilities, they owe an account that either excuses or admits to the offense and accepts the consequences. Without such accountability the notion of responsibility would be empty. For failure in responsibility would lack those consequences, the enforcement of which is an important aspect of the social recognition of roles. But, if the notion of responsibility is deprived of significant content, when responsibility is detached from accountability, what follows about the responsibility of moral agents qua moral agents? To whom are they to understand themselves as accountable? To at least two sets of individuals and groups: those with whom they have engaged together in critically informed deliberation and those whose hitherto unquestioning reliance on the established standards of the social order they challenge by their deliberation and their action. To the former they owe an account of why they take it that their reasons for action have been able to withstand the strongest criticisms so far directed against them. To the latter they owe an account of why their reasons for challenging the established standards are good reasons. In giving such accounts they are inviting those who have hitherto accepted the established standards to engage with them in critical deliberative conversation. And in understanding themselves and those others as accountable they understand themselves and those others as moral agents.

Accountability to particular others, participation in critical practical enquiry, and acknowledgment of the individuality both of others and of oneself are all then marks of the social relationships and mode of self-understanding that characterize the moral agent. Strip away those social relationships and that mode of self-understanding and what would be left would be a seriously diminished type of agency, one unable to transcend the limitations imposed by its own social and cultural order. Moral agency thus does seem to require a particular kind of social setting.

There must therefore be a place in any social order in which the exercise of the powers of moral agency is to be a real possibility for milieus in which reflective critical questioning of standards hitherto taken for granted takes place. These too must be milieus of everyday practice in which the established standards are, when it is appropriate, put to the question and not just in an abstract and general way. The necessary presupposition of such questioning is some more or less shared conception of what it is to be a good human being that focuses upon qualities which individuals possess or fail to possess qua individuals, independently of their roles, and which are exemplified in part by their capacity or their lack of capacity to stand back from and reconsider their engagement with the established role-structures. And we may remind ourselves that just this capacity to stand back was what J lacked.

Those qualities are the virtues and in different times and places the catalogue of the virtues is not always the same. But there is a core notion of the virtues as qualities of human beings as such and, central to it, there is an acknowledgment of two virtues, without which the other virtues cannot be possessed. To those virtues I give their traditional names of "integrity" and "constancy." To have integrity is to refuse to be, to have educated oneself so that one is no longer able to be, one kind of person in one social context, while quite another in other contexts. It is to have set inflexible limits to one's adaptability to the roles that one may be called upon to play.

Constancy, like integrity, sets limits to flexibility of character. Where integrity requires of those who possess it, that they exhibit the same moral character in different social contexts, constancy requires that those who possess it pursue the same goods through extended periods of time, not allowing the requirements of changing social contexts to distract them from their commitments. So individuals with these two virtues will learn not only how to occupy some determinate set of roles within their social order, but also how to think of their goods and of their character independently of the requirements of those roles. They will, that is to say, be inhabitants of not just one, but of two moral systems, that of the established social order with its assignment of roles and responsibilities and that developed within those milieus in which that assignment has been put to the question. The degree to which these two systems are at odds with each other varies in different social and cultural orders. Those whose social and cultural order is such that the two systems present requirements that it is difficult to render compatible will be forced either to think their way through a series of more or less painful choices or to find some strategy for evading these choices.

The thinking that is needed is practical thinking, thinking that may occasionally be driven to extend its resources by opening up theoretical questions, but even then always for the sake of practice. The milieus in which such thinking is at home are, as I have already said, those of everyday practice, of the everyday life of certain kinds of family and household, of certain kinds of workplace, of certain kinds of school and church, and of a variety of kinds of local community. And what their flourishing will always be apt to generate is tension, tension that may develop into conflict between the requirements of the established social and moral order and the attitudes of those educated in those social settings that make the exercise of the powers of moral agency possible. So to be a moral agent is to have the potentiality for living and acting in a state of tension or, if need be, conflict between two moral points of view. And this is never simply or mainly a tension or a conflict between points of view at the level of abstract and general theory. It is always primarily a tension or a conflict between socially embodied points of view, between modes of practice.

The history of moral philosophy has usually been written – except for those historians influenced by Augustine, Marx or Nietzsche – in such a way as to disguise this fact. Why does this matter? It is because it is from these tensions and conflicts, when and insofar as they are present, that morality gets an important part of its content. There are of course social and cultural orders in which tension, let alone conflict, between such rival moral systems has not yet been generated to any significant degree. But, whenever it has been so generated, it defines an area in which at least some moral agents find themselves with particular responsibilities to discharge. Consider how this might be so with regard to truthfulness, considered as one essential constituent of the human good. Both Aquinas and Kant hold that it is wrong to tell a lie in any circumstance whatsoever. But one could refrain from lying throughout one's life without having done what is required of one, if one is to achieve the good of truthfulness. For truthfulness requires of us that, when it is of peculiar importance that rational agents should understand some particular aspect of their lives, so that they are neither misled nor deceived, it is a responsibility of those who are truthful to disclose what is relevant to such understanding. What it is relevant to disclose is in key part determined by the limitations of the contemporary role structure and the ways in which it assigns responsibilities may obscure from view just that about which the virtue of truthfulness requires that we and others should be undeceived. Conflicts about whose responsibility it is to know about this or that are therefore among those that in some circumstances, especially the circumstances of distinctively modern societies, provide content for the requirements of morality. "Ask about any social and cultural order what it needs its inhabitants not to know" has become an indispensable sociological maxim. "Ask about your own social and cultural order what it needs you and others not to know" has become an indispensable moral maxim.

What degrees and kinds of tension and conflict are engendered by the incompatibilities of established role requirements and the demands of the virtues varies of course from social order to social order. There are societies in which the potentiality for such conflict has not yet been realized, societies in which conflict has been effectively contained, societies in which conflict has disrupted and fragmented, sometimes creatively, sometimes destructively. So that often a key moral question is that of how best to find our way through conflict. Notice also that the dimensions of moral conflict are more than moral, at least if morality is narrowly conceived: they are moral-cum-political, moral-cum-economic, moral-cum-religious, indeed sometimes moral-cum-religious-cum-political-cum-economic; and remember too that the established norms and values with which we may be invited to enter into conflict will commonly be to some large degree our own norms and values, the norms and values by which we have hitherto been guided. So that initially at least that conflict will be within each of us. (Such conflict is not only a matter of incompatibility between two sets of practically embodied norms and values. It is also a matter of a certain resistance to critical questioning that claims about the limitations and errors of the standpoint of the established order are apt to evoke. And we may in some cases be misled about the nature and degree of such resistance, if we are naive in our identification of the norms and values of the established order. For there are types of social order, including our own, in which those norms themselves not only legitimate but encourage questioning, criticism, and protest, so that the set of approved social roles includes such roles as those of the Indignant Protester and the Angry Young Person and activities of criticism and protest are themselves governed by prescribed routines. We need then to draw a line between conflict or apparent conflict that is internal to and in no way a threat to an established order and conflict that is more radical, conflict that genuinely raises the question of whether established roles and routines can or cannot be justified in the light of the best account we have of the human good. It is conflict of this latter kind that social orders may need to contain or suppress, if they are to continue functioning as they have done.)

Where then has the argument taken us? We began with the case of J, who asserted that he could not be justifiably held responsible for his part in making the massacre of Jews possible, because he did not know what or whom his trains were carrying and because it was not his responsibility to know this, given his social role and the standards defining the responsibilities of anyone occupying that role. To this it was replied that moral agents are responsible for critical scrutiny of the standards governing their practical reasoning about their responsibilities, including their responsibilities for knowledge of their actions. Therefore, if J, a psychologically normal human being, was capable of exercising the powers of moral agency, J was responsible for his lack of knowledge and so indirectly for his participation in massacring Jews. What then might have prevented J, even though a psychologically normal individual, from exercising the powers of moral agency?

How we answered this question depended upon an identification of three types of precondition for the exercise of the powers of moral agency. First, the powers of moral agency can only be exercised by those who understand themselves as moral agents, and, that is to say, by those who understand their moral identity as to some degree distinct from and independent of their social roles. To understand oneself thus is to understand that one's goodness as a human being, the answer that by one's whole way of life one gives to the question "How is it best for a human being in my circumstances to live?", is not to be equated with one's goodness at being and doing what this or that role requires.

Secondly, the powers of moral agency can only be exercised by those who are able to justify rational confidence in their judgments about the goodness and badness of human beings and this ability requires participation in social relationships and in types of activity in which one's reflective judgments emerge from systematic dialogue with others and are subject to critical scrutiny by others. Without milieus within which such relationships and activities are effectively sustained the possibility of the exercise of the powers of moral agency will be undermined. Those who participate in the relationships and activities of such milieus will always find themselves in potential conflict with, and often in actual conflict with, the requirements of established role structures and therefore with those who uphold those requirements. And it is in part by defining their relationship to those conflicts that they give content to what the virtues require of them in this or that particular situation.

Moreover it is only in and through such milieus that moral agents become able to understand themselves as accountable to others in respect of the human virtues and not just in respect of their role-performances. So all three preconditions can be satisfied only within social orders in which there exist milieus, spheres of activity, which sustain the relevant kind of understanding of the self, the relevant kind of critical discourse and reflection, and the relevant kind of accountability. The question therefore is: are there types of social structure that preclude the existence of such milieus, so that the very possibility of the exercise of the powers of moral agency might be threatened? The type of structure that I shall use as an example is very different in some respects from that inhabited by J. But it is worth beginning with a more extreme case.

THE STRUCTURES OF COMPARTMENTALIZATION

In the 1970s I was a minor participant in a study of the moral "dimensions of decision-making in the American electric power industry" (for the principal findings see *Values in the Electric Power Industry*, ed. Kenneth Sayre, University of Notre Dame Press, 1977). One incidental discovery in the course of that study was that power company executives tended to a significant degree to answer what were substantially the same questions somewhat differently, depending on whether they took themselves to be responding qua power company executive or qua parent and head of household or qua concerned citizen. That is to say, their attitudes varied with their social roles and they seemed quite unaware of this. I take this to be a mild example of a peculiarly modern phenomenon that I will call compartmentalization.

Compartmentalization goes beyond that differentiation of roles and institutional structures that characterizes every social order and it does so by the extent to which each distinct sphere of social activity comes to have its own role structure governed by its own specific norms in relative independence of other such spheres. Within each sphere those norms dictate which kinds of consideration are to be treated as relevant to decision-making and which are to be excluded. So in the power company case executives were unable even to entertain, as a serious policy alternative, reduction in the overall levels of power consumption, so long as they thought and spoke from within their sphere of activity as power company executives, but they did not suffer from the same inability when thinking and speaking as consumers or concerned citizens.

This relative autonomy of each demarcated sphere of activity is re-inforced by the degree to which in contemporary advanced societies individuals encountered in each particular sphere are often not the same as those whom one meets elsewhere. When one encounters each individual only within some particular sphere, in some role that is a counterpart to one's own role in that particular sphere, then one's responses are increasingly only to the-individual-in-this-or-that-role rather than to the individual who happens to be occupying this role at this time. So individuals as they move between spheres of activity, exchanging one role for another and one set of standards for their practical reasoning for another, become to some important extent dissolved into their various roles, playing one part in the life of the family, quite another in the workplace, yet a third as a member of a sports club, and a fourth as a military reservist. Within each sphere such individuals conform to the requirements imposed on their role within that sphere and there is no milieu available to them in which they are able, together with others, to step back from those roles and those requirements and to scrutinize themselves and the structure of their society from some external standpoint with any practical effect.

Consider the different forms that the ethics of deception may take in different spheres, the different answers given to such questions as "Who is justified in deceiving whom and about what?" and "Who has the authority to object to deception?" A first example is that of a business corporation whose chief executive officer decides to exaggerate the progress made by the corporation's scientists on a research project, with the aims both of not losing customers to rivals and of bolstering share prices. Here the scientists have no right to lie to or otherwise deceive the CEO – not to do so is a condition of their continuing employment – and they likewise have no right to speak out. The only objection to such deception that the ethics of the corporation recognizes as possibly well-founded is that in the longer run deception will fail to maximize corporate profits. (A former Chairman of the Securities and Exchange Commission explained his decision to endow a Chair in Business Ethics at Harvard by claiming that in the long run ethics pays.)

Contrast with this the situation of those same scientists when publishing their data in professional journals. The ethics of the scientific community is such that no end external to scientific enquiry is allowed to justify deception. The falsification of data warrants their exposure by other scientists and their consequent expulsion from the scientific community. So the individual who recurrently moves between the spheres of corporate activity and of independent scientific enquiry exchanges each time that he or she does so one ethics of deception for another, often without any consciousness of so doing.

That same individual will of course also move into yet other contexts with their own ethics of deception, for example, the kind of social occasion in which relative strangers meet, drink in hand, anxious to make a favorable impression on prestigious people and equally anxious to avoid garrulous and insistent bores. Here deception, including lying, is generally a sanctioned aspect of the work of self-presentation – without it I might not be able to make myself sufficiently interesting – and I may defend myself from aggressive conversational intrusions by further lies. Each of these three ethics of deception does of course need further elaboration, but that elaboration would only strengthen the grounds for concluding that the norms of deception are specific to social context and that to move from one role in one sphere of activity to another in another is to move from one context-based moral standpoint to another.

We encounter a similar range of differences in contemporary attitudes to death. Contrast the attitudes to death exhibited within the sphere of family life by those mourning the death of a child in an automobile accident, within that of the executives of the corporation that manufactured the automobile, and within that of the lawyers who urge the family to sue the driver of the automobile. For family members the death is a unique loss for which nothing can compensate, for the corporate executives it contributes to an annual death rate that is an acceptable trade-off for the benefits of automobile sales to their industry and to society, and for the lawyers it has a precise financial value calculable on the basis of recent jury awards. And it is possible to adopt the attitudes dictated by any of these three perspectives only by temporarily excluding those of the other two. So those who move from extending their condolences at the grave-side to a meeting of automobile company executives reevaluating their production goals to the offices of a law firm will find the same death evaluated in ways that are not only different, but to some degree incompatible.[1] and this often enough without any awareness of the incompatibility. Here again each sphere of activity has its own norms and values. But compartmentalization involves more than this in two respects: the degree to which each sphere of activity is insulated from others, so that considerations that would carry weight in some other sphere are deprived of it in this; and the absence of any accessible sphere of activity in which practically effective reasoning might be used to evaluate the norms and values of each particular sphere from some external point of view.

Insulation is provided by the prescribed standard responses to the introduction into the conversations within some particular sphere of considerations that are by its norms at best irrelevant, at worst distracting. So, if in a policy meeting of the Midwestern power executives one of them had proposed attempting to bring about an overall reduction in power consumption, or if at a social gathering someone were to insist that the standards of truthfulness required in scientific reports should also apply to party gossip, their remarks might be treated as a joke or ignored, but, if such a speaker persisted, they would find themselves deprived at least temporarily of their status in that sphere of activity, treated, that is, as a source of embarrassing background noise rather than a participant. And the effects of insulation are reinforced by the absence from everyday life of milieus in the home, the workplace, and elsewhere in which such agents might engage in extended critical reflection with others about, for example, what conflicts the virtue of truthfulness requires us to engage in and just how its requirements are at odds with the established ethics of deception in each sphere of activity or about what the significance of death is. Such milieus would provide agents with what they otherwise lack, an understanding of themselves as having a substantive identity independent of their roles and as having responsibilities that do not derive from those roles, so overcoming divisions within the self imposed by compartmentalization and so setting the scene for types of conflict that compartmentalization effectively suppresses.

1 I have treated this a little more fully in "Some Enlightenment projects reconsidered" in *Questioning Ethics: Contemporary Debates in Philosophy*, ed. R. Kearney and M. Dooley, London: Routledge, 1998, pp. 255–56.

This divided self has to be characterized negatively, by what it lacks. It is not only without any standpoint from which it can pass critical judgment on the standards governing its various roles, but it must also lack those virtues of integrity and constancy that are prerequisites for exercising the powers of moral agency. It cannot have integrity, just because its allegiance to this or that set of standards is always temporary and context-bound. And it cannot have the constancy that is expressed in an unwavering directedness, since it recurrently changes direction, as it moves from sphere to sphere. Indeed its conception of a virtue will generally be one of excellence in role performance rather than of excellence as a human being and hence what is judged excellent in one role-governed context may be very different from and at times incompatible with what is judged excellent in others. Lacking these, and lacking also an awareness that it lacks these, there is nothing about the self thus divided that is liable to generate conflict with what are taken to be the requirements of morality within the established order. So insofar as that self recognizes and aspires to conform to what it takes to be moral requirements, within each particular sphere of activity, it will be a morality from which the elements of potential and actual conflict are missing, a diminished morality that matches the diminished powers of agency.

It must therefore seem that so far as individuals approach the condition of this kind of divided self, they can no longer be justifiably held responsible for their actions in anything like the ways in which moral agents are held responsible. Here, it seems, there is indeed a type of social structure that warrants for those who inhabit it a plea of gravely diminished responsibility. And we may be tempted therefore to turn immediately to the question of whether the earlier twentieth-century society that J inhabited sufficiently resembled later forms of compartmentalized social and cultural order for us to enter a similar plea on J's behalf. But this would be a mistake. For we need first to consider some further dimensions of this divided self.

It is, I shall argue, a self that is to a significant degree responsible for its own divisions. It is indeed to be characterized negatively in terms of lacks or absences, but these lacks or absences are, so I will suggest, the expression of refusals, active refusals by that self. A number of aspects of its activity are relevant. First, it can never be dissolved nor dissolve itself *entirely* into the distinctive roles that it plays in each compartmentalized sphere of activity. It exhibits for one thing a quality that in a compartmentalized society is presented as a virtue of the individual as such and not just of the individual-in this-or-that-role, a virtue that is a newcomer to the catalogue of the virtues: adaptability, flexibility, knowing chameleon-like how to take on the color of this or that social background. And it exhibits this virtue in managing its transitions from one role to another, so that it appears, so far as possible, to be dissolved into its roles. But this appearance is, when well-managed, a dramatic feat, an expression of the actor as well as of the roles enacted.

Secondly, the individual qua individual appears not only in managing the transitions from one role to another, but also, as I suggested earlier, in the role-playing itself. There are some roles that may seem purely mechanical, since the individual who plays the role can always be replaced by a machine: where there was once a ticket-seller, there is now a ticket-machine. But the ticket-seller always faced choices that machines never confront: how to play her or his role, cheerfully or sullenly, carelessly or conscientiously, efficiently or inefficiently. And for all roles, the way in which the role is enacted presupposes not only an answer to a question posed to and by the role-player: "How is it best for me to play this role?," but also to such further questions: "By what standards am I to judge what is best?" and "Should I continue to play this role in this way?" It is the inescapability on occasion of such questions that suggests that practical reasoning that is adequate for doing what a particular role requires will itself generate reasons for acting beyond those requirements and even sometimes against those requirements. To resist asking such questions, to insist upon terminating one's practical reasoning whenever it directs one beyond one's role requires a peculiar kind of self-discipline. To be able to restrict one's practical reasoning to what will enable one to discharge the responsibilities of one's socially approved roles is to have imposed on one's thinking a set of artificial restrictions. It is to have arbitrarily closed one's mind to certain possibilities of action. And, although others may provide one with motives for effecting such a closure, it is only with one's own active cooperation that the habits of mind can be developed which make such closure possible.

What is true of practical reasoning generally holds with special force of those periods during which, but for avoidance strategies, one might find that one had committed oneself to incompatible judgments. The divided self of a compartmentalized social order, in order not to have to confront incompatible attitudes to, say, truthfulness or death has to have developed habits of mind that enable it not to attend to what it would have to recognize as its own incoherences, if it were to understand itself apart from its involvements in each of its particular roles in each distinct sphere. And to learn how to focus one's attention in this way once again requires one's active cooperation.

I conclude that what I earlier characterized as lacks or absences of the divided selves of a compartmentalized social order are better described as active refusals and denials. The divided self is complicit with others in bringing about its own divided states and so can be justly regarded as their co-author. It and those others can justifiably be called to account for what they have jointly made of themselves. They may indeed inhabit a type of social and cultural order whose structures to some large degree inhibit the exercise of the powers of moral agency. But they share in responsibility for having made themselves into the kind of diminished agent that they are. Their responsibility is that of co-conspirators, engaged together in a conspiracy that functions so that they can lead blamelessly compliant lives, able plausibly to plead lack of knowledge of as well as lack of control over outcomes for which they might otherwise be held jointly responsible. Their lack of knowledge and their lack of control are often real enough, an inescapable outcome of the structuring of roles and responsibilities in a compartmentalized social order. But they are, so I have argued, responsible and accountable for making it the case that they do not know and that they lack certain powers. They are not passive victims. To have understood this enables us to return to the case of J.

ONCE MORE THE CASE OF J

I take the social structures of compartmentalization, although peculiar to the late twentieth century, to be more generally instructive, just because they provide us with a case at the extremes, a case in which, after compartmentalization has progressed beyond a certain point, many agents exhibit no awareness of responsibilities beyond those assigned to them by their roles in each particular sphere of activity, while in their practical reasoning they admit as premises only those considerations sanctioned in each context by the norms defining and governing those roles. Their lives express the social and cultural order that they inhabit in such a way that they have become unable to recognize, let alone to transcend its limitations. They do not have the resources that would enable them to move to an independent standpoint.

Both their resemblances to and their differences from J and those like him are worth remarking. Both J and those who inhabit a compartmentalized society accept unquestioningly structures that give definition to their lives by prescribing a range of roles that they are to occupy and a range of responsibilities attached to each. And it is not only what they are to do in each type of social context that is prescribed. What kind of practical reasoning it is for each of them to undertake, qua enactor of this or that role, what it is the responsibility of each to know, and what is not matter for their concern or knowledge are also prescribed. And insofar as both are deprived of participation in milieus in which in the company of others they might have elaborated a standpoint external to their role-structured activities, they have become unable to pass judgment on the limitations of their judgments. These are the resemblances, but there are also striking differences.

For J and those like him exhibited a type of awareness of their situation that is absent from those who inhabit a compartmentalized society. J judged that this way of life was the best way of life for him and for others. It is true that he did not and perhaps could not open up this judgment to any extended reflective scrutiny. But he made it and was capable of making it proudly and defiantly. Judgments about compartmentalization and its effects upon the lives of those subject to it are necessarily third-person judgments delivered from some standpoint that has escaped those effects. J was able to deliver judgment on the organization of his social life in the first person. What kind of difference does this signify?

At least this: that, if those who inhabit a compartmentalized social order can be held responsible as co-authors of their social and moral situation, then the case for imputing such responsibility to J and those like him must be even stronger. For J actively chose not to move beyond the boundaries imposed by established role-definitions. He had made himself into what the roles said that he was. By so doing he had assented to doing, reasoning and knowing only as the standards governing his roles pre-scribed. And in so assenting he had excluded the possibility of moral conflict. He did not allow himself to pass judgment on the judgments that he made in accordance with those established standards and so rendered himself unable to raise the question of what it was about which he was required to know and required to be truthful. For truthfulness as a virtue was itself defined for J by the context-bound standards governing his role-performances, so that much that truthfulness requires had become invisible.

I argued earlier that "Ask about your social and cultural order what it needs you and others not to know" has become in the modern world an indispensable moral maxim. J, like those subject to the limitations of a compartmentalized social order, had cooperated in making it impossible to acknowledge the authority of this maxim. But J's refusal of such knowledge made him too responsible, in cooperation with others, for not knowing what he did not know. So J's later defense of his earlier actions failed.

It has been my assumption that when J defended himself by denying that he had had the relevant knowledge, he was sincere. Some commentators have insisted that J and those like him must have had that knowledge and that therefore they were guilty, thus implying that if they had not had that knowledge, then they would have been innocent. I have contended by contrast that, even if J and those like him did not have that knowledge, they remained guilty and that their guilt was not merely individual guilt, but, in a sense that I hope has been made clear, the guilt of a whole social and cultural order.

CHAPTER 12

Toleration and the goods of conflict

WHAT QUESTIONS SHOULD WE ASK?

When ought we to be intolerant and why? I pose this question in the first instance as one concerning the ethics of conversation and especially the ethics of one particular kind of conversation. That kind of conversation occurs when a group of individuals enquire together about how it would be best for them to act, so that some good can be achieved or some evil avoided, where that good is both an individual and a common good – the good of this or that household or neighborhood, this or that workplace or school or clinic, this or that orchestra or laboratory or chess or football club. The central aim of this type of conversation is to arrive at as large a measure as possible of agreement that will issue in effective practical decision-making. But it cannot achieve this aim unless it also achieves two subsidiary aims: that of enabling those who participate in it both to give voice to their own concerns and to understand those of others, and by so doing that of framing and cataloguing the best reasons for and against each alternative course of action.

Such conversations are a feature of any flourishing form of everyday social life. They are also characteristically and not surprisingly scenes of conflict. For they are most needed when significantly different alternative possibilities in its immediate future have opened up for some particular group and when there are at least prima facie good reasons for different and incompatible courses of action. And just this type of occasion is apt to elicit differences between individuals concerning their larger conceptions of their individual and common goods that had not hitherto been articulated. Disagreements over particular issues always may and sometimes do turn out to be rooted in more systematic disagreements.

Conflict is therefore as integral to the life of such groups as conversation. And in order for such a group to flourish it must be able to manage its conflicts, so that neither of two evils befalls it. The first of these is the evil of suppression, of thinking that one has avoided conflict by somehow or other depriving one party to it of the means for expressing its attitudes, concerns, and arguments. The other is the evil of disruption, of the kind of disagreement and the modes of expression of disagreement which destroy the possibility of arriving at the kind of consensus necessary for effective shared decision-making. Sometimes one of these evils is produced by those who are attempting to avoid the other. It is on occasion the prospect of disruption that leads to suppression. And it is sometimes the fear of suppression that engenders disruptive attitudes.

It is in this kind of local context where, although the conversation may be conducted in a variety of ways, it cannot but involve face-to-face encounters, that certain issues of toleration arise. For, when we are involved in debate with those who hold conflicting points of view, we may take any of four distinct attitudes to the utterances of others. We may welcome them as either reinforcing our own conclusions or as assisting in the reformulation or revision of those conclusions. Or we may welcome them equally as contributing to sharp, but constructive disagreement, by providing compelling reasons for adopting some point of view other than and incompatible with our own. In both these types of case we treat the utterances as contributing in a co-operative way to the achievement of the shared goods of conversational enquiry. In a third type of case we may regard the utterance as not so contributing, but as still requiring a reasonable answer, in order to convince the utterer, if possible, that, for example, the difficulty that she or he envisages is not going to arise or that the view expressed rests on some easily corrigible misunderstanding. But there is also a fourth type of utterance to which the only appropriate response is to exclude the speaker temporarily or permanently from discussion. This is not primarily a matter of suppressing the expression of some point of view within the debate. It is a matter of expelling someone from the debate. Either the matter or the manner – or both – of her or his utterance has been taken to disqualify the speaker as a participant. What she or he said or how she or he said it has destroyed her or his conversational standing. The utterance is intolerable.

My initial questions are: what is the line to be drawn that divides this fourth type of utterance from the other three? That is to say, what is the difference between justified intolerance and unjustified suppression? Who is to draw that line? And, when drawn, how is it to be enforced as a norm governing this kind of conversation? But before I can fruitfully ask these questions, I need to make three remarks. The first is that answers to these questions already inform, sometimes explicitly, often implicitly, the life of every social group. In practice every group sets a limit to its tolerance and in one way or another enforces that limit. My enquiry therefore takes it for granted that in the course of our disagreements and conflicts we are going to be intolerant and that the only questions are of what, of whom, and why. Secondly, we should note that disagreement and conflict occur not only within the kind of group that I have described, but also between groups. Some particular group with a well-worked-out conception of the goods to be achieved in its particular arenas of activity always may and often does encounter another such group whose conception of the goods to be conceived differs in important respects from its own. Where within each group rival arguments had proceeded from some set of more or less agreed premises and presupposed a shared understanding of the concepts involved, now in the debate between groups each has to attempt to find some further ground to which both may appeal and, in so doing, to re-examine the concepts upon which they have been relying. In the exchanges between such groups the same fourfold classification of utterances that applied to debate within groups will find application. So that once again the question will arise: what kinds of utterance, if any, ought to be found intolerable?

Secondly, it is in important part through disagreement and conflict that the common life of such groups is enriched. For it is only through disagreement and conflict, only through aiming at conclusions that emerge from being tested by the most powerful counter-arguments available, that such groups are able to embody in their shared lives the rational pursuit and achievement of the relevant goods. Therefore when we evaluate the argumentative contributions to some ongoing debate within a group in whose life we participate, we should do so with an eye to how far they do or do not contribute to achieving the goods of conflict. So what is to be treated as intolerable is anything the toleration of which would tend to frustrate or prevent the achievement of those goods. Particular practices of or proposals for the practice of toleration can only be adequately evaluated from within the context of conflict. And the line between what we are prepared to tolerate and what we refuse to tolerate always partially defines our stance in some set of conflicts.

LOCKE'S PROPOSALS CONCERNING TOLERATION AND THE STATE

In trying to answer these questions about the relationship between the goods of conflict and toleration in the context of certain kinds of conversation, what can we learn from the classical texts on toleration? Here I want to distinguish between what is to be learned from Locke and what is to be learned from Mill.[1] And I shall argue that we ought to agree with at least some of Locke's conclusions, or rather perhaps with conclusions drawn from lines of thought initiated by Locke, while deriving those conclusions from premises of a very different kind from Locke's, but that in Mill's case we should assent to some of his premises, while drawing very different conclusions. I begin with Locke.

It is a commonplace that what are now treated as the classical texts on toleration for the most part have as their context those seventeenth- and eighteenth-century European conflicts in which what was at stake was, on the one hand the relationship between groups that embraced a variety of incompatible versions of the Christian religion, and the power and authority of the state on the other. The single most influential position that emerged from those texts was that towards which Locke had moved as his thoughts on these issues developed: it is the function and duty of the magistrate to promote the security, order, and harmony of a people, but not to attempt to regulate or even to influence their beliefs, except when, as in the case, on Locke's view, of Roman Catholics and atheists, religious belief itself or the lack of it threatens such security, order, and harmony.

Locke's arguments exhibited a certain tension in his attitudes. On the one hand he seems to have held that genuine belief, interior assent, cannot be commanded, that coercion can produce at most the outward appearance of conformity. No one, he says, is able to "command his own understanding or positively determine today what opinion he will be of tomorrow," and therefore no one can give another power "over that over which he has no power himself."[2] So he draws a conclusion about religious belief from the nature of belief as such. On the other hand, when Locke had to reply to Jonas Proast's thesis that a moderate use of coercive power could in fact induce someone to consider arguments to which they would not otherwise have attended with care, Locke responded that we do not have sufficiently good reasons for asserting any one particular set of religious doctrines to justify us in using the power of the state on its behalf.[3] And in so saying he seems to distinguish religious beliefs from other types of belief.

1 What I say about both Locke and Mill on toleration is highly selective; for a broader account see Susan Mendus, *Toleration and the Limits of Liberalism*, London: Macmillan, 1989, chs. 2 and 3.
2 John Locke, *Essay on Toleration*, as quoted in John Dunn, *Locke*, Oxford: Oxford University Press, 1984, p. 26.
3 *A Third Letter Concerning Toleration*. See Maurice Cranston, *John Locke*, New York: Macmillan, 1957, pp. 331–32 and 366–38.

Each of these arguments anticipates a strain in subsequent liberal thought about toleration. On the one hand, so far as possible individuals are to be left alone to make up their own minds, free from interference by the prescriptions of political or religious authority. Each individual cannot but be the sole authority on how things appear to her or him to be and on her or his consequent beliefs. And this is true of all beliefs, not just of religious beliefs or of beliefs about the nature of the human good. On the other hand, religious beliefs and, more generally, beliefs about the nature of the human good are to be treated as unlike other beliefs in that they are indefinitely contestable. And for this reason their propagation and influence are to be subject to restriction in a way that other beliefs are not. The state may justifiably mandate curricula in the natural sciences by which belief in the theory of evolution by natural selection is inculcated. But it may not justifiably mandate curricula by which belief in the divine creation of the universe is inculcated. For on questions of religion and more generally on questions concerning the human good the state is to be neutral as between different points of view.

Toleration is therefore to be extended to the exponents of any and every point of view, provided only that they do not threaten the security, order, and harmony of society. Not only may the state not attempt to impose any one view, but no one else may either. The word "impose" is important here. What is excluded is coercion, especially coercive violence or the threat of coercive violence. But no limit, or almost no limit, is placed on the means of persuasion that may otherwise be allowed. Indeed the freedom extended to religious and other groups commonly includes a freedom to use whatever means of persuasion they choose, once again provided only that they do not threaten society's security, order, and harmony.

Locke himself of course, like those later liberals who developed and to some degree transformed his thought, was a participant in those very same conflicts which he proposed to resolve by, among other things, the legislative enforcement of toleration. That legislative enforcement was the work of what had first been a contending and then became a victorious party in the seventeenth-century conflicts over religion. And the modern state which originated as the instrument of that victorious party's purposes was itself never neutral in the conflicts that continued to divide the society over which it presided. Here we need only note that the conceptions which the state principally championed were particular and highly contestable conceptions of liberty and of property and of the relationship between them – conceptions which of course changed over time – and that it systematically favored those groups and parties whose understanding of the human good was consistent with the state's own conceptions of liberty and property, and systematically disfavored those whose understandings were antagonistic to the state. But, having noted that the modern state is never merely a neutral arbiter of conflicts, but is always to some degree itself a party to social conflict, and that it acts in the interests of particular and highly contestable conceptions of liberty and property, we need also to remember how very different our present condition is from that of the eighteenth century, and this in at least three respects.

THE NATURE AND VALUES OF THE CONTEMPORARY STATE

What are the relevant differences? First, in many areas of the West politics has been successfully secularized and the political importance of religion greatly diminished. There are of course still large parts of the world in which it is the persecution of religious believers by those invested with state power that makes issues of toleration so urgent. But for the advanced modernity of the West it is only relatively rarely that such issues concern religion. Sometimes of course they do, and not unimportantly, especially when they concern the rights of parents to bring up their children according to the tenets of some particular religion. But even here we will do well to extend our discussion more widely, so that from this point on I will speak only of rival conceptions of the human good, including religious conceptions under this heading.

Secondly, the contemporary state has become very different from the eighteenth-century state, and this in obvious ways. The scope of its activities has been greatly enlarged as has the effect of those activities on the economy. The number, size, and variety of its agencies have increased enormously. The complexity of its legislation, its tax codes, and its administrative regulations are such that to grasp their detail is now generally beyond the reach of ordinary citizens, a fact whose significance it is difficult to over-rate. And, while the modern state always was more and other than a set of instrumental means to realize the purposes of those who had achieved control of its mechanisms, it has become more and more a set of institutions which have their own values.

Thirdly, the contemporary state is to a remarkable degree united in an indissoluble partnership with the national and international market. It relies upon the operations of those markets for the material resources which taxation affords. And those markets rely on it for the provision of that social and legal framework without which they could not enjoy the stability that they need. It is true that there are often minor confrontations between this or that agency of government and the agents of this or that aspect of market operations. And it is true that there are ongoing ideological debates about where the boundaries between public and government corporate activity and private corporate activity are to be drawn. But the agreements underlying those conflicts and the shared presuppositions of those debates reflect the common needs of state and market for capital formation, for economic growth, and for an adequately trained but disposable labor force, whose members are also compliant consumers and law-abiding citizens.

Let us then think of the contemporary state and the contemporary national economy as a huge, single, complex, heterogeneous, immensely powerful something or other, noting that it gives expression to both its power and its values in two very different ways. On the one hand there is the mask that it wears in all those everyday transactions in which individuals and groups are compelled to deal with a heterogeneous range of public and private corporate agencies: paying their taxes, applying for employment and welfare, buying a house, being arrested, getting an education. Here, what individuals and groups encounter in the first instance is the administrative application of rules to instances. Those rules are part of those codes of laws and regulations whose complexity makes them more or less inaccessible to the vast majority of individuals and groups. If individuals or groups are to question the application of the rules in their particular case, they generally therefore have to put themselves into the hands of experts. If they go further and try to put the rules in question, they find themselves able to do so effectively only in so far as they learn how to employ the same idioms and types of argument with which the representatives of state and market justify their rules and their decisions. The concepts central to those idioms and arguments are those of *utility* and of *rights*.

Consider how such justificatory argument proceeds through three stages. There are first of all those cost-benefit analyses designed to provide good reasons for preferring one set of decision-making procedures or one policy alternative to another. In constructing such analyses there are always questions of whose preferences are to be included in the analyses, of what time scale it is over which costs and benefits are to be measured, and of who is to decide the answers to the first two questions. And the answers to these questions determine where power lies. Next a second type of argument has to be advanced, which proceeds by first identifying those individuals and groups who may have grounds for claiming that to maximize utility in accordance with the conclusions of the cost-benefit analysis will be to violate some right of theirs, and then enquiring what grounds there are for agreeing with their claim. What the first and second types of argument yield are conclusions which in a third type of argument have to be weighed against one another to provide an answer to the question: what weight in this particular context is to be given to the conclusions concerning the rights of those involved, and what weight to the conclusions concerning what course of action will maximize the relevant utilities? How is the one set of considerations to be balanced against the other?

The metaphors of weighing and balancing are indispensable to this stage of argument. But what their use obscures is a salient fact: there are no scales. That is, not only is there no rationally justifiable general rule by which claims about utilities can be evaluated as over-riding or as failing to over-ride claims about rights, but in each particular context what decides how such claims will be adjudicated will always depend upon who it is that in that particular context has the power to adjudicate, and how this power to adjudicate is related to the distribution of economic, political and social power more generally. But this is not the only rhetorical mode in which state and market present themselves.

For they wear quite another mask and speak with quite another voice when they justify their policies and actions in their role as custodians of society's values, presenting the state as the guardian of the nation's ideals and the caretaker of its heritage, and the market as the institutionalized expression of its liberties. It is in this guise that the state from time to time invites us to die on its behalf and that the market fosters through its advertising agencies fantasies about well-being. This type of rhetoric relies not on the idioms of utility and rights, but on the persuasive definition and redefinition of such terms as "liberty," "democracy," "free market," and the like. And it is a prerequisite for achieving certain kinds of status within the apparatus of state and market that one should be able to move effectively between the one rhetorical mode and the other.

What the modes of justification employed in and on behalf of the activities of state and market cannot give expression to are the values that inform just those ongoing argumentative conversations through which members of local communities try to achieve their goods and their good. The values of state and market are not only different from, but on many types of occasion incompatible with, the values of such local community. For the former, decision-making is arrived at by a summing of preferences and by a series of trade-offs, in which whose preferences are summed and what is traded off against what depends upon the political and economic bargaining power of the representatives of contending interests. For the latter, a shared understanding of the common good of the relevant type of activity or sets of activities provides a standard independent of preferences and interests, one by reference to which individual preferences and group interests are to be evaluated. For the former there is no consideration that may not under certain circumstances be outweighed by some other consideration. For the latter, there are conclusive considerations, those that refer us to goods that cannot be sacrificed or foregone without rendering the activity in which the community is engaged pointless. For the former, a gift for flexibility and compromise, for knowing when and how to exchange one set of principles for another, is accounted a central political virtue. For the latter, a certain moral intransigence of a kind that is apt to prevent success in the larger worlds of the state and the market economy is accounted among the political virtues.

TOLERATION AND THE CONTEMPORARY STATE

It is a consequence of these features of the social life of advanced modernity that there is always tension and sometimes conflict between the demands of state and market on the one hand and the requirements of rational local community on the other. Those who value rational local communal enterprise are therefore wise to order their relationships with state and market so that, as far as possible, they remain able to draw upon those resources that can only be secured from state and market, while preserving their own sufficiency, their self-reliance, and their freedom from constraint by either. They must treat the agencies of the state with unremitting suspicion.

So by a very different route we have arrived at very much the same conclusion as that reached both by classical liberals and by modern liberals: the state must not be allowed to impose any one particular conception of the human good or identify one such conception with its own interests and causes. It must afford tolerance to a diversity of standpoints. But liberals generally have arrived at these conclusions because they believe either that the state ought to be neutral between different rival conceptions of the good or that states ought actively to promote the liberty and autonomy of individuals in making their own choices. I have argued by contrast first that the contemporary state is not and cannot be evaluatively neutral, and secondly that it is just because of the ways in which the state is not evaluatively neutral that it cannot generally be trusted to promote any worthwhile set of values, including those of autonomy and liberty.

What has most often been feared in the past was that the state, by favouring one point of view exclusively, would damage the interests of those who gave their allegiance to other standpoints. The harm done by the legally sanctioned hegemony of an established church would be a harm done to dissenters and to the liberty to dissent. But although this kind of harm is still to be feared, grave harm would also be done to the cause of those whose point of view the state had made its own. For the contemporary state could not adopt a point of view on the human good as its own without to a significant degree distorting, degrading and discrediting that point of view. It would put those values to the service of its own political and economic power and so degrade and discredit them. The principal harm that was done by the hegemony accorded to the Roman Catholic Church by regimes as different as those of Franco's Spain and de Valera's Ireland was after all to the Roman Catholic religion.

I have now given a partial and negative answer to one of my initial questions. Whoever is to draw the line between those points of view concerning the human good whose expression is to be tolerated and those points of view whose expression is not to be tolerated, it should not be the agencies of the state. It is very much to be desired that those agencies should provide for the equal protection of all the state's subjects from a wide variety of harms, and that this protection should be characterized so that it preserves an ostensible neutrality on the part of the state. Even although that neutrality is never real, it is an important fiction, and those of us who recognize its importance as well as its fictional character will agree with liberals in upholding a certain range of civil liberties.

THE EXCLUSIONS AND INTOLERANCES NECESSARY FOR RATIONAL COMMUNAL DIALOGUE

The state, however, must not be allowed to impose constraints that would prevent local groups from ordering their own conversations concerning their common goods as practically rational dialogue. And the conditions for promoting and maintaining such practically rational dialogue require certain local exclusions and intolerances. Consider five such conditions.

The first concerns *who* is to participate in the conversation. If some group aiming at a common good is engaged in practically rational conversation aimed at reaching a decision that will be genuinely its own decision, it must ensure that all its members are able to voice their concerns and evaluate the arguments that are advanced, so that what is arrived at is the reality and not merely the appearance of consensus. But it must also ensure that those with irrelevant or conflicting aims do not subvert their shared enquiry. So, for example, in discussion designed to identify how the goods of health are to be defined concretely for some particular community with a particular age distribution and a particular set of threats to its health, the contribution of physicians, nurses, therapists of various kinds, actual and potential patients and those who have responsibility for children or for the aged are all germane to the enquiry, while those of the representatives of insurance companies or of bureaucratic managers of healthcare organizations are not. The latter do indeed have an interest in how the goods of health are defined, but the kind of interest that should render them not participants in this discussion, but objects of suspicion and candidates for exclusion.

Of course once the members of a given community have decided how the goods of health are to be defined correctly for them in their circumstances, they themselves must then face the further question of how much of their resources they are able and prepared to make available to achieve those goods, what other types of good they will consequently be unable to achieve and how they should use those resources as efficiently as possible. And at this later stage of discussion some kinds of contribution that were irrelevant or even corrupting at an earlier stage may well become relevant.

Let me put this point in another way. The more open a discussion is to anyone and everyone, so that multifarious interests of indefinitely many kinds may find expression, and there are few, if any, widely shared presuppositions, then that discussion can only have a direction and an ordered agenda that will issue in the making of decisions if such a direction and agenda, and the form of decision-making, are imposed upon the discussion by those with the power so to impose. That power in the liberal democracies of advanced modernity rests with the elites of the political parties and of the mass media and it is they who largely decide the direction of discussion and its agenda, so determining not what the public chooses, but what the alternatives are between which public choices are made.

If the participants themselves are not only to engage in, but to control the direction of genuinely rational discussion that determines practical outcomes, there has to be some large measure of initial agreement about what it is that needs to be decided, about what the standards are by which better reasons for decision and action are to be discriminated from worse, and about what goods are at stake. The rational resolution of disagreement thus requires some measure of prior agreement, agreement which can itself always be put in question, if there turns out to be good reason to question it. And the initial agreement that is needed can only be secured by exclusions, exclusions that must themselves be agreed and be open to question.

Secondly, rational discussion and enquiry in which all the relevant voices are to be heard is incompatible with certain modes of expression. Threatening and insulting utterance, utterance that brings certain others in the discussion into contempt or makes them feel insecure, that addresses their motives, their persons, their ethnic characteristics or their gender, rather than their arguments or their conclusions, are so much a violation of the norms of rational discussion that they should be treated as a kind of self-expulsion from the discussion, an expression of a will to be expelled. The group should consent to and enforce this self-imposed withdrawal, perhaps temporarily. Local rationality mandates local intolerance.

To this it will be replied that I seem to have an absurdly unrealistic and sterile view of how local communal debate proceeds when it is genuinely informed by its members' concerns. Jokes, mockery, and indignation are after all only a few of the forms taken by the rhetoric of reason-informed passion, and reason-informed passion is what moves those who participate in such debate. How then are we to draw a line between jokes and insults, between legitimate mockery of a view and illegitimate mockery of those who hold that view? How can we possibly legislate against the clever sneer and the subtle act of condescension?

The answer is that rationality compels us to admit the force of both sets of considerations and that there can indeed be no hard and fast rule by which such a line can be drawn. What is required is the exercise of judgment and the cultivation of those virtues necessary for the exercise of judgment. That the members of a rational community have to educate themselves and each other into these and other virtues, and that such an education takes time, draws our attention to the fact that any particular community that exhibits rationality does so as a result only of an extended self-education into the virtues of practical rationality and that any particular community will have made more or less progress in this education. A capacity for judgment has to emerge. We have to learn how to be rationally intolerant of certain kinds of utterance.

To these already catalogued exclusions and intolerances we need to add another. It is a condition of rational discussion and enquiry that certain questions should be understood by the participants to have been settled conclusively. More than this, an insistence that certain kinds of question remain open may be a sign of a type of character that disqualifies those who possess it from further participation in discussion. Consider first an absurd example. Dr. Rumpelstiltskin is an apparently intelligent and well-informed person. He has a doctorate in the humanities from a leading university. His range of opinions resembles those of other such persons, with one notable exception: he is deeply and passionately convinced of the truth of the phlogiston theory of combustion. He publishes at his own expense pamphlets denouncing Priestley and Lavoisier for having diverted chemistry from its true course. He advances explanations for their successes, explanations that display a certain ingenuity, but are likely to convince only those who are almost completely ignorant of chemistry. How do we in fact treat such as Rumpelstiltskin?

The answer is that we all of us tacitly agree to silence him by ignoring him, and among other measures that we take we exclude him from any discussion in which the truth or otherwise of particular chemical theories is taken in any way seriously. The essays that he prepares for delivery at scientific meetings are never accepted. His letters to journals and newspapers go unpublished. At public lectures, once the chair knows who he is, he is deliberately ignored at question time. His pamphlets are unread, except as jokes. But are we prepared to allow Rumpelstiltskin to teach in schools or colleges subjects other than chemistry – ancient history, say?

No one reasonable will say "No" to this, unless it is discovered that his prestige with his students in his ancient history classes may be making some of them take his views on chemistry seriously, so that some students who would otherwise have chosen to take classes in chemistry elect other alternatives to their own detriment. This would certainly provide some grounds for denying Rumpelstiltskin a position as a teacher. How strong these grounds would be taken to be would, I suggest, be very generally a matter of how great the influence on his students was. But there would be some degree of influence that would make it appropriate no longer to employ him as a teacher, to exclude his views and with them him, not only from the scientific but also from the larger academic community. That is, our position on such as Rumpelstiltskin is in fact that we do nothing to hinder the expression of their views, so long as we are assured that no one gives them serious consideration.

Consider now what Mill asserts in chapter 2 of *On Liberty* (the chapter entitled "Of the Liberty of Thought and Discussion"), namely that we should not only tolerate but also welcome the expression of all and any opinions that deviate from whatever in a particular society is taken to be the accepted norm. "If all mankind minus one were of one opinion, and only one person were of the contrary opinion, mankind would be no more justified in silencing that one person, than he, if he had the power, would be justified in silencing mankind."[4] Mill, we should remind ourselves, was envisaging the silencing of opinions by government, government which had made itself the instrument of public opinion, of what Mill calls "the general intolerance of the public." And I have already agreed that we ought not to allow government – or at least the governments of modern states – to suppress opinions. But what I hope the example of the fictitious Dr. Rumpelstiltskin shows is that we do not have to invoke the powers of government to silence the expression of opinions. They can be and often are effectively silenced at a range of local levels by the tacit or even explicit agreement of the relevant communities. It is true that what is involved here is not that "general intolerance of public opinion" which Mill had in mind. But it is a form of suppression that is flagrantly at odds with Mill's ringing and unqualified declarations.

What I am suggesting here is that there is a class of opinions which many of us, liberals and non-liberals alike, agree in exempting from Mill's ban on suppression, although often without acknowledging that we do so. And our reason for disagreeing with Mill is that we take it not to be true of this class of opinions that its suppression involves what Mill took to be "the peculiar evil" of suppression, that:

It is robbing the human race; posterity as well as the existing generation; those who dissent from the opinion, still more than those who hold it. If the opinion is right, they are deprived of the opportunity of exchanging error for truth: if wrong, they lose, what is almost as great a benefit, the clearer perception and livelier impression of truth, produced by its collision with error.[5]

What is deeply implausible in this is the suggestion that the serious reassertion of the phlogiston theory of combustion in any mode whatsoever could do anything to produce a "clearer perception and livelier impression" of those truths of modern chemistry that displaced it two hundred years ago.

To this it may be said that it is the example that is misleading and that it is significant that I have employed a fictitious example. No one does in fact now hold, because no one could now hold, the phlogiston theory of combustion. And more generally the class of opinions that would provide

4 John Stuart Mill, On *Liberty*, Harmondsworth: Penguin, 1978, p. 76.
5 Ibid.

counterexamples to Mill's generalization is empty. Moreover, if such opinions were held, their expression would be self-discrediting. Their suppression is either unnecessary or pointless. There are, however, real-life examples of scientific opinions uncomfortably close to Rumpelstiltskin's that have flourished in some quarters very recently – I have in mind not only the beliefs of members of Flat Earth Societies, but also some kinds of rejection of Darwinism. But the type of example that it is most important to consider as a possible counterexample to Mill's claims is of a different kind.

Consider the assertion and the attempted justifications of the assertion that the Holocaust – the intended and to a horrifying extent achieved destruction of the Jewish people by those acting under the orders of Hitler and Himmler or collaborating with them, and with it the intended and to a horrifying extent achieved destruction of the Romany people, the gypsies – never happened and that the belief that it happened is a fabrication of anti-Nazi propaganda. How should we stand on the freedom to express this opinion?

So far as the intervention of government is concerned, we have the opposing examples of the United States and of Germany. In the United States twentieth-century interpretations of the First Amendment have made it quite clear that the liberty to express this opinion, like the liberty to express any other opinion, has to be guaranteed by the state. It would indeed be open to a university to deny an appointment in, say, modern German history to someone holding this opinion, on the grounds that it exhibited gross incompetence in the evaluation of evidence. But to deny some individual well qualified in some other field, in one of the natural or applied sciences say, a professorial appointment just because he or she held and expressed this opinion, and just because his or her holding a professorial appointment enhanced the credibility of this opinion among certain types of people, would be an infringement of that individual's First Amendment rights. In Germany, by contrast, the utterance of this opinion is, I understand, a punishable crime. How are we to decide between these rival views?

Two features of the denial of the Holocaust are relevant to answering this question. First of all, the denial of the Holocaust is certainly an intervention in the debates between the protagonists of different and rival conceptions of the human good. For what some particular conception of the human good amounts to is always a matter in part of what allegiance to it amounts to or would amount to in practice. What would it be like to live in a society informed by this particular conception? It is not of course a conclusive objection to a particular conception of the human good that those whose practice has been directed to it as their supreme end have in fact been guilty of many and great evils. For the source of those evils may not have been in that conception of the good, but rather in its distortion or in the imperfections of its realization, or in some contingent features of the history of its adherents that are only related *per accidens* to that conception. Nonetheless the history of how some particular conception of the human good has been embodied in practice is always of great relevance in evaluating it. And for anyone who is concerned to evaluate all those conceptions of the human good that have played a central part in European history – those of Catholic Christianity, of different types of Protestant Christianity, of a variety of doctrines and movements stemming from or reacting to the Enlightenment – the relationship of their history to the history of European antiSemitism has to be of immense importance.

It follows that were the state to proscribe and punish utterances that afford expression to a denial of the Holocaust, the state would be actively intervening in the debates between protagonists of rival conceptions of the human good. And it was my conclusion earlier that such interventions by the state are bound to be pernicious. I am therefore bound to side with the law of the United States rather than that of Germany; as I do. But it does not follow that utterances that afford expression to a denial of the Holocaust ought to be tolerated generally. Why not?

Local communities engaged in systematic conversation about their own good have to treat certain questions as already decided. And among these by now are questions about the evils of antiSemitism. Indeed the poisons of anti-Semitism are such that no conception of the human good can be treated as rationally defensible whose defenders cannot show not only how allegiance to it can be dissociated from antiSemitism, but also how it can provide or acquire resources for neutralizing those poisons. And that can be done only by those who recognize the facts of the Holocaust. I do not mean by this that there are not many other facts that also need to be recognized. But I take the facts about the Holocaust to be a paradigm case of historical facts the denial of which precludes a rational evaluation of an important range of conceptions of human good. I conclude that this is an opinion that ought not to be tolerated in any local community, that to tolerate it is a form of vice, and that those who express it ought to be silenced.

George P. Fletcher has argued against this conclusion by remarking that:

"If it is a crime to deny the Holocaust, then perhaps it should be a crime to question the reigning view of historians about other troubling historical events. What if someone could show that Lincoln did not care about emancipating the slaves, that he was interested only in the economic value of the Union? Should this view be suppressed? This is the slope that becomes too slippery to stop the slide towards ever more censorship."[6]

The argument is a familiar one and about it two things need to be said. The first is that it would be a good deal more compelling if its protagonists were able to supply a number of historical examples of slopes down which this kind of slide had in fact taken place, instead of merely asking "What if?" questions. Without such examples the slippery slide into intolerance of the otherwise tolerant is in danger of seeming no more than a phantom of the liberal imagination. Secondly, Fletcher has indeed warned us of a danger of which we need to be aware and about which we need to be vigilant. But this kind of vigilance is one aspect of the virtue of prudence, a virtue required in all rational debate and practice. I conclude therefore that the slippery slope argument does not warrant the conclusion that those who deny the Holocaust ought to be allowed to voice their opinion. But how then should they be silenced, if not by government?

The answer is that they should be silenced by the same methods or by a further and more extreme development of those methods by which those real individuals whose opinions resemble those of the fictitious Rumpelstiltskin are silenced. That is to say, it should be the mark of any form of local discussion or enquiry that has any pretension to genuine practical rationality that its participants exclude the expression of this thought. And they should also treat the will to make such assertions as a sign of a character that has unfitted itself for participation in rational discussion or enquiry. Those who make them should be excluded, so far as is possible, not only from decision-making discussion, but also from holding any position in such types of local community as schools or colleges. But of course whether or not to enforce such an exclusion, whether or not to refuse to tolerate the expression of this belief, is itself something open to rational debate and enquiry for any group for whom this issue arises. It is their reasoning about particular cases, not my generalizations, which has to be conclusive.

6 George P. Fletcher, "The Instability of Tolerance," in David Heyd (ed.), *Toleration: An Elusive Virtue*, Princeton, N.J.: Princeton University Press, 1996, p. 167.

It does of course follow from what I have said that, although the state must tolerate, it must not be allowed to impose tolerance on others. Local communal autonomy requires the freedom to make one's own decisions about where the line is to be drawn between tolerable and intolerable utterance. Such local autonomy has to extend to those institutions that are integral to local community, among them schools and colleges. And so I reiterate a conclusion plainly at odds with some of Mill's most heartfelt convictions. Yet in fact the relationship of this exclusionary and intolerant view to Mill's plea for tolerance is a little more complex. For these disagreements with Mill, fundamental though they may be, not only coexist with but possibly derive from even more fundamental agreements. Mill rightly laid great stress on what he called "the intelligent and living apprehension of truth," and he understood that such intelligent and living apprehension can only emerge from some systematic process of enquiry in the course of which we are held accountable by others for the reasons which we give for asserting our conclusions. The examples that Mill gives of such processes of enquiry are the dialectical interrogations of Socrates and the process of arguments and counter-arguments in medieval scholastic disputations. (Mill's praise for the latter is qualified by his disapproval of the part played by appeals to authority in such disputations; I suspect, however, that he had misunderstood what was involved in such appeals.) What is important about such face-to-face encounters is that in them we cannot evade responsibility for our assertions; we show ourselves as deserving of a hearing only insofar as we have made ourselves accountable in this way. And Mill himself provides an admirable example of someone who in very different contexts exhibited the virtues of conversational and argumentative accountability.

One mark of the possession of those virtues is that of taking pleasure in having been shown to be mistaken, something notoriously difficult to achieve. Another closely related mark is that of being both able to recognize and willing to admit that one has been shown to be mistaken. Conversely it is a failure in respect of those virtues to be unable to recognize or unwilling to admit this, a failure in respect of accountability and therefore something that prima facie disqualifies one from further participation in rational discourse and enquiry. Whether in a given case this should be more than a prima facie verdict, whether an offender's exclusions should be from only one type of discourse and enquiry or should instead extend more widely, and whether it should be a temporary or a permanent exclusion will all vary with the circumstances of the case. But it is because accountability is important in just the ways on which

Mill lays emphasis that there are some beliefs failure to abandon which in the face of the evidence justifies, so long as it is continued, exclusion from the company of rational human beings.

Toleration then, so I have argued, is not in itself a virtue and too inclusive a toleration is a vice. Toleration is an exercise of virtue just in so far as it serves the purposes of a certain kind of rational enquiry and discussion, in which the expression of conflicting points of view enables us through constructive conflict to achieve certain individual and communal goods. And intolerance is also an exercise of virtue when and in so far as it enables us to achieve those same goods. But such intolerance has perhaps to extend somewhat further than I have so far suggested.

The rationality of local communities, when it exists, is always an achievement, the outcome of a history in which a variety of difficulties and obstacles has had to be overcome. And rationality in such communities is always threatened by the seductive and coercive forces that are so powerful in the wider arenas of the civil society of advanced modernity. The rational making of decisions in everyday life has to be undertaken for the most part in milieus in which individuals and groups are exposed by the technologies of the mass media to too much information of too many different types of doubtful provenance, often misleadingly abbreviated, and designed in any case to arouse short-term interest or excitement that can easily be displaced by the next targeted stimulus. It is a commonplace that the use of slogans, the shortening of the public's attention span, and the manipulation of feelings are now carried through in the media, in political debate, and in advertising with extraordinary professional expertise. So a set of further problems has been created. The rhetorical modes of rational enquiry and discussion are deeply incompatible with the rhetorical modes of the dominant political and commercial culture. And we cannot confront this incompatibility and the conflicts that it generates, and the goods that it threatens, without rethinking even further some well-established notions of freedom of expression and of toleration. But about how to do this constructively in defence of the rational politics of local community no one has yet known what to say. Nor do I.

Index